Hebre

Good News Commentaries

Hebrews

Donald A. Hagner

A GOOD NEWS COMMENTARY

New Testament Editor

W. Ward Gasque

1817

HARPER & ROW, PUBLISHERS, SAN FRANCISCO

Cambridge, Hagerstown, New York, Philadelphia
London, Mexico City, São Paulo, Sydney

FIRST EDITION

Designed by Design Office Bruce Kortebein

Library of Congress Cataloging in Publication
Data
Hagner, Donald Alfred.
    HEBREWS.
    (A Good News Commentary)
    Bibliography: p.
    Includes index.
    1. Bible. N.T. Hebrews—Commentaries. I. Bible
N.T. Hebrews. English. Today's English. 1983.
II. Title. IH. Series
BS2775.3.H33   1983   227'.87077   82-48410
ISBN 0-06-063555-X

83 84 85 86 87 10 9 8 7 6 5 4 3 2 1

About the Series

This is the first major series to use the popular Good News Bible, which has sold in the millions. Each volume is informed by solid scholarship and the most up-to-date research, yet each is biblically faithful and readily understandable to the general reader. Features include:

Introductory material highlighting authorship, dating, background information, and thematic emphases—plus a map

Full text of each Good News Bible Book, with running commentary

Special end notes giving references for key words and concepts and providing suggestions for further reading

Full indexes for Scripture and Subjects/Persons/Places

Series Editor W. Ward Gasque is Vice-Principal and Professor of New Testament at Regent College in Vancouver. A former editor-at-large for *Christianity Today*, he is the author of numerous articles and books and has edited *In God's Community: Studies in the Church and Its Ministry, Handbook of Biblical Prophecy, Apostolic History and the Gospel,* and *Scripture, Tradition, and Interpretation.* Dr. Gasque's major involvement is in the provision of theological resources and education for the laity.

Contents

Foreword

The Good News Bible Commentary Series

Although it does not appear on the standard best-seller lists, the Bible continues to outsell all other books. And in spite of growing secularism in the West, there are no signs that interest in its message is abating. Quite to the contrary, more and more men and women are turning to its pages for insight and guidance in the midst of the ever-increasing complexity of modern life.

This renewed interest in Scripture is found outside of, as well as in, the church. It is found among people in Asia and Africa as well as in Europe and North America; indeed, as one moves outside of the traditionally Christian countries, interest in the Bible seems to quicken. Believers associated with the traditional Catholic and Protestant churches manifest the same eagerness for the word that is found in the newer evangelical churches and fellowships.

Millions of individuals read the Bible daily for inspiration. Many of these lay Bible students join with others in small study groups in homes, office buildings, factories, and churches to discuss a passage of Scripture on a weekly basis. This small-group movement is one that seems certain to grow even more in the future, since leadership of nearly all churches is encouraging these groups, and they certainly seem to be filling a significant gap in people's lives. In addition, there is renewed concern for biblical preaching throughout the church. Congregations where systematic Bible teaching ranks high on the agenda seem to have no difficulty filling their pews, and "secular" men and women who have no particular interest in joining a church are often quite willing to join a nonthreatening, informal Bible discussion group in their neighborhood or place of work.

We wish to encourage and, indeed, strengthen this worldwide movement of lay Bible study by offering this new commentary series. Although we hope that pastors and teachers will find these volumes helpful in both understanding and communicating the word of God, we do not write primarily for them. Our aim is, rather, to provide for the benefit of the ordinary Bible reader reliable guides to the books of the Bible, representing the best of contemporary scholarship presented in a form that does not require formal theological education to understand.

The conviction of editors and authors alike is that the Bible belongs to the people and not merely to the academy. The message of the Bible is too important to be locked up in erudite and esoteric essays and monographs written for the eyes of theological specialists. Although exact scholarship has its place in the service of Christ, those who share in the teaching office of the church have a responsibility to make the results of their research accessible to the Christian community at large. Thus, the Bible scholars who join in the presentation of this series write with these broader concerns in view.

A wide range of modern translations is available to the contemporary Bible student. We have chosen to use the Good News Bible (Today's English Version) as the basis of our series for three reasons. First, it has become the most widely used translation, both geographically and ecclesiastically. It is read wherever English is spoken and is immensely popular with people who speak English as a second language and among people who were not brought up in the church. In addition, it is endorsed by nearly every denominational group.

Second, the Good News Bible seeks to do what we are seeking to do in our comments, namely, translate the teaching of the Bible into terms that can be understood by the person who has not had a strong Christian background or formal theological education. Though its idiomatic and sometimes paraphrastic style has occasionally frustrated the scholar who is concerned with a minute examination of the original Greek and Hebrew words, there can be no question but that this translation makes Scripture more accessible to the ordinary reader than any other English translation currently available.

Third, we wish to encourage group study of the Bible, particularly by people who have not yet become a part of the church but who are interested in investigating for themselves the claims of Christ. We believe that the Good News Bible is by far the best translation for group discussion. It is both accurate and fresh, free from jargon, and above all, contemporary. No longer does the Bible seem like an ancient book, belonging more to the museum than to the modern metropolis. Rather, it is as comprehensible and up-to-date as the daily newspaper.

We have decided to print the full text of the Good News Bible—and we are grateful for the kind permission of the United Bible Societies to do this—in our commentary series. This takes up valuable space, but we believe that it will prove to be very convenient for those who make use of the commentary, since it will enable them to read it straight through like an ordinary book as well as use it for reference.

Each volume will contain an introductory chapter detailing the background of the book and its author, important themes, and other helpful information. Then, each section of the book will be expounded as a whole, accompanied by a series of notes on items in the text that need further clarification or more detailed explanation. Appended to the end of each volume will be a bibliographical guide for further study.

Our new series is offered with the prayer that it may be an instrument of authentic renewal and advancement in the worldwide Christian community and a means of commending the faith of the people who lived in biblical times and of those who seek to live by the Bible today.

W. WARD GASQUE

ITALIA

Rome
Aricia
Puteoli • Neapolis
Pompeii

MACEDONIA

Thessalonica
Beroea
Philippi

GREECE

Delphi
Corinth
Athens
Sparta

Heraclea

PONTUS

Sinope

GALATIA

Ancyra

PHRYGIA

Adramyttium
Pergamum
Sardis • Philadelphia
Ephesus • Laodicea
Trolles
Miletus • Halicarnassus
Cos

Lesbos
Samos

Delos
Paros
Melos

CRETE

Gortyna

Rhodes

CAPPADOCIA

Iconium

Antioch
Apamea

PAMPHYLIA

Derbe • Tarsus
Perge • Side

COMMAGENE

MESOPOTAMIA

Tigris River

Euphrates River

Pumbeditha
Nehardea •
Babylon

• City
with
Jewish
community

Palmyra

Damascus

SYRIA

Antioch
Seleucia • Apamea

Aradus
Tripolis
Berytus
Sidon
Tyre
Ptolemais

Salamis

CYPRUS

Paphos

Jerusalem

JUDEA

ARABIA

Mediterranean Sea

Alexandria

CYRENAICA

Pelusium

Athribis • Bubastis
Memphis • Leontopolis
Philadelphia • Philadelphia
ArsinoE • Heracleopolis
Tebtynis
Oxyrhynchus

Nile R

E G Y P T

0   50   100 miles
0 50 100 150 km

Used with permission of Macmillan Publishing Company from *The Macmillan
Bible Atlas*, Revised Edition, by] Yohanan Aharoni and Michael Avi-Yonah.
Copyright © 1964, 1966, 1968, 1977 by Carta Ltd.

Introduction

As distinctive among the writings of the NT as Hebrews is, we know in fact very little about its origin, its author, and its first readers. The traditional and ancient designation of the book as "The Epistle of Paul the Apostle to the Hebrews" found, for example, at the head of the book in the KJV is not a part of the original document, but rather an opinion of the early church that first comes to expression in the Eastern church (Alexandria) late in the second century, and in the Western church two centuries after that. Moreover, this information appears to have been inferred from the document itself, much in the manner of modern scholarship, rather than derived from any independent tradition about its origin. The result is that we are left to draw such conclusions as we can from the actual contents of Hebrews.

The author, however, writing to circumstances well known to his readers and himself, assumes much that we would like to know. As is often true in the interpretation of the epistles of the NT, it is as though we were listening to one side of a telephone conversation, having to supply in our mind what the other party has said in order to make intelligible what we are able to hear. It must be admitted, then, that the conclusions we draw about the readers, the author, and the circumstances that gave rise to this extraordinary book can only be tentative, not final. The truth of these conclusions is not based upon, nor is it to be assessed solely by, particular statements in the book considered in isolation from the work as a whole. The most convincing conclusions are those that best explain the total document.

The Addressees

Hebrews, of course, does not begin with an identification of the author and the addressees, as do most of the letters of the NT. Nor, indeed, does it begin like a letter at all, despite its typical epistolary ending. Nowhere in this letter, furthermore, are the original readers referred to as Hebrews or Jews. The title "To the Hebrews" is first attested at the end of the second century (by Clement of Alexandria and Tertullian). Although it is also found in the oldest manuscript of the Pauline epistles (P^{46}) from about the same time, this may only reflect the opinion that was emerging.

Nevertheless, the early church was very probably correct in understanding the first readers to have been Jewish Christians. The vast majority of modern scholars has agreed with this conclusion from analysis of the content of the book. The OT is of very great importance: it is quoted often and expounded in "midrashic" fashion,* and the argument of the epistle to a large extent depends upon the use of the OT. More specifically, the stress on the levitical liturgy and priesthood, the sanctuary of the wilderness tabernacle, and the Mosaic covenant, which in such a detailed manner are contrasted with the fulfillment brought by Christ, point to the high probability of Jewish readers.

The same is true of the book's interest in Christology (the doctrine of the person of Christ) and fulfillment of OT promises, as well as the way in which the experiences of Israel are used by the author as warnings for the community. Certain passages seem particularly appropriate for Jewish readers. For example, the opening words "In the past God spoke to our ancestors [lit., "fathers"] many times" (1:1) refers most naturally to physical fathers. Again, this is a compelling conclusion from 2:16, "For it is clear that it is not the angels that he helps. Instead, as the scripture says, 'He helps the descendants of Abraham.' " In this passage the incarnation is explained as due to Christ's identification with humanity (and not angels), yet this is expressed through the allusion to Isaiah 41:8 f., where it is specifically Israel that is in view. This would have special relevance to Jewish readers. And it is particularly Jewish readers more than any others who, because of the intrinsic excellence of Judaism, would have been tempted to return to their earlier religious faith—something our author warns against repeatedly in the book. They more than any others would have been forced to grapple with the relation between the old and new covenants.

That the first readers of the book were Jewish Christians remained the unanimous conviction of scholars until the end of the nineteenth century. Since that time some scholars have argued that the first readers were Gentiles, and not Jews. Since the title "To the Hebrews" is traditional, rather than original, the determination of whether the readers were Jews or Gentiles can only be made from the book itself. These scholars argue that nothing about the content of the book necessitates Jewish readers. Although this assertion is quite true in itself, the question remains as to which hypothesis is most successful in accounting for the phenomena of the book as a whole.

The objections raised to the identification of the readers as Jewish (and some responses) follow. The potential apostasy described in 3:12,

---

* A *midrash* is a type of writing based on a distinctively Jewish use of the OT. For additional information, see below, pp. 25 and 28.

"My fellow believers, be careful that no one among you has a heart so evil and unbelieving that he will turn away from the living God," seems difficult if it is a return to Judaism that is contemplated. If Gentiles return to their paganism they can indeed be understood as turning away from the living God. And yet, given our understanding of the author's larger argument, to turn away from the fulfillment brought in Christ is indeed so grievous that, even for Jewish readers, it would be to "turn away from the living God." From our author's perspective, the old covenant is passé; to return to it could in no way have been thought by him to be a return to a valid religion in which the living God was active.

Similarly, although some are of the opinion that the reference to "dead works" in 6:1 and 9:14 is a more appropriate description of paganism than Judaism, our author's perspective may well make such a description of Judaism possible. Further, the references to "Gnostic"-related views in 13:4, 9 need not imply a Gentile readership; Diaspora Judaism was subject to such "Gnostic" influence (cf. Col. 2:16, 21 f.).* The elegant Greek of the book and the regular citation of the OT from its Greek translation (LXX) also does not necessarily point to Gentile readers. Again, the fact that it is not Judaism and the Temple but rather the levitical ritual and the wilderness tabernacle that are the focus of the author's arguments does not necessitate Gentile readers. The author's appeal to the past and to what is recorded in Scripture comes from his desire to stress the motif of promise and fulfillment. Thus the new that has come in Christ succeeds not simply the present manifestation of Judaism but also its ideal statement in the Torah (Genesis–Deuteronomy). If the readers are Jewish, we are very probably to conceive of them as Hellenistic, or Greek-speaking, Jews whose Judaism was of a nonconformist variety (i.e., other than the typical rabbinic Judaism, though not necessarily uninfluenced by it).

It must be admitted that just as nothing in the book necessitates that the original readers were Jews, despite strong probability in favor of such a view, so nothing in the book excludes the possibility of a Gentile readership. Some scholars, indeed, argue for a mixed readership of both Jews and Gentiles! Such is the nature of the book's contents that it possesses a universal applicability.

If, as we have argued, the most natural explanation of the book, taking

---

Gnosticism refers to a constellation of Oriental and Greek religious-philosophical ideas common in the early Christian era. Traditionally, it was regarded as a Christian heresy, but most scholars today consider it to be a broader phenomenon. Cf. below, pp. 10 and 221.

into account its total contents, is that the original readers were Jewish Christians, can anything more specific be said about them? An increasingly popular view is that the readers were themselves converts from the Essene community at Qumran, known to us through the discovery of the Dead Sea Scrolls, or at least had been under the influence of that perspective. Although there are some striking similarities between the content of our book and that of the Dead Sea scrolls, upon closer analysis the similarities can be shown to be more superficial than substantial (see F. F. Bruce, " 'To the Hebrews' or 'To the Essenes'?" *NTS* 9 [1962–63], pp. 217–32.) Furthermore, the stress on the levitical priesthood and ritual in our book need not indicate that the readers were former priests (cf. Acts 6:7). The author's argumentation is not so technical as to be beyond Jews who had been converted to Christianity. Similarly, the author's criticism of the readers when he says that they ought to have been teachers (5:12) does not necessarily indicate professionals in contrast to laity. It could well mean that they as Jewish Christians, with their intimate understanding of the OT, ought to have been in a superior position to teach others (especially Gentiles) about the full significance of Christianity.

Although the hypothesis that the readers were Jewish Christians remains at best only highly probable, there are some things about the readers that are certain. First, it is plain that the recipients of the letter formed a specific community with a specific history. We learn that although they had been Christians for some time, they remained immature in their understanding of the Christian faith (5:11–6:3). The reason for this seems to have been their fear of persecution and their reluctance to separate from their Judaism rather than mental dullness on their part. This failure is all the more striking given their earlier history, in which they demonstrated their love of their fellow Christians through service to them (6:9 f.); in a time of persecution during which they themselves suffered considerably, they nevertheless identified with those whose sufferings were worse and thereby suffered all the more, including losing personal property (10:32 ff.). But despite this honorable past, there seems to have been evidence that they were weakening in their commitment, perhaps in the face of the threat of new persecution. Although hitherto they had apparently not suffered martyrdom, perhaps this now loomed as a threatening possibility (10:35 f.; 12:4).

We may further say of the readers that the author did not simply know them but was somehow related to them, perhaps as a former leader of the community (13:18 f., 22 ff.; cf. 13:7, 17).

It is less certain, but nevertheless a good possibility, that this community of Jewish believers was, or at least had once been, part of a larger Christian community, perhaps the Jewish wing of a larger congregation (cf. the reference to "all your leaders" in 13:24). They may have met together as a house church, but the new pressures upon them appear to have discouraged them from meeting this way (cf. 10:25). Indeed, perhaps the imminence of persecution caused them to separate themselves from the main body of Christians.

Can we say with any certainty where this group of Jewish Christians lived? Jewish converts to Christianity were found throughout the Mediterranean world as well as in Palestine. The only geographical clue at all in the epistle is found in 13:24, and it is a somewhat ambiguous one. The words "The brothers from Italy send you their greetings" most probably mean that Italian compatriots, away from home and with our author, send greetings to their brethren in the homeland. This is more natural than to conclude that Christians in Rome (in which case we would not expect the preposition "from") send their greetings elsewhere. Furthermore, our first knowledge of Hebrews—and a very early one at that—comes from Clement of Rome in A.D. 95 (1 Clement). Clement quotes from Hebrews extensively but unfortunately gives us no hint of its author, whose identity he probably knew if the letter was addressed to Jewish Christians in Rome. Also to be noted is that the Roman church, like the first readers of Hebrews, had suffered persecutions and was known for its generosity (cf. Heb. 6:10 ff.; 10:32 ff.). Timothy, mentioned in 13:23, was also known to the Roman church (cf. Rom. 16:21).

Some scholars maintain, however, that the letter was sent to Jewish Christians in Palestine. Would not Jewish Christians there be under the greatest pressure to return to their former religion? They had suffered persecution from their unbelieving brethren (but, contrary to 12:4, *had* suffered martyrdoms), and the imminent crisis they seem to face in Hebrews could be the destruction of Jerusalem by the Romans. Against this view, however, is the strongly Hellenistic character of the book, which does not fit well with, for example, a Jerusalem readership. It is further to be noted that the Jerusalem church was poverty-stricken and therefore hardly capable of the generosity for which our author compliments his readers (6:10, 10:34, 13:16).

Because of apparent signs of an Alexandrian perspective in the epistle—for example, the dualism between heavenly archetypes and earthly copies, the use of the OT, similarities with the Jewish scholar Philo—some scholars have postulated Alexandria as the destination of the epistle. This evidence, however, is possibly more pertinent to the author's background than that of the readers. It would also be strange that the Alexandrian church would not remember the name of the author, for it is in Alexandria late in the second century that Hebrews was first attributed to Paul. But there it was also believed that the letter had originally been sent to Jewish Christians in Palestine, and not to Alexandria!

T. W. Manson, a distinguished British theologian, suggested that Hebrews was directed to Jewish Christians who faced the same problems as those addressed by Paul in his letter to the Colossians, and thus that Hebrews also had been sent to the churches of the Lycus Valley. Both Colossians and Hebrews refer to scruples about certain foods (Col. 2:16; Heb. 13:9; cf. Col. 2:20–23; Heb. 9:10), as well as to the veneration of angels (Col. 2:18; Heb. 1:4 ff.). Yet there is no reason to believe that these manifestations of an early form of Jewish Gnosticism would have been limited to the Lycus Valley.

A number of other places, such as Ephesus, Syria, Asia, Galatia, Corinth, and Cyprus, have also been suggested as the location of the readers, but these involve an even higher degree of speculation than those previously mentioned. When all the data have been considered, Rome remains the most attractive hypothesis concerning the destination of the letter. But this view necessarily remains only a hypothesis.

Date

If, then, it is tentatively accepted that the original readers of Hebrews were Jewish Christians forming a part of the larger Christian church in Rome, what may be said concerning the date of its composition? Because of the use of Hebrews by Clement of Rome, we can be certain that it was written earlier than A.D. 95. The most important factor in determining the approximate date of the epistle is the identification of the persecution referred to in 10:32 ff. According to this passage, sometime "in the past" the readers had suffered abuse, public insult, and the loss of possessions. There are three conspicuous Roman persecutions to consider: that under the Emperor Domitian in the eighties and nineties of the first century, that under Nero beginning in A.D. 64, and that under Claudius in A.D. 49. The first two of these, however, involved considerable loss of life, whereas our readers seem clearly not to have suffered a persecution that involved martyrdom (12:4). The persecution under Claudius, on the other hand, fits well the description given in 10:32 ff. Claudius expelled the Jews from Rome, and this included Jewish Christians (among whom were Priscilla and Aquila; cf. Acts 18:2). Indeed, according to the Roman historian Suetonius (*Life of Claudius* 25.4), the expulsion was due to riots having to do with one named "Chrestus" (probably a misspelling of *Christus* [or Christ]). These riots likely had to do with the recent conversion of Jews to faith in Christ and with the consequent turmoil caused within the Jewish community. The difficulties of this time would have afforded the readers ample opportunity to demonstrate the love and service for which the author compliments them.

A second important issue involved in dating Hebrews is whether it was written before or after the fall of Jerusalem and the destruction of the Temple in A.D. 70. The sacrificial ritual and the work of the levitical priesthood are described in the present tense throughout the book. Yet it must be remembered that what is described in this way is not the contemporary ritual but that described in the OT. Hence the description is set forth in ideal terms. It is furthermore the case that Christian writers after A.D. 70 can still describe the temple ritual using present tenses (e.g., Clement of Rome and Justin Martyr). Despite these observations, however, the present tense could be a sign that Hebrews was written before A.D. 70. It is highly remarkable—indeed, unbelievable—that had our author written after the destruction of the Temple he could have failed to mention it. For this historical fact could have been seen as the divine authentication of the author's central argument that the levitical ritual was outmoded and hence without significance (cf. 8:13). Indeed, it would have provided the perfect capstone to his attempt to persuade his readers not to return to their Judaism. It is, therefore, especially the silence about the events of A.D. 70 that lead us to the probability of an earlier date for the writing of the book. And if Nero's persecution had not yet taken place, as seems to be the case, then we are drawn to a date somewhere in the early sixties. Such a date seems compatible with the statement in 2:3 that the readers heard the gospel from those who had heard Jesus, assuming this statement to be literal and not simply a general statement about the integrity of the tradition. When and by whom in particular this message first came to the readers remain beyond our reach, however, as does knowledge about the founding of the church at Rome.

Author

A secure place in the NT canon came early for Hebrews with the attribution of the book to Paul in the Eastern church by the end of the second century. Clement of Alexandria (c. A.D. 200), following his teacher, held to Pauline authorship of Hebrews, but found it necessary because of the different character of its Greek to postulate that Paul had written the letter in Hebrew (Aramaic) and Luke had translated it into Greek. Several decades later Origen, although denying Pauline authorship (even of a Hebrew original), affirmed the content of the book to be essentially Pauline. After Origen, Pauline authorship of Hebrews remained unchallenged in the East, where by the middle of the third century it was placed immediately after Romans in the midst of the Pauline corpus in P^{46}, the earliest papyrus copy of that corpus to survive in the modern era.

Pauline authorship of Hebrews was disputed in the Western church until the late fourth and early fifth centuries. Only with Jerome and Augustine was Pauline authorship accepted, and then more because of the strong tradition confirming it in the Eastern church, as well as canonical considerations, than because of any genuine conviction on their part. This conclusion remained established in the West until the Reformation period, when Erasmus, Luther, and Calvin again challenged it.

It is difficult to accept Paul as the author of Hebrews for the following significant reasons. First, unlike all the undisputed Pauline letters, this writing is anonymous. There are, furthermore, no personal allusions in the letter that would lead us to the conclusion that Paul was the author. Nowhere does the personal experience of the author intrude into the content of the letter, and yet this was frequently the practice of Paul. Second, the author puts himself with those who have only a secondhand knowledge of the Lord (2:3), something that Paul vehemently denies (e.g., Gal. 1:12; 1 Cor. 9:1). He will admit no inferiority to the twelve apostles, the more so because exactly this charge was repeatedly leveled at him. Third, as was already noticed in the early church, the style of the Greek in this book—the most elegant in the NT—is unlike that of any of the Pauline epistles. It is, of course, possible to attribute this to the use of a different secretary, although this seems unlikely. Fourth, and most important, there are considerable theological differences between Hebrews and the Pauline letters. Most prominent among these is the major significance of the high priesthood of Christ for our author, something absent altogether from Paul's writings. In addition, several emphases common in Paul's letters are not found in Hebrews: union with Christ ("in Christ"), justification by faith, the opposition of faith and works, and the tension between flesh and spirit are lacking; the resurrection of Christ (mentioned only in 13:20) has given way to repeated emphasis on the exaltation to God's right hand; and Paul's common stress on the redemptive character of Christ's work is subordinated to an emphasis upon Christ's cleansing and sanctifying of his people. All the same, nothing in

Hebrews is contradictory of Paul; indeed there are many things in common between Paul and our author. This fact led Origen to conclude that although the book itself was not by Paul, much of its contents were of a Pauline character. This, together with the mention of Timothy (13:23), suggests that the author was associated with the Pauline circle.

Since, therefore, the ancient tradition that Paul was the author of Hebrews cannot be relied upon, we are left to speculate concerning the author's identity from the content of the book. An increasingly popular proposal, first made by Luther, is that the author was Apollos, that Jewish convert from Alexandria who is described in Acts 18:24 as "an eloquent speaker," possessing "a thorough knowledge of the Scriptures." It is also said of him that "with his strong arguments he defeated the Jews in public debates by proving from the Scriptures that Jesus is the Messiah" (Acts 18:28). Both his background and his abilities thus accord well with what we know of the author of Hebrews. Further, it is clear that Apollos knew Paul and indeed had indirectly through Priscilla and Aquila been instructed by him. He would also have been acquainted with Timothy. The only drawback to the suggestion that Apollos was the author of Hebrews is the lack of any ancient testimony supporting it. Because we know so little, Apollos can only be a guess. But it is a very good guess, and perhaps the best that can be offered.

Another name proposed is Barnabas, who does have the support of the early church father Tertullian (c. A.D. 200). Barnabas (see Acts 4:36) was a Levite and therefore would have been interested in, and knowledgeable about, the levitical system. He was from Cyprus, where he would have been influenced by Hellenistic culture and Greek of a high caliber. Another striking point, if of minor importance, is the translation of Barnabas' name (Acts 4:36) as "one who encourages" (lit., "son of encouragement") and the corresponding description of Hebrews as a "message of encouragement" (Heb. 13:22). The suggestion of Barnabas as the author of Hebrews is thus tenable, but it is still worth wondering whether Tertullian's view depended on an inference from the contents of the letter, as did Luther's, rather than any authentic tradition to that effect.

Several other names—all speculative—have been put forward at one time or another as supplying the identity of our author. These may be mentioned briefly with the main claim made in their support: Luke (similarities in style and in the content of Acts, especially Stephen's speech); Silvanus (similarities in style between 1 Peter and Hebrews); Philip (commending Paulinism to Jewish Christians of Jerusalem); Clement of Rome (nearly identical wording in places); Epaphras (in connection with the similarities with Colossians); Priscilla (based on the anonymity of the letter and her tutelage of Apollos; but see note on 11:32); and even the Virgin Mary (a "feminine" touch plus affinity with Luke 1–2)!

This multitude of candidates itself reflects the difficulty of discovering the identity of the author. It was Origen in the third century who, after surveying a list of possible authors, uttered the famous words: "But who wrote the epistle, in truth God knows" (quoted by Eusebius, *Ecclesiasti-calHistory* VI,25). Whoever he or she was, the author had an exceptional knowledge of the OT, interpreted the OT in terms of Christ, was probably acquainted with the Platonic idealism popular in Alexandria, enjoyed the best training in the use of the Greek language, and shared the universal perspective of the early Hellenistic Christians. He or she was probably a member of the Pauline circle and was very probably a converted Jew. The author's burden for the situation and plight of the readers is manifestly evident throughout the letter. He or she writes as one of them, who apparently has had previous contact with them in the form of some kind of ministry. More than this is difficult to say. If Origen was unable to establish the author's identity in the third century, it is unlikely that we shall be able to succeed where he failed.

Purpose

Discernment of the author's purpose in this letter of course depends to a very large degree on the identification of the addressees. There can be no question but that it is a major and probably *the* major purpose of the book to warn the readers of a danger and to exhort them to faithfulness (thus the frequent applications, e.g., 2:1–3; 3:6, 12–14; 4:1, 11–13; 6:1–12; 10:26–31, 35–39; 12:3–17; 13:9). If the argument presented above is correct, then it is the author's concern to warn Jewish Christian readers against apostasy to their former Judaism. It is in the accomplishing of this purpose that other basic emphases in the letter find their significance. Thus, the author understands that if the readers are to be motivated to remain faithful, they must come to an understanding of the true significance of Christianity. Accordingly, the author sets forth the incomparable superiority, together with the utter finality and definitive nature, of God's work in Jesus Christ. Christianity rightly understood is thus absolute in character and universal in scope. It is indeed nothing less than the fruition of God's intended purposes from the beginning and therefore the fulfillment of what "God spoke . . . many times and in many ways through the prophets" (1:1). The inescapable conclusion that must be drawn from this fact is that a turning away from Christianity to any other way—regardless of how excellent in itself—is altogether ruled out. The answer to any such tendency is to be found in an understanding of the true significance of Jesus Christ and his work. It is this, therefore, that accounts for the high Christology of the book together with its full explanation of his priestly work. Christianity by its nature is far more than a new Jewish sect. It is of absolute and universal significance.

All other motifs in Hebrews are subordinate to this central purpose of the author. Although there is evidence in the book that the author intends to combat heretical teachings of what was probably a form of Jewish Gnosticism (e.g., 9:10; 13:9; 1:4–2:16), this is secondary to his main concern for the readers.

Form and Structure

The literary genre of Hebrews is that of an exhortatory sermon. It begins, not with the usual identification of author and readers followed by a salutation and thanksgiving, but with an impressive christological prologue that in many respects resembles the prologue to the Gospel of John. Nevertheless, it is plain, as we have seen, that Hebrews is directed to a specific community. Moreover, the book does end like an epistle, including some items of personal information about the author's circumstances and those of a mutual friend, Timothy, as well as greetings and benedictions. (Some scholars have regarded chapter 13 as not originally belonging with the first twelve chapters but only added later to give the treatise the appearance of a letter. Admittedly it is not a part of the argument of the book and consists mainly of various ethical injunctions. Nevertheless, much of the content of chapter 13 is closely related to the emphases of chapters 1–12, and the way in which Pentateuchal material [i.e., material from Genesis and Deuteronomy] is elaborated and applied in 13:10–15 is quite similar to the use of the OT throughout the book.)

What we apparently have in the book of Hebrews, then, is a sermon-treatise that the author sent to a particular community as a letter. It is a sermon-treatise because of its distinctive combination of exhortation and argumentative discourse, but a letter because it is written for and sent to a specific community of Jewish Christians, probably in Rome.

Although the central purpose of Hebrews is clear, it is precisely this mixture of discourse and exhortation that sometimes makes the structure of the book and the sequence of the argument difficult to discern. In addition to the frequent insertion of exhortations, sections of the discourse are often bridged by no more than a common word, the same argument can be restated often with only slight variations, and summarizing sections can obscure the flow of the argument.

Scholarly study has shown that the literary style of the author involves an impressive artistry. Often, upon close examination, a concentric symmetry can be discovered. As examples, it may be noted that 2:1–4 is symmetrically shaped; the sequence of Christ–angels–Christ in 1:5–8 is repeated in 1:13–2:4; and 3:1 is found again in nearly symmetrical form in 4:14.

A further mark of the author's artistry (which in this case would seem to reveal a Jewish background) is his utilization of the OT and especially his midrashic treatment (i.e., practical exposition of the quotation, employing words taken from the quotation) of many of the quotations. The use of the OT is prominent throughout the book. Chapter 1, after the opening sentence, consists of an argument concerning the superiority of the Son to the angels based on seven OT quotations that are presented with virtually no comment. In 2:5–8 a quotation from Psalm 8:4–6 is presented followed by a midrashic commentary. Probably most impressive in this regard is the author's artistic construction of 3:12–4:11, which is based on the quotation (with several refrains) of Psalm 95:7–11 together with a midrashic application of the passage to the situation of the readers. The next major section of the book may be said to depend upon the citation of Psalm 2:7 and Psalm 110:4 in 5:5–6. The argument about the Melchizedekan priesthood, interrupted by a lengthy digression (5:11–6:12), resumes in 7:1, where (in addition to the use of Gen. 14) Psalm 110:4 is cited twice again. The argument of chapter 7 consists of a skillful elaboration of OT texts. Chapter 8 in turn depends upon the lengthy quotation from Jeremiah 31:31–34. In chapter 9 we again encounter a midrashlike presentation of material drawn from the Pentateuch, but with no explicit quotation. Chapter 10 combines a quotation of Psalm 40:6–8 with a brief midrashic commentary, followed by the requoting of Jeremiah 31:33–34 and an exhortation that concludes with the citation of Habakkuk 2:3–4. Chapter 11, of course, depends heavily upon the OT in its description of the heroes of the faith. In chapter 12 we again encounter in the midst of exhortation the quotation and midrashic treatment of OT material (Prov. 3:11–12 and Hag. 2:6).

Thus practically the entire argument of Hebrews rests on OT passages. Indeed, the author seems to have structured his argument around key quotations. His favorite practice is to quote an appropriate passage and then to comment on the passage in the manner of Jewish midrash, applying its truth to the readers in a most practical way. In this regard his procedure is reminiscent of the commentaries on Scripture produced by the Qumran community (cf. the commentaries on Habakkuk, Micah, Nahum, and Psalm 37 found among the Dead Sea Scrolls).

Interpretation of the Old Testament

The book of Hebrews is, then, very dependent upon the OT (about thirty actual citations and over seventy allusions have been counted). In his quotations the author regularly follows the Greek (LXX) rather than the Hebrew (or Masoretic) text that has come down to us. It is primarily this that accounts for differences between the citations as found in Hebrews and in our English OT.

In his interpretation of the OT our author uses what may be called a *Christocentric* hermeneutic. That is, Christ is seen to be the key to the real meaning of the OT as it can now be understood in this era of fulfillment. From this point of view, all of the OT points directly or indirectly to Christ, who is by definition the *telos* (goal) of God's saving purposes.

Obviously this kind of interpretation involves going beyond the meaning of the text in a literal sense—that is, beyond what the original writers of those texts meant by them. Yet because of the unity of God's saving purposes and the basic relationship of the past to the present as promise to fulfillment, the OT texts may be said to have a deeper or fuller sense (what theologians call *sensus plenior*), beyond what the Hebrew authors could be aware of because of their early position in the history of salvation. Only from the standpoint of fulfillment can the ultimate significance of the OT be seen. The dawning of eschatology* in Christ and the experience of fulfillment through his death and resurrection provide the writers of the NT, including the anonymous author of Hebrews, with a dramatically new point of orientation from which the OT can be read with new understanding.

This new perspective on the OT does not amount to the sanctioning of an arbitrary, frivolous, or allegorical interpretation of the OT. Although this kind of abuse of the OT did occur in the second-century church, as in forms of Judaism contemporary with the NT, the NT by comparison is

---

*Eschatology (from Gk. *eschaton*, "last thing") refers to the biblical teaching that God will act decisively "in the last days" to reveal himself, save his people, judge the world, and consummate his divine purposes.

relatively restrained and sober in its interpretation of the OT. It does not bring something alien to the text in its attempt to interpret it (as Philo did by interpreting Moses through Plato) but looks at the text in the light of its intended fulfillment. Thus, in the view of the early church and our author, a Christocentric interpretation of the OT entails the determination of the ultimate intention of the divine inspirer of Scripture and the recognition of the underlying unity of God's work in history.

Before Christ, no key was available to arrive at the ultimate intention and unity of Scripture. But now in Christ, God has disclosed the true goal of the OT promises (cf. 2 Cor. 1:20). Now the NT writers are able to understand the OT retrospectively and to conclude "This is that" (cf. Acts 2:16). (This type of interpretation was known in Jewish circles as *pesher* and is found amply in the writings of the Qumran community. The Qumranites, however, used *pesher* interpretation to portray their time as that immediately prior to eschatological fulfillment, whereas the NT writers used it to express the fulfillment that had already occurred in Christ. This is very clearly the viewpoint of the author of Hebrews, as can be seen, not only from his use of the OT, but from the entire content of his letter.)

Only from a perspective such as this can the fundamental importance of the OT and the interpretive procedure of our author be appreciated. In this he is not as distinctive among NT writers as he is, for example, in his midrashic utilization of the OT texts. For with the others he shares the excitement of the joy and fulfillment of the gospel.

Theological Perspective

In its broader outlines, the perspective of our author is in accord with other writers of the NT. In his high Christology and his use of "dualistic" language of the world above and the world below, he agrees with John. His similarities with Paul have often been noted. We mention only the high view of Christ, the centrality of the obedient suffering of Christ, the substitutionary atonement accomplished by Christ, and the contrasting of old and new covenants.

Certain theological emphases of the book, however, may stem from the Hellenistic Jewish circle represented by Stephen. Stephen (Acts 7) was to our knowledge the first in the early church to begin to articulate the true, and hence universal, significance of Christianity and the implications of this for the Jerusalem temple and Judaism. Our author's stress on these matters is very similar. There is, of course, a sense in which the OT is upheld in Hebrews. The OT is repeatedly appealed to and cited as the very oracles of God, who continues to speak through these ancient writings. Yet the authority of these writings is not self-contained but is recognized only in the sense that they point to what has occurred in and through Christ. For the old order, pointing to what yet lay in the future, was intrinsically incomplete. It was valid as preparation, but as one of its own authors admitted, something new was needed (Jer. 31:31 ff.). And thus our author, with a courage resembling Stephen's, points out the invalidity of the old now that the new has come. Like all NT writers, he works within the tension existing between the continuing authority of the OT, as a witness to the truth of Christianity, and the obvious sense in which the old must give away to the new. Indeed, for him the old no longer finds meaning in itself but only in that to which it points, God's definitive revelation in his Son.

The language and theology of Hebrews is that of a Christian who was a Hellenistic Jew. But how much was he influenced by his Hellenism? In particular, to what degree, if at all, does he owe his unique perspective about heavenly archetypes and earthly copies to the Alexandrian Jew Philo? Philo's view of reality was derived from the dualistic idealism of Plato, in which for every object perceived with the senses there is a corresponding perfect, changeless archetypal "Idea" or "Form" that can be known only through the intellect. There is an obvious similarity between this perspective and that of our author when he speaks of earthly copies of heavenly realities (e.g., 8:1, 5; 9:11, 23, 24; 10:1; 11:1, 3). The language of 8:5 may indeed seem Platonic in tone, yet it must be noted that this view of the earthly sanctuary of God as a copy of his heavenly sanctuary antedates Plato, being found within the Pentateuch (Exod. 25:9, 40; 26:30; 27:8; cf. 1 Chron. 38:19; Wisd. of Sol. 9:8). But more important is the fact that the dualism in Hebrews is not oriented toward the metaphysical questions of the philosophers. The author's basic framework is a temporal or eschatological one in which Christ and his work bring a fulfillment that corresponds with God's perfect and eternal purpose. The earthly copies and the heavenly realities correspond as promise and fulfillment. The promise is the shadow or copy; the fulfillment is the good things that have come. Christ on the cross, and thus in the historical process, accomplished what the earthly prototypes pointed toward. Because of its glorious nature and its definitive character, the fulfillment brought by Christ in history is expressed in the exalted language of the spiritual realm, the language of eternal reality. But this is far removed from the perspective of Plato and Philo.

The theology of Hebrews reflects the perspective of a Hellenistic Jew.

His style and vocabulary are clearly Hellenistic, but his orientation is much more that of a Jewish Christian with an overarching paradigm of promise and fulfillment. As a Hellenistic rather than a Palestinian Jew, he is more open to the radical consequences for the old now that the new has come. The theology of Hebrews is at the same time in basic accord with other NT writings. Thus, in agreement with Paul and others, Hebrews stresses the definitive, eschatological character and the universal significance of Christ.

It is apparent from the foregoing discussion that we are unable to provide more than tentative answers to such basic questions as the original readers, destination, date, and authorship. Fortunately, the greater part of the epistle can be interpreted effectively without solid information on these matters. Since the content of the book is what we do have, it must remain normative, and all hypotheses must be subject to its test.

Hebrews, like every book of the NT, must be understood in its own historical context, even if that must be, to some degree, a matter of inference. Yet there is also a sense in which the message of Hebrews transcends its own historical situation. This message has a universal applicability and an ongoing relevance to every generation of Christians whatever their cultural context. For *the main themes of this book*—the incomparable superiority and finality of Christ, the fulfillment of the old covenant, the establishment of the new covenant, the universal significance of the Christian faith—*must always be central wherever authentic Christianity is to be found.* But more than that, this book with its rich theological content is at the same time wonderfully practical. From its pages Christians of every era can learn of the pilgrimage of faith and of the great personal resources available to them through the finished work of Christ.

Note: A list of the abbreviations used in the commentary is found at the end of the book (see pp. 241–42). When an author's name is followed simply by a page number (rather than a book title or abbreviation), reference is to that author's commentary. Full bibliographical information for the commentaries can be found beginning on p. 243.

1

God's Definitive Revelation

In the past God spoke to our ancestors many times and in many ways through the prophets, ²but in these last days he has spoken to us through his Son. He is the one through whom God created the universe, the one whom God has chosen to possess all things at the end. ³He reflects the brightness of God's glory and is the exact likeness of God's own being, sustaining the universe with his powerful word. After achieving forgiveness for the sins of mankind, he sat down in heaven at the right side of God, the Supreme Power.

The magnificent opening verses of this passage provide an immediate expression of the author's theological perspective: he moves from past revelation to definitive revelation, from God's word to the OT "fathers" to his final word through his Son, Jesus Christ. He gives first his doctrine of Christ in order to set the tone for the entire book. The introductory christological prologue in these verses is thus similar to the prologue of the Fourth Gospel (John 1:1–18) in its function as well as in its Christocentric theology. The author, however, does not want to present such an exalted Christology without first indicating that God's word spoken in his Son is continuous with, and not alien to, what has preceded. What God has done in Christ is the climax of what he had begun to do in earlier times.

1:1 / God has spoken **many times and in many ways** in the past. This serves as a good characterization of what we call the Old Testament—the account of God's revelation of himself to Israel through not only his words, but also his acts. Moreover, our author identifies himself and his readers with those to whom God spoke in the past, **our ancestors** (lit., "fathers"). This statement is an affirmation of what the Jews have always been committed to: God has indeed spoken to us in the past **through the prophets. Prophets** here are to be understood as God's spokesmen, his representatives to people in every era and therefore as all the writers of Scripture, not just those referred to in the literature we designate as "the Prophets." This affirmation provides a strong sense of continuity, of reaching back; it says God began with Israel but is even now at work in the church and in what the church believes. A unity of revelation can be seen as we move from the past into the incomparable present.

1:2 / **In these last days** (lit., "at the end of these days") God has spoken through his Son. The writer uses eschatological language, that is, language of the last or end time, thereby affirming that we have entered the era of eschatology. In other words, God's plan has now come to fruition; we have entered a new age (cf. 9:26). A fundamental turning point has been reached as God speaks climactically, definitively, and finally through his Son. Any further speaking about what remains to happen in the future is but the elaboration of what has already begun. All that God did previously functions in a preparatory manner, pointing as a great arrow to the goal of Christ. This is the argument our author so effectively presents throughout the book. Christ is the *telos*, the goal and ultimate meaning of all that preceded.

But in what sense was the writer, or any of the writers of the NT for that matter, justified in referring to his time as the **last days**? The key to understanding this kind of statement (see also 4:3; 6:5; 9:26; 12:22 ff.), is found in the theological ultimacy of Christ. There is no way our writer can have recognized the reality of Jesus Christ—who he is and what he has done—and not have confessed this to be the last time. The sense in which it is "last" is not chronological but theological. The cross, the death, and the exaltation of Jesus point automatically to the beginning of the end. Theologically we have reached the turning point in the plan that God has had all through the ages, so by definition we are in the last days. Eschatology is of one theological fabric: when God has spoken through his Son eschatology has begun and we are necessarily in the last days theologically. These are the last days because of the greatness of what God has done. The surprise is, of course, that this period of eschatological fulfillment is so prolonged that these last days are not necessarily (though for any age it may turn out that they are) the last days chronologically.

This book, this opening passage, and particularly this verse point to the centrality of the Son and the superiority of the Son to all that preceded, all that exists now, and anything that might exist in the future. God has now spoken to us climactically **through his Son**, the one, as Paul puts it, "who is the 'Yes' to all of God's promises" (2 Cor. 1:20). The very mention of the Son has strong OT messianic overtones, as is evident immediately in the quotations in verse 5 of Psalm 2:7, "You are my Son; today I have become your Father," and 2 Samuel 7:14, "I will be his Father, and

2

he will be my Son." Indeed, the remainder of the chapter, with its numerous OT quotations, points to the unique identity of the Son as the Promised One, the Messiah designated by God to bring about the fulfillment of God's great plan and purpose.

The true nature of the Son is then expounded by our author in seven glorious phrases that portray his incomparable superiority. He is, in the first instance, **the one through whom God created the universe**. (In the original text this is the second clause. GNB transposes the first two clauses for the clarity of logical sequence, moving from creation to eschatological possession, though thereby weakening the connection between sonship and inheritance.) The Son is God's agent in the creation of the universe of all space and all time—in short, of all that exists. This view of Christ is found also in the Fourth Gospel (John 1:3, "Through him God made all things; not one thing in all creation was made without him"), and in Paul (Col. 1:16, "God created the whole universe through him"; 1 Cor. 8:6, "through whom all things were created"). The background of this view is possibly to be found in the concept of Divine Wisdom, which, personified, is instrumental in creation according to Proverbs 8:27–31 (cf. Wisd. of Sol. 9:1 f., 9).

Secondly, the Son is described as the one **chosen to possess all things at the end**. In the Hebrew culture, to be a son means to be an heir, especially when one is the only or unique son. Therefore, the Son of God, by virtue of his sonship, is appointed literally "the heir of all things." To the messianic Son of Psalm 2:7 (quoted above) are also spoken the words "Ask, and I will give you all the nations; the whole earth will be yours" (Ps. 2:8). The Son is thus of central significance at the beginning, in creation, and at the end, in inheritance. Paul's language is parallel: "God created the whole universe through him and for him" (Col. 1:16).

1:3 / The third and fourth clauses in this characterization of Christ turn to the manner in which the Son is a true expression of the father. **He reflects** (lit., "is") **the brightness of God's glory**. The word **brightness** (occurring only here in the NT) can also be translated "radiance" or "radiant light." Barclay effectively paraphrases: "The Son is the radiance of his glory just as the ray is the light of the sun." Again a parallel is found in the personification of wisdom, this time in the apocryphal book The Wisdom of Solomon (7:25 f.): "For she is a breath of the power of God and pure emanation of the glory of the Almighty . . . she is a reflection of eternal light, a spotless mirror of the working of God, and an image of his goodness." Other NT writers hold a similar view of Christ. In the prologue of the Gospel of John, Christ is designated "the real light—the light that comes into the world and shines on all mankind" (John 1:9), in whom "we saw his glory, the glory which he received as the Father's only Son" (John 1:14). For John, as for our author, Jesus expresses the brilliant glory of God. Paul, too, speaks of the light that Christ brought, referring to "the knowledge of God's glory shining in the face of Christ" (2 Cor. 4:6; cf. 4:4).

The next clause, **he . . . is the exact likeness of God's own being**, is simply a more explicit way of expressing what the author has just said. The Son is a perfect representation of God's being "just as the mark is the exact impression of the seal" (Barclay). The thought is again reminiscent of Christology elsewhere in the NT, for example in Paul's statements that Christ is "the exact likeness of God" (2 Cor. 4:4) and "the visible likeness of the invisible God" (Col. 1:15), although in these two instances the Greek word (*eikōn*, from which comes the English word "icon") is different from that used here. John expressed the same idea in the words "whoever has seen me has seen the Father" (John 14:9). It is to be noted further that it is **God's own being** that is expressed so accurately, the word **being** here to be understood as "substance" or "essence." These two parallel clauses at the beginning of verse 3 very obviously speak of the uniqueness of the Son. They also point to the extraordinary connection between the Father and Son. In order for the Son to be the kind of direct, authentic, and compelling expression of the Father described in these clauses—for him to be the radiance of God's glory and the impress of His very essence—he must participate somehow in the being of God itself, that is, he must himself be deity to accomplish the wonderful mission described here. Our author would have us conclude, without denying the distinction between Father and Son, that the Son is of the same order of existence as God, and so with God over against all else that exists.

As the Son was instrumental in the creation of the universe (v. 2), so the continuing significance of the Son is seen, in the fifth clause, in his **sustaining the universe with his powerful word**. Philosophers of every age are prone to ask what it is that underlies reality—that is, what dynamic sustains and makes coherent all that exists. Our author, further revealing his Christocentric perspective, finds the answer in the mighty word of the Son. This view also finds parallels in Paul and John. When John uses "Word" (*logos*) to describe Jesus, he uses a term that has both Jewish and Greek associations. For the Greek philosophers *logos* was the underlying principle of rationality that made the world orderly, coherent, and intelligible. Without using the technical term *logos*, Paul argues in similar fashion: "He is before all things, and in him all things hold together" (Col. 1:17, RSV). Although the author of Hebrews does not use the specific term *logos* in this passage, the idea that Christ sustains the universe, is behind it all, and keeps it all going (as the present participle **sustaining** indicates), is parallel.

Our author, however, is not content simply to mark off the incomparable character of the Son against all others and all else, as he has done in the first five clauses. He wants also to get to one of the main points of the epistle, the atoning work of the Son, for this too is vitally a part of and dependent upon the Son's uniqueness. What makes these the last days is the "once-and-for-all" (to borrow language that will be encountered later in the epistle) **achieving of forgiveness for the sins of mankind**. This indeed is the pre-eminent work of the Son. The "cleansing of sins" (a literal translation) may seem strange in the midst of glorious clauses pointing to the deity of the Son. This phrase, after all, describes the work of the high priest and, though impressive in itself, would seem familiar enough to a Jewish reader. With the insertion of this clause, however, the author anticipates a main argument of the book (cf. chaps. 9 and 10): the work of the high priest is not efficacious in itself but rather foreshadows the priestly work of the one who alone can make atonement for sins. Only God in the Son can accomplish the sacrifice that makes possible the cleansing and the forgiveness of sins (see Rom. 3:24–26). Thus the cleansing of sins rightly belongs with phrases that describe the uniqueness of the Son in his relationship to God.

When he had thus accomplished the purpose of his incarnation, **he sat down in heaven at the right side of God, the Supreme Power** (lit., "the majesty on high"). The words of this seventh and final clause convey a sense of completion and fulfillment of God's purpose. They are drawn from a messianic psalm of the OT (Ps. 110) that is exceptionally important to our author's argument. Psalm 110:1 is cited or alluded to here and in 1:13 (more fully); 8:1; 10:12–13, and 12:2. Psalm 110:4, the Melchizedek passage, is cited or alluded to in 5:6, 10; 6:20; and throughout chap. 7 (vv. 3, 11, 15, 17, 21, 24, 28). Why is this psalm so important to our author? Two main arguments of the epistle can be supported by Psalm 110: the incomparable superiority of Christ (as revealed in his exaltation to the right hand of God) and the extraordinary high priesthood of Christ (as paralleled and prefigured by Melchizedek). The ascension of Christ to the position of power and authority at the side of the Father is the vindication of the true identity of the one who suffered and died in accomplishing the forgiveness of sins. This view is found often in the NT and is

5

regularly associated with the ascension of Christ. "So the one who came down is the same one who went up, above and beyond the heavens, to fill the whole universe with his presence (Eph. 4:10); "Christ who has gone to heaven and is at the right side of God, ruling over all the angels and heavenly authorities and powers" (1 Pet. 3:22). Jesus alludes to Psalm 110:1 in the Synoptic tradition (see Mark 12:36 and 14:63, both with parallels in Matthew and Luke). What the psalmist promised now had come to pass—hence the note of completion and finality. That he has **sat down** signifies the completion of his atoning work (cf. 10:11–12).

We have come to the end of this important christological prologue. It sets the tone of the book and has been put first by the author in order that it may inform our understanding of all that follows. The Son is set forth as the embodiment of the three main offices of the OT: prophet (speaking for God), priest (accomplishing forgiveness of sins), and king (reigning with God at his right hand). But he is even more than this marvelous combination of traits can express. He is the one through whom and for whom all that exists has been created, the one who sustains it, and who is the very expression of God's glory and essence.

The person of Christ is the key to understanding this epistle.

Additional Notes

1:1 / The opening sentence in the Greek is skillfully constructed from the literary standpoint, beginning with effective alliteration and measured cadence. See D. W. B. Robinson, "The Literary Structure of Hebrews 1:1–4," *Australian Journal of Biblical Archaeology* 1 (1972), pp. 178–86. **Many times** (lit., "in many parts") . . . **many ways** are two Greek words occurring only here in the NT, whose nuance is captured nicely in NEB: "in fragmentary and varied fashion." On **prophets** as spokesmen of God, see Friedrich, *"prophētēs," TDNT*, vol. 6, pp. 830 ff.

1:2 / **In these last days** is language of the Greek translation of the OT (the LXX) commonly used for describing the eschatological expectation of the prophets (e.g., Jer. 23:20; Ezek. 38:16; Dan. 10:14). The First Coming of Christ and the Second Coming of Christ are closely related theologically in that both are eschatological in character. This being so it is normal to expect that the second will quickly follow the first. The theological interconnectedness of Christ's work implies (but does not necessitate) the chronological imminence of the Second Coming. Christians must be careful to preserve the eschatological character of Christ's first work without weakening their expectation of his future work. For a masterly description of the tension of this as the time of the end yet not *the* end, see O. Cullmann, *Christ and Time*, trans. F. V. Filson (Philadelphia: Westminster Press, 1964). On the eschatology of Hebrews, see C. K. Barrett, "The Eschatology of the Epistle to the Hebrews," in *The Background of the New Testament and Its Eschatology* (Festschrift for C. H. Dodd), ed. W. D. Davies and D. Daube (Cambridge: Cambridge University Press, 1964), pp. 363–93.

On the designation of the Messiah as the Son of God, see Lohse on *hyios* in *TDNT*, vol. 8, pp. 360 ff.; see too M. Hengel, *The Son of God* (Philadelphia: Fortress, 1976), pp. 85–88; on the Christology of Hebrews see V. Taylor, *The Person of Christ* (London: Macmillan, 1958), pp. 89–98.

Universe is literally "the ages"; hence Barclay's translation, "the present world and the world to come" (cf. 6:5). For "age" as a spatial term meaning "world" see Sasse on *aiōn* in *TDNT*, Vol. 1, pp. 203 f.

The eschatological dimensions of "inheritance" and its connection with sonship are important not only for Christ, but for his people who enjoy their sonship by adoption and are made fellow-heirs with Christ according to Paul (Rom. 8:17) and Peter (1 Pet. 3:7). For our author the inheritance of the saints is important. See 6:12, 17; 9:15; 10:36; 11:8.

1:3 / Some scholars have argued that v. 3 was originally part of a confessional hymn. The opening relative pronoun "who" (*hos*), the characteristic participles, and the content all point to this possibility. (On these points see the similarity in other "hymns" in New Testament epistles, e.g., Col. 1:15, Phil. 2:6 ff., and 1 Tim. 3:16.) See further J. T. Sanders, *The New Testament Christological Hymns*, SNTSM no. 15 (Cambridge: Cambridge University Press, 1971), pp. 19 f. and pp. 92 ff. It is a striking fact that the major christological passages of the NT bear marks of being adapted from hymns. The best theology, after all, is better sung than spoken.

This verse contains two key words that are found only here in the entire NT, "brightness" (*apaugasma*) and "exact likeness" (*charaktēr*). The former has the active sense of "effulgence" as well as the passive sense of "reflection" in its occurrences in Philo, who uses the word to describe what God breathed into man at his creation. The active is probably the nuance here. (See R. P. Martin in *NIDNTT*, vol. 2, pp. 289 f.) The latter word, also found in Philo, means accurate representation in the manner of an "impress" or "stamp," as of a coin to a die. (See Wilckens in *TDNT*, vol. 9, pp. 418–23.) The Greek word *katharismos* that underlies **forgiveness** in our translation is a technical term for cultic cleansing and is so used in the LXX and even within the NT, where it can signify "ritual washing" (John 2:6; 3:25) or, more generally, "purification" (Luke 2:22; 2 Pet. 1:9). The use of the word here is no accident given the central argument of our author about the sacrificial ritual of the temple finding its goal in the work of Christ. **Forgiveness** for **sins** is used in an absolute sense, and thus the added words of our translation of **mankind**, though not in the original text, are appropriate.

Ps. 110 is of very great importance in the early church. Understood widely as bearing messianic significance by Jewish interpreters before the time of Jesus, this psalm was seen to be vividly fulfilled in the risen and ascended Christ whom the Church now confessed as sovereign Lord. See the excellent study by David M. Hay, *Glory at the Right Hand: Psalm 110 in Early Christianity*, SBLM no. 18 (Nashville and New York: Abingdon, 1973). The extensive use of Ps. 110 by the author of Hebrews is striking and is to be explained by the effective way in which its content supports the arguments of the epistle. G. W. Buchanan, however, probably goes too far in describing Hebrews itself as "a homiletical midrash based on Ps. 110." *To the Hebrews*, Anchor Bible (New York: Doubleday, 1972) p. xix.

The Greek text of the prologue studiously avoids unnecessary use of the word "God" (*theos*), as is befitting a document addressed to Jewish readers who regarded the word as very holy. Thus, apart from the initial use in v. 1, the word does not occur again. Our translation uses it six times, supplying it for pronouns and circumlocutions. Two circumlocutions may be noted in v. 3: "the glory" and "the majesty on high," the latter represented in GNB by **the Supreme Power**.

Christ Is Superior to the Angels in His Deity

HEBREWS 1:4–14

---

[4]The Son was made greater than the angels, just as the name that God gave him is greater than theirs, [5]For God never said to any of his angels,

"You are my Son;
today I have become your Father."

Nor did God say about any angel,

"I will be his Father,
and he will be my Son."

[6]But when God was about to send his first-born Son into the world, he said,

"All of God's angels must worship him."

[7]But about the angels God said,

"God makes his angels winds
and his servants flames of fire."

[8]About the Son, however, God said:

"Your kingdom, O God, will last[a] forever and ever!
You rule over your[b] people with justice.

[9]You love what is right and hate what is wrong.
That is why God, your God, has chosen you
and has given you the joy of an honor far greater

than he gave to your companions."

[10]He also said,

"You, Lord, in the beginning created the earth,
and with your own hands you made the heavens.

[11]They will disappear, but you will remain;
they will all wear out like clothes.

[12]You will fold them up like a coat,
and they will be changed like clothes.

But you are always the same, and your life never ends."

[13]God never said to any of his angels:

"Sit here at my right side until
I put your enemies as a footstool under your feet."

[14]What are the angels, then? They are spirits who serve God and are sent by him to help those who are to receive salvation.

a. Your kingdom, O God, will last; *or* God is your kingdom.
b. your: *some manuscripts have* his.

With verse 4 the author turns to the first important point he wishes to establish, the superiority of Christ to the angels. The great concern given to this issue, which occupies the remainder of chapter 1 and most of chapter 2, probably strikes us as odd since we do not have the same consciousness of angels as the ancient world.

So important was the idea of angels in the first century that one encounters it in both Greek and Jewish religious thinking. In the former we have to do with Gnosticism, which stressed a special knowledge leading to the experience of salvation. Fundamental to the Gnostic perspective is a dualism between spirit and matter. God is pure spirit and therefore good; we, on the other hand, have physical bodies that involve us in the evil that is intrinsic to matter (salvation consists in the escape of the soul from the body). Mediating between God and us are his emanations in the form of a host of spiritual beings who are God's agents of rule, and who thereby elicit worship. These spiritual beings, having no material bodies, are regarded as intrinsically superior to Jesus (unless it be argued, as it was by Christian Gnostics, that Jesus never had a real, physical body, but only appeared to have one).

Even within the realm of Jewish thought, which affirmed the goodness of matter and shunned the dualism of the Gnostics, God was perceived as remote in his transcendence, and the need for angelic intermediaries was felt. Thus, in much of the intertestamental and rabbinic literature the role of angels is considered vitally important. We do not know whether the situation addressed in Hebrews stems primarily from Gnostic or Jewish circles or from some indeterminate mixture of the two. If, however, we are correct in arguing that the recipients of the epistle are Jews who are in danger of lapsing back into their Judaism, it may well be that they found it expedient to regard Christ as an angel and thereby to avoid the stumbling-block of Christ as deity. For our author it is intolerable that Christ be regarded as less than the angels or even that he be regarded as an angel himself. The only acceptable view is that which sees the Son as superior to the angelic host—one who belongs on the side of God against all else that exists, incomparable in his splendor.

1:4 / **The Son was made greater than the angels** refers not to the character of the Son from the beginning, but to the last clause of verse 3, which refers to the ascension of Christ. In this exaltation to the right hand of the Father, the Son comes to hold a position that indeed was always his by virtue of his identity, but which was set aside during the incarnation. The ascension is a dramatic attestation of the true identity of the Son and thus also of his superiority to angels. By so much has the son been **made greater than the angels**. In this statement the author employs one of his favorite words in describing the definitive and final character of the Son and his work, the comparative **greater** (lit., "better").

Since in the ascension the Son assumed the position that was in fact rightfully his, he also in this event was given the name that is rightfully his. In the NT the ascension is regularly associated with the bestowing of a name upon the ascended Christ. Behind this association lies the Hebrew view of names as more than labels, but as actually connected with the nature and character of what is named. Thus the name "Son," which is the name referred to here (see the next verse), although in a sense always appropriate to describe Jesus Christ, assumes a special appropriateness in the event that newly installed him at the right hand of God. This installation, following the completion of the work of the incarnate Son wherein he revealed God and accomplished redemption, now afforded the actual reality that coincided with the meaning of the name. In Paul's epistles the ascension is also linked with the granting of a name. In the classic passage Paul writes, "for this reason God raised him to the highest place above and gave him the name that is greater than any other name" (Phil. 2:9; see also Eph. 1:20–21). In this instance the name is "Lord" (*kyrios*), a title comparable in meaning to "Son." Our author's argument is that the ascension of the Son to the right hand of God gives him a unique position and name, marking him out as far superior to the angels.

1:5 / In order to strengthen this argument, the author now gives a series of seven OT quotations, the meaning of which he regards as rather evident, since he does not, apart from an occasional introductory note, bother to interpret them for us. His approach to the OT is here, and throughout the book, manifestly Christocentric. That is, regarding Jesus Christ as the goal of all the preceding works and words of God, the author finds in him the ultimate meaning of it all and thus the key to its proper understanding. In light of the fulfillment that has come, a deeper and truer meaning of the OT may now be perceived. (A discussion of the author's hermeneutics may be found in the Introduction).

The first quotation is drawn from Psalm 2, a psalm that has its own historical setting. Psalm 2 was originally a royal psalm composed for the coronation of some Israelite king of the past. Yet such is the content of the psalm that Jewish interpreters before the NT era saw a deeper meaning in the words than a straightforward historical reading can establish. Though not directly prophetic, the psalm is nonetheless seen to anticipate that special Anointed One who would bring with him judgment and blessing—judgment for the wicked and blessing to Israel in the deliverance that she longed for. The historical king is thus a foreshadowing of the King to come. And the psalm is thus appropriately designated as "messianic." By "messianic" is simply meant that this "anointed" deliverer is in view (the Hebrew word "Messiah" and the Greek word "Christ" mean "the Anointed One"). Psalm 2 specifically refers to such an "anointed" one (2:2, RSV) who will be given all the nations of the earth and who will bring judgment (2:8–9). This Anointed One, or Messiah, is identified as uniquely related to God: **you are my Son; today I have become your Father** (Ps. 2:7). It is indeed pre-eminently from the background of this psalm, identifying God's Messiah as his Son, that our author can use the title "Son" in the absolute sense in which it occurs in the christological prologue (see vs. 2). Psalm 2:7 is cited again by our author in Hebrews 5:5, and alluded to in 7:28. It is an important text in the early church (see Acts 13:33) and, combined with Isaiah 42:1, is applied to Jesus both at his baptism (Mark 1:11 and parallels) and at the transfiguration (see Mark 9:7 and parallels; cf. 2 Pet. 1:17). The **today** is understood most appropriately as referring to the resurrection (see Rom. 1:4), or especially the ascension, given the context of our verse. God never spoke so gloriously of angels.

The second of this chain of quotations also refers to a special Son, this time with words drawn from the Davidic covenant: **I will be his Father and he will be my Son** (2 Sam. 7:14; see also the parallel, 1 Chron. 17:13). Again a king is in view, a descendant of David, whom grammatico-historical exegesis most naturally defines as Solomon. He will build a temple and with David will be at the head of a dynasty that lasts forever (2 Sam. 7:13, 16). But such is the glorious nature of this promise that this "son of David" comes to merge with the expectation of a messianic king who will bring the fulfillment of God's promises. The passage accordingly was seen by Jewish interpreters before the time of Jesus to have a deeper meaning than had yet been realized in any descendant of David. This passage, like Psalm 2:7, was regarded as having a distinctly eschatological significance. Indeed, the combination of these two texts in just such a perspective is encountered in the literature of the covenant community at Qumran on the shore of the Dead Sea, just prior to the NT era. The repeated references to Jesus in the Gospels as the "Son of David" identify him at once with the Messiah and with the Davidic covenant (for the latter see Luke 1:32, 69 and Rom. 1:3). In these first two quotations the author establishes the unique sonship of the Son and thus the superiority of the Son on the basis of the authority of Scripture (which he can presuppose in writing to Jewish readers).

1:6 / The third quotation consists of words contained only in the LXX (Deut. 32:43). All of God's angels must worship him, although there is also a parallel in Psalm 97:7, "bow down all the gods before the Lord" (GNB, margin), where the LXX has "all his angels." Most probably our author here as elsewhere depends upon the LXX version of the OT and thus upon Deuteronomy 32:43. What is remarkable in this passage (also in Ps. 97:7) is that the one who is worshipped is the Lord, or Yahweh (i.e., the personal name of God, consisting of the consonants YHWH), and thus the Son is identified with Yahweh of the OT. This quotation is utilized primarily for the reference to the worshiping angels. But if the Son is in mind in words spoken to the Lord then the deity of the Son is clearly implied and thus, obviously, his superiority to the angels.

1:7 / The fourth quotation presents a description of the function of angels that itself puts angels in a decidedly subservient position. The source of the quotation is again the LXX (Ps. 104:4). Angels are likened to the natural elements that function at God's bidding and thus are also his messengers. Angels are spirits who serve God, as our author will put it in verse 14. There is also an implied contrast between the changeability and transitoriness of wind and fire (and hence of the angels) and the unchanging character and permanence of the Son in verse 12, "you are always the same and your life never ends" (see also 13:8). The angels are indeed God's agents, but they are distinctly subordinate agents, not of central significance, not to be likened to God or the Son.

1:8–9 / In a fifth quotation, Psalm 45:6–7, words originally used at a royal wedding are understood to have their fullest application to the Son of God. The king originally in view was an Israelite monarch, but so glorious are the words spoken to him that their ultimate fulfillment can only be in the messianic King, the Son of David, the Son now at the right hand of the Father. The opening words of the quotation are ambiguous both in the Hebrew and the LXX. Either **God** is to be understood as vocative, "O God," and God is thus the addressee, or "God" is the subject and **kingdom** (lit., "throne") is a predicate nominative, "God is your kingdom" (as in margin of GNB). The latter does not make much sense but is sometimes preferred because of the difficulty of God speaking to another as God (as in v. 9), as well as the difficulty of understanding the original historical context wherein a king of Israel is addressed as God. The latter difficulty can be explained as hyperbole for the king who functions as God's representative in his office. In understanding these words as applying to Christ, however, our author takes the words literally and not hyperbolically. He thus affirms the deity of the Son (as we have

13

seen him do also in v. 6). The Son is not simply the representative of God; he *is* God by virtue of his nature and function. The **kingdom** that **will last forever and ever** and will be characterized by **justice** is the promised messianic kingdom with its eschatological overtones.

In verse 9 the word **God**, as it first occurs, may possibly mean "O God," thus continuing the address to God in this passage. (Thus the NEB: "therefore, O God, thy God has set thee above thy fellows.") The one addressed has an unrivaled position of honor. The messianic dimensions of this passage are heightened by the words **God has chosen you** (lit., "God has anointed you"). The appropriateness of this passage for the Son who is the Messiah was not lost to our author or his readers. The Anointed One who is the consummation of God's purposes is rightly addressed as God. He is thus without peer, having been given **honor far greater** than any of his **companions**. This last word may contain an allusion to the reality of the incarnation for it is the cognate to the verb "shared" in 2:14; more specifically it may refer to all other anointed kings in whose lineage the Son stands. Although there is no specific reference to angels in this quotation, the link with the preceding quotation is such that a contrast to the angels remains the intention of the author. If this Son is who this psalm says, the superiority of the Son is transparently obvious.

1:10-12 / The longest in this chain of quotations is the sixth (Ps. 102:25–27). In the midst of his troubles the psalmist praises the LORD (Yahweh) as providing the permanence and security that he so painfully lacks. It is understood that these words are meant by our author to apply to the Son. What is in view is the eternality of the Son as over against all that is transitory. The opening lines, **you, Lord, in the beginning created the earth . . . made the heavens**, echo the statement of the prologue that the Son is "the one through whom God created the universe" (v. 2). The Son is identified as the LORD (Yahweh). So far as the created order is concerned, the time is coming when it will be revamped, altered completely. In metaphorical language of the last times, the LORD **will fold up** the heavens and earth **like a coat, and they will be changed like clothes**. But in the midst of eschatological crisis with all else appearing to fail, **you are always the same, and your life never ends**, the psalmist affirms. There is nothing else of which it can be said that it will remain forever, except God and what he chooses to sustain. Angels are even less in view in this passage than in the preceding one. The Son is being extolled as God. And the christological prologue is thus undergirded by the quotation of these OT passages.

1:13 / The seventh and climactic quotation introduces Psalm 110:1, that passage of such fundamental importance to our author, which we first encountered at the end of verse 4 in the seventh and climactic clause of the christological prologue. Here, however, we have the verse quoted in full. Again in mind is the ascension of Christ to the position of unparalleled honor and authority at the right hand of the Father. There he exercises his present reign, yet strangely, in a period when his enemies are not yet a **footstool under your feet**. This aspect doubtless enhanced the meaningfulness of this verse for the early church, grasping as it does the tension between realized (the fulfillment that has already occurred) and future (the wrapping up that still remains) eschatology. For our author the psalm is doubly meaningful because of the reference to the priesthood of Melchizedek and the utility of this reference for the author's main argument (see below, 5:6–10 and chap. 7). The words that introduce this quotation again raise specifically the superiority of the Son to the angels. This verse, describing the vindicating capstone of the Son's completed ministry, serves as one of the basic weapons in our author's arsenal of arguments concerning the superiority of the person and work of the Son.

1:14 / What then is a realistic estimate of angels and their function? **They are** indeed **spirits**; but, as has been shown, they have a subordinate role of serving God. God's concern is not with angels, but with us, and he accordingly sends them to bring help to **those who are to receive salvation**. God and the Son are the source of our salvation, as the author will demonstrate so boldly in this epistle. By God's grace, his servants serve us in and toward this end. The idea of personal aid from angels builds on an OT motif (e.g., Ps. 91:11), recalls the ministry of angels to Jesus (Matt. 4:11; compare 26:53), and is meant as a note of personal comfort and encouragement in the face of real difficulty for these Jewish Christians.

Additional Notes

The major concern with angels in the opening chapters of Hebrews has helped some scholars to reach conclusions about the addressees of the epistle. T. W. Manson saw a correlation between the argument of the author of Hebrews and that pursued by Paul against the Jewish-Gnostic, Colossian heresy in which, among other things, the worship of angels is mentioned as a specific problem (Col. 2:18, cf. 2:15). He concluded that Apollos (as he argues) wrote Hebrews to the church at Colossae. (See "The Problem of the Epistle to the Hebrews," *Studies in the Gospels and Epistles* [Manchester: Manchester University Press, 1962].) Hughes finds the concern with angels supportive of his tentative conclusion that the addressees were inclined toward the teaching of the Dead Sea Sect wherein angels played an exceptionally important role (p. 52 f.). Montefiore, on the other hand, points out convincingly that the concern with angels need point to nothing more specific than the probability that the Jewish readers would have found it easier to retain their Jewish presuppositions and a form of Christian experience if they were able to regard Jesus as merely an angel (p. 41 f.). Angelology, after all, was in full flower in the intertestamental and rabbinic literature.

1:4 / This verse introduces the author's favorite word in drawing the contrast between new and old, "better" (*kreissōn*, alternately spelled *kreittōn*). The word occurs thirteen times, being used in reference to the Son (1:4), Melchizedek (7:7), salvation (6:9), covenant (7:22; 8:6), sacrifice (9:23; 12:24), promises (8:6), present possession (10:34), and future expectation (7:19; 11:16, 35, 40). The frequent use of this word is exactly in line with the central argument of the book.

On the theological significance of the ascension, see J. G. Davies, "Ascension of Christ," in *DCT*, pp. 15 f.

1:5 / There is a good possibility that the author borrows this chain of quotations (vv. 5–13) from a previously existing collection. Evidence from Qumran indicates that collections of Scripture texts were used in the first century and, indeed, suggests that Ps. 2:7 and 2 Sam. 7:14 had been combined long before the writing of Hebrews. (See J. M. Allegro, "Further Messianic References in Qumran Literature," *JBL* 75 [1956], pp. 174 ff.; J. A. Fitzmyer, "4Q Testimonia and the New Testament," *Theological Studies* 15 [1957], pp. 513–37.) The dependence of our author on such a source is of course speculative and it remains possible that he was himself the collector of these OT passages. See J. W. Thompson, "The Structure and Purpose of the Catena in Heb. 1:5–13," *CBQ* 38 (1976), pp. 352–63. More generally on the subject of OT quotation in Hebrews (in addition to the material in the Introduction), see R. N. Longenecker, *Biblical Exegesis in the Apostolic Period* (Grand Rapids: Eerdmans, 1975), pp. 158–85; G. B. Caird, "Exegetical Method of the Epistle to the Hebrews," *Canadian Journal of Theology* 5 (1959), pp. 44–51; S. Kistemaker, *The Psalm Citations in Hebrews* (Amsterdam, 1961); S. Sowers, *The Hermeneutics of Philo and Hebrews* (Zurich, 1965).

Ps. 2 is an exceptionally important messianic text in the first century both in Jewish and Christian interpretation. For the former we have mentioned its presence in the Dead Sea Scrolls and may add Psalms of Solomon 17:23–27. For the latter, in addition to the three occurrences of 2:7 in Hebrews (see 5:5 and 7:28), see also Matt. 3:17, 2 Pet. 1:17, and especially Acts 13:33. Also noteworthy in the early Christian proclamation is the citation of Ps. 2:1–2 in Acts 4:25–26. Finally, several allusions to other verses of Ps. 2 are also found in Revelation.

Ps. 2:7 is a fundamental text for our author, whose Christology is expressed pre-eminently in the concept "Son of God" (4:4; 6:6; 7:3; 10:29). Son, used absolutely as in the prologue, of course carries the meaning "Son of God." In this sonship lies the uniqueness of Jesus, who participates fully in the deity of the

Father. To be the "Son of God" is to be one with God. See O. Cullmann, *The Christology of the New Testament* (Philadelphia: Westminster Press [ET], 1959) pp. 303–305.

The citation of 2 Sam. 7:14 implies the title "Son of David," with its clear messianic connotation. That the "Son of David," the Messianic Descendant, signified the dawning of eschatology was plain, but that he was also to be the Son of God was not understood prior to the fulfillment experienced by the church in the resurrection and exaltation of Jesus.

1:6 / The fact that our author regularly quotes the LXX is nowhere more evident than in the present quotation from Deut. 32:43, which is not found in the Hebrew Bible. The LXX is a pre-Christian translation of the OT (by a number of translators from the third century B.C. to the Christian era) and thus rests upon earlier Hebrew manuscripts than those that were handed down as canonical authority by the Masoretes (Jewish scholars who added vowels to the consonantal text and faithfully transmitted the text into the Middle Ages). The fact that in the first century divergent Hebrew manuscripts of the same book were occasionally available is demonstrated by the discovery of the present quotation in a Hebrew manuscript of Deuteronomy among the scrolls at Qumran (cave 4). The LXX translator apparently had this verse in the Hebrew manuscript that he translated. (See F. M. Cross, Jr., *The Ancient Library of Qumran*, [New York: Doubleday, 1958], pp. 181 ff.) The LXX is important for our author's theology and argument throughout the book. Here, for example, it may be pointed out that the LXX's translation of YHWH as *kyrios* (LORD) in the context of our quotation, serving as the antecedent of "him," has facilitated our author's use of this quotation in applying it to Christ. Since *kyrios* is the favorite title given to Christ in the early church, it becomes easy to identify Christ with the *kyrios* (YHWH) of the LXX. In v. 10 ("You, Lord") the identification is explicit. See further, K. J. Thomas, "The Old Testament Citations in Hebrews," *NTS* 11 (1964-65), pp. 303–25; T. F. Glasson, "Plurality of Divine Persons and the Quotations in Hebrews 1, 6 ff.," *NTS* 12 (1966), pp. 270–72.

In the words that introduce this quotation, **when God was about to send**, the time of the sending of the Son into the world is unclear, that is, whether this refers to his earthly ministry or his second advent. For the former, one may note the reference to angels in Luke 2:13 f. (or possibly Matt. 4:11); angels are of course regularly associated with the eschatological advent. Omitted from our translation is the word "again." If "again" is taken with reference to the sending, the second advent is indicated. More probably, however, the "again" simply refers to the adding of another quotation in which God speaks concerning the Son.

The important word **first-born**, applied to the Son, is to be understood in a special sense, referring not to the creation of the Son but to his supremacy of rank. He stands at the apex of all that exists, not as one who was born first, but rather with God over against the entire created order, which indeed exists only by the agency of the Son. The pre-eminence of the Son is thus conveyed by the word, as also in Paul (Col. 1:15, 18). The two other occurrences of the word in Hebrews (11:28; 12:23) do not refer directly to the Son. See further, L. R. Helyer, "The *Prōtotokos* Title in Hebrews," *Studia Biblica et Theologica* 6.2 (1976), pp. 3–28.

1:7 / The apocryphal book 2 Esdras (8:21) contains this interesting parallel, "who art attended by the host of angels trembling as they turn themselves into wind and fire at thy bidding" (NEB), which is itself probably dependent upon Ps. 104:4.

1:8–9 / **Your people** in some manuscripts reads **his people**. The weight of manuscript evidence slightly favors **your**, as does the sense of the passage, which, if **his** is accepted, demands acceptance of the more difficult "God is your kingdom."

1:10–12 / The LXX has inserted "Lord" (*kyrios*) in the first line of this quotation, thereby making our author's application of this passage to the Son (who is Lord) much easier. Although, however, the Hebrew lacks the vocative just at this point, it is found in the immediately preceding line: "O LORD [YHWH], you live forever."

1:13 / For the importance of Ps. 110 for our author and the early church, see comment and note on 1:3.

1:14 / The expression **spirits who serve** (*leitourgika pneumata*) is not found in the OT, but bears considerable resemblance to the description of the angels as "servants" (*leitourgos*) in Ps. 104:4, which is quoted by the author in v. 7. Underlying GNB's *to help* (lit., "for service") is the common NT noun *diakonia*, which occurs only here in Hebrews. The word "inherit" (*klēronomeō*), which GNB translates **receive**, is important to the author (cf. 6:12, and cognate nouns in 6:17; 9:15; 11:7 f.). This language reflects the reception of the fulfillment of the OT promises and is therefore particularly suitable for the author's purpose when he writes of the salvation received by Christians. See Foerster, TDNT, vol. 3, pp. 776–85. On **salvation** (*sōtēria*), see note to 2:3.

3

A Call to Faithfulness

That is why we must hold on all the more firmly to the truths we have heard, so that we will not be carried away. ²The message given to our ancestors by the angels was shown to be true, and anyone who did not follow it or obey it received the punishment he deserved. ³How, then, shall we escape if we pay no attention to such a great salvation? The Lord himself first announced this salvation, and those who heard him proved to us that it is true. ⁴At the same time God added his witness to theirs by performing all kinds of miracles and wonders and by distributing the gifts of the Holy Spirit according to his will.

These four verses provide a parenthetical exhortation, the first of a series of such exhortations following the author's well-designed style and method. He will not discuss theology in the abstract, but constantly calls his readers to its practical significance and to the appropriate response. He writes indeed as an accomplished theologian but also as a preacher with distinct pastoral concerns.

2:1 / If the Son is the One of incomparable splendor, then the message of salvation that the readers **have heard** is to be held **all the more firmly**, lest they **be carried away** (lit., "drift," or "slip away"). There were pressures working upon them to cause them to compromise the truth of the gospel. See 10:29; 12:25. Our author's argument is that a proper assessment of the Son (this is the force of **that is why**) will result in the recognition of the truth and the supreme importance of the Christian message, **the truths we have heard**, and will also encourage faithfulness to that message.

2:2 / With this verse the author begins an *a fortiori* argument, that is, one from the accepted truth of one matter to another that has even stronger reason for being accepted as true: if the one is convincing, how much more the other. The lesser matter involves **the message given to our ancestors by the angels**. What is in view is the Mosaic Law received on Mount Sinai through angelic intermediaries. This message was, of course,

shown to be true in many ways (our author accepts the validity of God's message to his ancestors, see 1:1), but the particular way that our author has in mind is in the reality of judgment upon those who **did not follow it or obey it**. It was God's word and therefore punishment came upon those who were not obedient.

2:3 / If the preceding is true with respect to God's word spoken to our ancestors, how much more it must be true that the reality of judgment will come upon those who fail to hear God's definitive word spoken in his Son! Implicit in the argument is the superiority of God's message spoken "in these last days." If indeed they received judgment in that earlier situation, **how shall we escape** if we disregard **such a great salvation**? The last words point up the glorious salvation that the Son accomplished, something our author will take up at length later in the epistle. Exactly the same *a fortiori* argument is found in 12:25.

The truth of **this salvation** is now stressed in order to strengthen the warning to the readers. The Son, who has already been described so effectively in the prologue, **the Lord himself**, is the one who **first announced** it (cf. Mark 1:1, 15). It is thus initiated by the authority of the One who stands with God over against all else that exists. There can be no greater authority than this to certify the truth of the church's message. And this message has furthermore been carefully attested to both authors and readers (**proved to us that it is true**) by those who actually heard the proclamation from the lips of Jesus. The evidence of eyewitness is highly regarded and our author clearly separates himself from those who were privileged to witness the words and works of Jesus, thus placing himself in the second generation of disciples. In this regard he may be likened to Luke (Luke 1:2).

2:4 / This message of salvation is no less true than the earlier message spoken by God on Sinai, and as that event was accompanied by glorious signs (which, although our author only mentions the angels, were surely in the mind of the readers) so also **God added his witness** to this, His definitive message. **All kinds of miracles and wonders** were performed by Him through the apostles. But the climactic sign of authenticity is the new outpouring of **the gifts of the Holy Spirit**. Thus, like Peter at Pentecost (see Acts 2:14–18) our author finds the Holy Spirit as the ultimate indicator of the fulfillment of God's promises and the dawning of the new era. All of this taken together points inescapably to the incomparable superiority and finality of the message proclaimed by the apostles and the church. It can only be foolish and dangerous for the readers to let themselves drift away from the truth.

Additional Notes

The exhortation and admonitions in this epistle are not incidental; they are integral to the argument of the book and the purpose of the author, who himself describes his work as "this message of encouragement" (13:22). Although there is more exhortation in the epistle than this listing of passages indicates, the following deserve special notice: 2:1–4; 3:7–19; 4:14–16; 5:11–14; 10:19–39; 12:12–17, 25–29. These exhortations are sometimes addressed to the readers in the second person plural, "you," but also frequently occur in the first person plural, "we" or "us," wherein the author identifies himself with the readers, hence reflecting the unity of all in the church. Thus, although the readers are in special need, the message has a wider application to all Christians.

2:1 / The Greek word for **be carried away** (*pararrheō*) occurs only here in the NT. The idea of drifting away is aptly expressed in Barclay's translation "otherwise, we may well be like a ship which drifts past the harbour to shipwreck."

2:2 / The idea of angels as intermediaries in the giving of the Law at Sinai was accepted both by rabbis (references in Marmorstein, *EJ*, vol. 1, p. 643) and Christians in the first century, despite the slim OT warrant (Deut. 33:2). Thus in Stephen's defense reference is made to "the angel who spoke to [Moses] on Mount Sinai" and to the Jews as those "who received God's law that was handed down by angels" (Acts 7:38, 53). Paul, too, writes "the Law was handed down by angels" (Gal. 3:19). Indirectly this reference supports our author's thesis about the servant role of angels and thus their inferiority to the Son. The angels are of instrumental importance in the lesser matter; the Son is of central importance in the greater matter.

Behind the words **did not follow it or obey it** are two nouns (*parabasis* and *parakoē*) that cover all violation of the Law, the former referring to specific transgression or cutting across the commandments, the latter more generally to all forms of disobedience.

2:3 / **Proved to us that it is true** translates the verb "make firm" or "establish" (*bebaioō*) in the sense of providing a guarantee, and corresponds to the cognate (derived) adjective (*bebaios*) **true** or "valid," applied to the Law in v. 2. **Salvation** (*sōtēria*) is an important word for our author. It is at once the salvation promised in the OT, fulfilled in the present time (cf. 2:3, 10; 5:9) and to be consummated in the future (cf. 1:14; 6:9; 9:28). See Foerster, *TDNT*, vol. 7, pp. 989–1012.

2:4 / The **miracles and wonders** referred to are those of the early apostolic age rather than those of the ministry of Jesus. GNB's translation involves a slight telescoping of three terms (cf. "signs and wonders and various miracles," RSV) into two, which is justifiable in that the terms refer to the same thing. The same three terms become virtually formulaic in describing the phenomena of the early church (see the same three words in RSV of Acts 2:22 and 2 Cor. 12:12). Even more common is the occurrence of the first two terms ("signs and wonders") in describing the early church (see Acts 2:43; 4:30; 5:12; 6:8; 14:3; 15:12). In Rom. 15:19 the two terms are associated with "the power of the Spirit of God" as in the present passage.

The reference to the distributing of **the gifts of the Holy Spirit according to his will** recalls the identical Pauline view expressed in 1 Cor. 12:4, 11: "It is one and the same Spirit who does all this; as he wishes, he gives a different gift to each person." For both writers the very presence of these gifts of the Holy Spirit conveys the message of eschatological fulfillment, and thus testifies to the truthfulness of the Christian gospel.

Christ Is Superior to the Angels Despite His Humanity

God has not placed the angels as rulers over the new world to come—the world of which we speak. [6]Instead, as it is said somewhere in the Scriptures:

> "What is man, O God, that you should think of him;
> mere man, that you should care for him?
> [7]You made him for a little while lower than the angels;
> you crowned him with glory and honor,[c]
> [8]and made him ruler over all things."

It says that God made man "ruler over all things"; this clearly includes everything. We do not, however, see man ruling over all things now. [9]But we do see Jesus, who for a little while was made lower than the angels, so that through God's grace he should die for everyone. We see him now crowned with glory and honor because of the death he suffered. [10]It was only right that God, who creates and preserves all things, should make Jesus perfect through suffering, in order to bring many sons to share his glory. For Jesus is the one who leads them to salvation.

c. *Many manuscripts add:* You made him ruler over everything you made (*see Ps. 8:6*).

Without question the greatest obstacle to the author's argument about the superiority of the Son is the authentic humanity of the Son which involved him in both suffering and death. For the first time our author uses the name of the Man from Nazareth, **Jesus** (v. 9). The humanity, the suffering, and the death of Jesus all seem to point with unmistakable clarity to his inferiority in comparison with the angels. The matter obviously demands attention, if the author's argument is to stand; and rather than shrinking from the problem, he effectively turns it to his advantage.

2:5 / Although in Jewish thought the present world was regarded as in some sense subject to angels, this is not the case in **the new world to come**. When our author adds that this is **the world of which we speak**, we encounter the tension between fulfillment and consummation that runs through all of Christian theology. That is, there is a sense in which **the new world to come** has come already and yet also a sense in which it is yet **to come**. We have already encountered this tension in considering the meaning of the phrase "these last days" (1:2) and the quotation in 1:13. The Son has been exalted to the right hand of God, the position of all power, and yet some time is to elapse before his enemies are put under his feet. The reality of the Son's finished work, the essence of the gospel, has nevertheless brought **the new world to come** in the present and to the church. Thus our author has both a future eschatology and a realized eschatology. The latter is vividly expressed in 6:5 where he describes Christian experience as a tasting of "the powers of the coming age." (See too the "you *have* come" of 12:22–24.) In point of fact, **the world** of which the author has been speaking is that new reality already brought into existence by the exaltation of the Son but the end result of which remains yet to be experienced; hence it remains that world yet **to come**. This tension is further manifested in the following verses.

2:6–8a / This quotation from Psalm 8:4–6 provides another indication of our author's christological understanding of the OT. As originally written, the psalm extols the glory of the created order, in comparison with which mankind looks woefully insignificant: "When I look at the sky . . . the moon and the stars . . . what is man?" At the same time, however, according to the Genesis narrative (1:26, 28) mankind was given dominion over the rest of creation, over all animals, birds, and fish, and this position of honor is celebrated by the psalmist. Our author understands the psalm to refer to Christ, as well as to humanity, in this instance not merely because of the possible messianic associations of the psalm (i.e., in the last two lines of the quoted material) but, rather, because he regards the Son as the Archetypal Man. That is, Jesus is the true embodiment of humanity, the Last Adam who realizes in himself that glory and dominion that the first Adam and his children lost because of sin. In him the words of the psalmist have their fulfillment. If the words were meant originally to apply to mankind, they find their fullest realization in the one who is pre-eminently Man, who reveals mankind as mankind was meant to be.

The application of the psalm to Jesus was clearly facilitated by the words "son of man," the title that Jesus himself preferred during his ministry. This title is rendered by GNB as **mere man**, which is indeed the nuance of the original Hebrew (as can be seen by the parallel **man** in the preceding line), but which has the disadvantage of concealing what must have jumped out at our author and his readers. For him, the son of man was understood to be Jesus. Once the mind turns to Jesus in verse 6, the temporal sequence of incarnation and exaltation can readily be perceived in verse 7. The last line of the quotation has a much closer tie with the author's favorite exaltation text (Ps. 110:1, quoted in 1:13) than can be seen from the translation **and made him ruler over all things**, which reads more literally, "having put everything in subjection under his feet." Thus the OT passage is effectively utilized by the author in his argument. The Son was indeed made man, and accordingly, **lower than the angels**. But only **for a little while**, for he has been exalted (to the right hand of the Father), **crowned with glory and honor**, thus having everything put in subjection under his feet. What man once had, but lost, has now been gained by the One who became Man for that very purpose. In him humanity has begun to realize its true inheritance.

2:8b–9 / In these verses we encounter the first instance of our author's midrashic treatment of an OT passage—that is, where he presents an interpretation of the quotation, utilizing specific words drawn from the quotation itself. (See the same phenomenon in 3:7–4:11; 10:5–14; 12:5–11.) The result may fairly be described as a Christian commentary (i.e., seen from the perspective of the fulfillment brought by Christ) on the passage that enables the author to drive home his point and thereby also to demonstrate the continuity he finds between old and new.

When in verse 8b GNB specifies **man** as the one made ruler over all, and **man** as not yet realizing that rule, it goes beyond the simple "him" of the Greek text. This is a correct interpretation and reflects the parallelism of the OT text. But it obscures the allusion to Christ probably intended by the author—that is, that the masculine pronoun refers to mankind *and* Christ (just as the quotation itself may be understood to refer to both). It is clear that the author understands the quotation from Psalm 8 to refer to Christ as well as to mankind by his application of specific words from the quotation to **Jesus** in verse 9: **who for a little while was made lower than the angels ... now crowned with glory and honor**. Jesus, already so crowned, is in principle "ruler over all things" (v. 8a). We do not, however, yet see that reign in the present world. Indeed, the delay is already alluded to in a key text previously quoted (1:13): "Sit here at my right side *until* I put your enemies as a footstool under your feet" (Ps. 110:1). In fact, now we see neither man nor Christ ruling over all things; but Christ's rule will in the future be fully consummated, and when that occurs, mankind will experience the full realization of the rule spoken of in Psalm 8 (cf. Phil. 3:21). **This clearly includes everything**. Our author does not specify the obvious exception noted by Paul in 1 Corinthians 15:27: "It is clear, of course, that the words 'all things' do not include God himself, who puts all things under Christ."

But we do see Jesus. This is the first mention of the personal name Jesus, which is used deliberately here to focus attention upon his humanity. It is the incarnation that makes Jesus temporarily **lower than the angels**, and the purpose of the incarnation is to make possible his death on behalf of all, for **everyone**, **through God's grace**. The incarnation and its goal, the cross, are the glorious expression of God's free mercy and favor. The exaltation of Jesus, his being **now crowned with glory and honor**, is **because of the death he suffered**. Since it was from an exalted position that Jesus was temporarily made lower than the angels, we should not press the causal aspect too far (cf. 12:2). What is primarily in view is the sequence *exalted status–humiliation–exaltation* (as, e.g., explicitly in Phil. 2:6–11). At the same time, the exaltation that follows the humiliation does have a new dimension of joy and triumph, standing as it does at the end of the accomplishment of God's plan of salvation.

2:10 / **It was only right** refers to the full appropriateness of the way in which God accomplished his will through the death of Jesus. It was indeed the will of God, the sovereign Creator of all, that brought about the incarnation and death of his Son. The Creator thereby becomes also the Redeemer of his creation. The death of Jesus involves, therefore, not weakness and inferiority, but strength and superiority. Jesus fulfilling the plan of God becomes **the one who leads them to salvation** (lit., "originator" or "founder" of salvation). But the real point of the appropriateness referred to at the beginning of the verse is that the Son should become fully like human beings, sharing their **suffering**, which here means identification with mankind to the point of death, in order that mankind may become fully **sons** and with Jesus **share his glory**. Jesus became like us that we may become like him. (For a similar exchange, see 2 Cor. 5:21.) Making **Jesus perfect through suffering** refers primarily to the accomplishment and fulfillment of God's purposes. The perfection is not a moral or ethical perfection, for Jesus in this sense was always perfect. Jesus was made **perfect** in the sense of being brought to a certain "completeness" associated with the fulfillment of God's plan. In his suffering and death there is therefore a completeness to his humanity that corresponds to his completeness as God's Son. **Who creates and preserves all things** (lit., "for whom are all things and through whom are all things") applies to God—language that is applied to the Son in 1:2 ("through whom"; cf. 1 Cor. 8:6; Col. 1:16; John 1:3). **In order to bring many sons to share his glory** (lit., "to glory") expresses at once the purpose of the incarnation, suffering, and death of Jesus. **Glory** and **salvation** stand as parallel terms describing the goal that Christians attain through Christ's work. The One who "brings" them to this blessed state is thus the "pioneer of salvation" (RSV).

The full humanity of the Son, therefore, involves the greatest of advantages, including the superiority of the Son to angels as the One who makes salvation possible by fulfilling the will of God in suffering and death. Further benefits of the humanity of Jesus are explored by our author in the remainder of this chapter.

Additional Notes

2:5 / It is presupposed that angels have an important role in the present age. Evidence indicates the widespread belief that angel-princes under God ruled the nations. Philo says that the Creator employs angels as his assistants and ministers for the care of mortals (*On Dreams* 1:22); according to Enoch (89:59) seventy guardian angels have charge over the seventy nations (cf. Deut. 32:8 [LXX]; Dan. 10:20–21; Sirach 17:17). See Kohler, JE, vol. 1, p. 594. This vice-regency, however, apparently does not hold true when the Son of Man, Jesus, has accomplished his work.

2:6–8a / The formula that introduces the quotation is unusual: **it is said somewhere in the Scriptures** (lit., "somewhere someone testified, saying"). Other indefinite introductory formulae are found in 4:4 ("somewhere . . . this is said"), and 5:6 ("He also said in another place"). This usage of indefinite introductory formulae is unique in the NT. Elsewhere, the author clearly introduces Scripture as spoken by God, Christ, or the Holy Spirit. In only two places is a human speaker referred to (9:20; 12:21), and in both we encounter Moses as the speaker in the OT narrative. See R. Longenecker, *Biblical Exegesis in the Apostolic Period* (Grand Rapids: Eerdmans, 1975), pp. 164–70. It is especially appropriate that the Son of man be understood as the representative of humanity. The title includes readily the idea of the community of the faithful, as it does in one of the sources of the concept, Dan. 7:13 f., 22. (Cf. John 1:51, which some apply to the Son and the community of believers.) For "Son of Man," see O. Michel, *NIDNTT*, vol. 3, pp. 613–34; P. Giles, "The Son of Man in the Epistle to the Hebrews," *ExpT* 86 (1975), pp. 328–32. (The translation **mere man** is apparently intended to reflect Ps. 8:4 as translated in the OT of GNB. Yet consistency with the OT of GNB is not held to in the translation of the next verse of Hebrews.)

The OT of GNB translates the first line of Ps. 8:5: "Yet you made him inferior only to yourself," rightly reflecting the Hebrew *'lōhim*; cf. RSV: "Yet thou hast made him little less than God." Hebrews depends on the LXX, whose translators indeed translated *'lōhim* by *angelous*, "angels." (A similar rendering of *'lōhim* by a plural may be seen in Ps. 82:6, "you are gods" [John 10:34], which was probably understood as "angels.") It is obvious that our author's argument benefits from the LXX reading at this point, although *'lōhim* could be understood also to substantiate the point being made. Although the Hebrew of Ps. 8:5 refers to the smallness of degree to which man is inferior, "thou hast made him little less than God" (RSV), the LXX quoted in Heb. 2:7 can also be understood in a temporal sense, hence **you made him for a little while lower**. The temporal understanding of the phrase is supported by the argument of v. 9. See *brachys*, BAGD.

Many manuscripts add to v. 7 the words "you made him ruler over everything you made" (which is not as synonymous with the first line of v. 8 as GNB makes it appear). Despite the textual witness in favor of its inclusion (but it is missing from P[46] and B), the line is almost certainly an adaptation to the LXX, and therefore the shorter reading is to be preferred.

2:8b–9 / Four key phrases are picked up from the preceding verses in a midrashic exposition of the quotation from Ps. 8. Only the first appears in quotation marks in GNB, "**ruler over all things**," but the others could well be put in quotation marks too: **ruling over all things**; **for a little while was made lower**; and **crowned with glory and honor**. In midrashic exposition the author constructs his argument by using phrases from the quotation, and hence produces a kind of commentary on the passage before him. The author of Hebrews is a master of this technique, and in his frequent use of it he reflects his basic theological conviction that Christ and his work represent the fulfillment of the OT, not only as the fulfillment of direct prophecy, but as the fulfillment that occurs in corresponding patterns of events that find their *telos*, or goal, in Christ. The author of Hebrews makes extensive use of midrashic commentary on OT texts in his treatise; indeed, he seems eager to derive his arguments from the Scriptures, and this doubtless reflects the importance of the OT to his readers.

Commentators are almost equally divided concerning whether the pronoun "him" (**man**) in v. 8b refers to man or to Jesus. But, as F. F. Bruce correctly points out: "the *crux* is only a minor one, because in any case Christ is in view as the representative Man" (p. 37, n. 35). In v. 9 GNB correctly links **so that** (*hopōs*) . . . **he should die** with the statement that Jesus **was made lower than the angels**, despite the fact that the clauses are not consecutive in the Greek text (cf. the awkwardness of NASB for example). The fact that a few manuscripts and some early fathers witness the more difficult reading *chōris theou* ("without" or "apart from God") for *chariti theou* (**through God's grace**) has produced much discussion. Although it is difficult to explain the origin of the former reading, and although generally the more difficult or awkward reading is to be preferred in textual criticism, here the manuscript evidence for **through God's grace** is overwhelming (including the very early P[46]), the phrase makes good sense as it stands and therefore is to be accepted as the original reading. On **grace** (*charis*), see note to 4:16. In **he should die for everyone**, we have the clear teaching of substitutionary atonement, a doctrine central to Hebrews (cf. 5:1; 7:27). On this use of the preposition **for** (*hyper*), see M. J. Harris, *NIDNTT*, vol. 3, pp. 1196 f. **The death he suffered** correctly interprets the more literal "might taste death" (RSV), as a full rather than only partial experience of death (cf. Mark 9:1).

2:10 / Although the expression occurs in Jewish literature outside the Bible, this is the only place in the Bible where **it was only right** (*eprepen*) describes God's action. **Should make Jesus perfect** brings the first occurrence of *teleioō* in the epistle. This is an important word which occurs frequently in Hebrews (verb also found in 5:9; 7:19, 28; 9:9; 10:1, 14; 11:40; 12:23; other forms of root: 5:14; 9:11; 6:1; 7:11; 12:2). Although some see the verb in Hebrews as often carrying a cultic significance (following its use in LXX), i.e., "being fit to approach the presence of God," the verb more generally carries the idea of "bringing to perfection" in the sense of fulfillment or completeness. M. Silva argues persuasively that the idea of fulfillment is behind the various occurrences of the word in Hebrews. See "Perfection and Eschatology in Hebrews," *WTJ* 39 (1976–77), pp. 60–71. See also Delling, *TDNT*, vol. 8, pp. 49–87.

Those who participate in the salvation Jesus has accomplished are here called **sons** and thus they share in Jesus' own title (cf. v. 11). The only other place in the book where "sons" is used absolutely is in 12:5–8. The author shares this concept with Paul (e.g., Rom. 8:14, 19; Gal. 3:26; 4:6 f.). To be "sons" means to be those who enjoy and are on the way to **salvation** and **glory**. It is ambiguous in the Greek whether God or Jesus is to be understood as the one who brings the sons to glory, although a slight probability favors God as the subject (see Hughes, pp. 101 f.).

Jesus' central role in the procural of salvation gives him the special title *archēgos tēs sōtērias*, which has variously been translated "captain of salvation" (KJV), "pioneer of salvation" (RSV, NIV), "author of salvation" (ASV), "leader of salvation" (Moffatt). On **salvation** (*sōtēria*), see note to 2:3. The word *archēgos* has two related meanings: (1) leader, ruler, prince, and (2) originator, founder. "Pathfinder" or "trailblazer" are sometimes suggested as distilling the meaning of the word. It occurs also in Heb. 12:2, where it refers to Jesus as the author or pioneer of faith and is linked with "perfecter" (RSV). The only other references are Acts 3:15, "the Author of life" (RSV) and Acts 5:31, absolutely, "Leader." See G. Johnston, "Christ as Archēgos," *NTS* 27 (1981), pp. 381–85; Bietenhard, *NIDNTT*, vol. 1, p. 168.

The Benefits of Christ's Humanity

He purifies people from their sins, and both he and those who are made pure all have the same Father. That is why Jesus is not ashamed to call them his brothers. [12]He says to God,
"I will tell my brothers what you have done;
I will praise you in their meeting."
[13]He also says, "I will put my trust in God." And he also says, "Here I am with the children that God has given me."
[14]Since the children, as he calls them, are people of flesh and blood, Jesus himself became like them and shared their human nature. He did this so that through his death he might destroy the Devil, who has the power over death, [15]and in this way set free those who were slaves all their lives because of their fear of death. [16]For it is clear that it is not the angels that he helps. Instead, as the scripture says, "He helps the descendants of Abraham." [17]This means that he had to become like his brothers in every way, in order to be their faithful and merciful High Priest in his service to God, so that the people's sins would be forgiven. [18]And now he can help those who are tempted, because he himself was tempted and suffered.

Pursuing his argument that Christ's humanity makes possible the fulfillment of God's saving plan and therefore involves no inferiority of Jesus to the angels, the author now focuses on the full reality and benefits of the Son's humanity.

2:11 / The work of Jesus, the purifying of **people from their sins**, is accomplished by his death, which in turn depends upon his humanity (cf. the words of 10:10: "we are all purified from sin by the offering that he made of his own body once and for all"). In his humanity Jesus is fully one with us and therefore we **all have the same Father** (lit., "are all from one"). Jesus has identified with us to the extent that he is our brother and is **not ashamed to call** us **his brothers**. Three OT quotations are provided by the author to support this claim.

2:12 / Again the author's Christocentric interpretation of the OT emerges. The first quotation he presents is from Psalm 22. The opening words of this psalm were quoted by Jesus from the cross: "My God, my God, why have you abandoned me?" (Mark 15:34; Matt. 27:46). Certain details in the psalm correspond strikingly with the Gospel narratives concerning the crucifixion (e.g., the physical agony, 14–17; the mocking, 6–8; the gambling for and dividing of Jesus' clothes, 18); and the evangelists allude to the psalm in this connection. It is obvious that the early church regarded the whole of Psalm 22 as exceptionally appropriate on the lips of Jesus. If Jesus speaks the psalm to God, then—much to the delight of our author—he refers to the people in the assembly as his **brothers**. It is a man among mankind who speaks concerning God. **What you have done** is literally "thy name" (RSV). Thus our author has found an ideal passage to buttress his argument about the full humanity of Jesus.

2:13 / Jesus is also seen to be the speaker in the next two brief quotations, each of which the author introduces with the simple "and again." These quotations are from consecutive verses in Isaiah 8 (17 [LXX] and 18). Here, unlike the preceding quotation, we do not encounter an immediately evident rationale as to how Jesus may be understood to be the speaker of these words. Since in the OT Isaiah is the speaker, it is commonly argued that similarities between Isaiah and Jesus, as well as the "messianic tone" of the larger passage (which is, however, difficult to see in these verses), explain how Jesus can be thought of as the speaker. This type of argument, however, is much too weak to establish our author's point. Instead, the solution is to be found in the fact that according to the LXX, which is obviously being used here (cf. the first quotation with Isa. 8:17), the Lord, and not Isaiah, is the speaker of the words in question. Accordingly, the references to "Lord" in the LXX of Isaiah 8:17 are changed to "God." Thus it is the "Lord" (*kyrios*) who speaks to "God" (*theos*). It was of course very common in the early church to identify "the Lord" in the OT as Jesus, especially when the context favored such an identification. Indeed, we have already encountered this identification of Jesus with Yahweh in the quotations in 1:6, and 1:10–12. If the Lord speaks to God, reasons our author, what else are we meant to understand but that Jesus here speaks to his Father. If this is true, then here are places where Jesus identifies himself with humanity over against God. He, like them, puts his **trust in God**; he associates himself with **the children that God has given me**.

31

2:14 / As the word *brothers* at the end of verse 11 anticipates its occurrence in the quotation in verse 12 (it occurs again in v. 17), so, similarly, here the word **children** is obviously drawn from the preceding quotation. There is no new thought in the first half of this verse, but only a higher degree of specificity: as humans are **people of flesh and blood**, so he also **shared their human nature** (lit., "partook of them," i.e., of flesh and blood.) Again, as the aorist tense (in Greek, that tense which usually refers to completed action in the past) indicates, what is in view is a pre-existent being who at a particular point in time took upon himself human nature. The second half of the verse consists of a purpose clause that again links the incarnation with its goal, **his death**. But whereas in the previous statements of this purpose the goal is stated positively as salvation or the purifying from sins, here it is expressed negatively, that **he might destroy the Devil, who has the power over death**. Again it is necessary to distinguish between fulfillment and consummation. The Devil has been defeated in principle in and through the ministry of Jesus (Luke 10:18) and especially through the cross (cf. John 10:31), and yet he is not yet destroyed, but continues to have real, if limited, power (cf. Eph. 4:27; 6:11; 1 Tim. 3:7; James 4:7; 1 Pet. 5:8). In a similar way, the NT can say that Christ has "ended the power of death" (2 Tim. 1:10), and yet death continues to be a reality with which mankind must reckon. The Devil and death are clearly overcome in Christ's work, even if in this interim period between the cross and the return of Christ we do not see the full effects of Christ's victory. The Devil's **power over death** is related to his role in introducing sin into the world, for death is the fruit of sin (cf. Rom 5:21).

2:15 / It is significant in light of the preceding comments that the deliverance now experienced, to which our author makes reference, is described not as deliverance from death, but from the **fear of death**. Death, indeed, may still occur, but it need no longer be feared. Its sovereignty, like the Devil's, is limited and soon to come to an end. Through the death of Jesus, and all that this means, Christians are **set free** from the fear that perpetually enslaves others. Our author would agree with Paul's questions: "Where, Death, is your victory? Where, Death, is your power to hurt?" (1 Cor. 15:55). Jesus has come "to destroy the works of the devil" (1 John 3:8, RSV), and presents himself to John in Revelation 1:18 in these words: "I am the living one! I was dead, but now I am alive forever and ever. I have authority over death and the world of the dead."

2:16 / Jesus was not concerned with the angels, but with humankind. This serves as a reminder of the reason that Jesus became "for a little while lower than the angels" (v. 7); had he come to redeem angels, it is implied, he might have assumed the nature of angels. Far from reflecting any inferiority in Jesus, the humility of Jesus demonstrates the faithfulness of God to his saving purposes for his people, here identified as the **descendants of Abraham**. Although it may well be that we have an allusion to Isaiah 41:8 f. here, this is a far from necessary conclusion. There is nothing in the Greek text corresponding to GNB's **as the Scripture says**. The author may well deliberately refer to **the descendants of Abraham** to focus attention upon his Jewish readers. But since the church is the heir of the OT promises in Christ, it is not wrong to understand the expression in a wider sense as referring to the entire community of faith (cf. Gal. 3:7).

2:17 / In order to help **his brothers** (alluding to the quotation in v. 12), by which the author means "to save them from their sins," Jesus had to become fully like them, **in every way** (cf. v. 14). These last words, of course, are not to be taken literally since Jesus was not a sinner, an observation made by our author in 4:15 (cf. 7:26 f.). The full humanity of Jesus enables him to perform the functions of a **High Priest**. This is the first occurrence of what for the author is a most important title of Jesus, and one indeed that in the NT is applied to him only in Hebrews. A priest is one who represents humanity before God (cf. 5:1) and, in order for a priest to accomplish his task, he must be one with those whom he represents before God. When our author thinks of Jesus as performing a high priestly **service to God**, he has in mind, as we shall see in chapters 9 and 10, the all-important work of the high priest on the Day of Atonement. This work of this High Priest, like those before him whose work foreshadowed his, is in fact done **so that the people's sins would be forgiven** (cf. v. 11).

2:18 / Although it is not strictly pertinent to our author's argument at this point, he cannot resist a brief pastoral note about the practical benefit of having Jesus as our High Priest. Jesus, because of his full humanity and because of his suffering, is in a special position to **help those who are tempted** and who call upon him. This application is made more explicit in 4:15, and almost certainly is prompted by the actual difficulties faced by the readers.

Additional Notes

2:11 / **Purifies ... from sins** is an interpretation, probably correct (because drawn from the context), of the word usually translated "sanctify" (*hagiazō*). This word in Hebrews can mean "to make holy" or "to consecrate" (as in 10:14, 29), but even in these instances the context speaks of an "offering" or of "blood." Elsewhere in Hebrews the word comes close to being a synonym for "make atonement" (9:13; 10:10; 13:12). See Procksch, *TDNT*, vol. 1, p. 112. **All have the same Father** is an interpretation of an indefinite Greek phrase, "from one" (*ex henos*). It is equally possible to construe the phrase to mean "one origin" (RSV), "of one stock" (NEB), or "same family" (NIV). GNB appropriately opts for **the same Father** in connection with the reference to **brothers**. Although according to the Gospels Jesus calls his disciples "brothers" (Matt. 12:49 f.; 25:40; 28:10), and although "brothers" is the most common designation for the Christian community in the NT, this is the only passage outside the Gospels where the community is called brothers of Jesus (apart, of course, from his actual siblings). See Günther *NIDNTT*, vol. 1, pp. 254–58. **Not ashamed** is an example of a rhetorical device called litotes, whereby an affirmative statement is expressed by a negative (cf. 11:16; Rom. 1:16). On this passage, see G. W. Grogan, "Christ and His People: An Exegetical and Theological Study of Hebrews 2, 5–18," *VoxEv* 6 (1969) pp. 54–71.

2:12 / **What you have done** extends the literal meaning of the Greek for "your name." The "name" connotes not only who the Lord is, but what he has done. See Bietenhard, *NIDNTT*, vol. 2, pp. 648–55. **In their meeting** is literally "in the midst of the *ecclēsia*" or "church" (see KJV). Although in the LXX the "congregation" or "assembly" of Israel is meant, the author and his readers would quite naturally have had their minds turned to the church by this particular Greek word.

2:13 / The readiness with which the early Christians identified the *kyrios* ("Lord") of the LXX (for YHWH) with Jesus is evident throughout the NT (see e.g., Acts 2:21, 34 f.; Rom. 10:13; Phil. 2:9–11; 1 Pet. 3:14 f; Rev. 19:16), and accounts for the OT quotations in this verse which the author attributes to Jesus. See I. H. Marshall, *The Origins of New Testament Christology*, (Downers Grove: InterVarsity, 1976), pp. 104–8. It is of no concern to our author that in the quotation of Ps. 22:22 in the preceding verse it is the one who is addressed, and not the speaker, who is *kyrios*. (The "Lord" addressed in the psalm is called God in its opening verses.) The focus of our author at this point is obviously on the humanity and not the deity of Jesus.

2:14 / The stress on the **flesh and blood** in which Jesus shared puts Hebrews, along with the Johannine writings, among the strongest opponents of Docetism in the NT writings. Docetism stressed the deity of Christ and argued that Christ was not really, but only appeared to be, human. This is a totally impossible view so far as the argument of Hebrews is concerned. (Cf. John 1:14; 1 John 1:1; 4:2.) See G. S. Hendry, "Christology," *DCT*, p. 56. Nothing in the Greek text strictly corresponds to **became like them**, but this probably derives from the adverb *paraplēsiōs* ("similarly") which modifies **shared**. **Devil** and Satan are the two main designations for the supernatural enemy of God. They are used about equally often in the NT. **Devil** means "slanderer"; Satan, a Hebrew word, means "adversary." The **Devil** is "the prince of this world" (John 12:31; 14:30; 16:11). The connection between the Devil and death was well known in the Judaism of the intertestamental period (see Wisd. of Sol. 1:13 f.; 2:23 f.). The Devil and death are thrown into "the lake of fire" consecutively according to Rev. 20:10, 14. This is the only occurrence of either word in Hebrews. See H. Bietenhard, *NIDNTT*, vol. 3, pp. 468–72.

2:15 / The Greek word underlying **set free** is *apallassō* (elsewhere in the NT only in Luke 12:58 and Acts 19:12) and not the more common word *eleutheroō*. In pursuing this argument about Jesus setting us free from the fear of death, it is remarkable that our author fails to refer to the resurrection of Jesus. The author knows the doctrine of the resurrection of the dead (6:2), but in the entire epistle the resurrection of Jesus is referred to only in 13:20, and even then the usual word for resurrection, *anastasis*, is not used. So far as our passage is concerned, it may be said that any reference to the death of Jesus as a victory, wherein the Devil is destroyed and believers are delivered from the fear of death, necessarily carries with it the implication of his resurrection. Although not stated by our author, the resurrection of Jesus and its significance for the present argument cannot have been overlooked by any of the Christian readers of this book. The resurrection of Jesus, after all, was the cornerstone of the early church's faith and preaching.

2:16 / It is difficult to be certain about the meaning of the verb twice translated as **helps** in this verse. The LXX (Isa. 41:8 f.) which may underlie the verse uses the verb *antilambanō*, which in its context means "take" (i.e., "from the ends of the earth"). The verb in the present verse is *epilambanomai*, "to take hold of." The latter verb can connote "to help" (hence NIV agrees with GNB in rendering the verb "helps"). It may be, however, that to opt immediately for an evident connotation rather than the basic meaning is to avoid something important to the author. The meaning "take hold of" may be understood in the sense of Jesus taking upon himself the nature of man, which as we have seen is our author's main point. NEB translates appropriately: "It is not angels, mark you, that he takes to himself, but the sons of Abraham." Similarly, Phillips: "It is plain that for this purpose he did not become an angel; he became a *man*, in actual fact a descendant of Abraham." RSV's "is concerned with," however, is too weak. "Take hold" finds its fullest meaning in the present context, namely, "to become like in order to give help" (cf. the same verb, with the note of implied help, in "took" in 8:9).

2:17 / The title **High Priest** is applied to Jesus ten times in Hebrews. The development of this title and application of it to Jesus is, so far as we can tell from the other writings of the NT, our author's original work. Obviously, the primary significance of the title has to do with the sacrificial ritual for atonement, as in the present verse (cf. 7:26, 8:1). The author, however, takes up opportunities for further application in such areas as help for those in difficulty (4:14 f.; 6:20) and the good things brought by Christ (3:1, 9:11). Since the significance of the title composes an important, indeed central, part of the argument of Hebrews, there is no need to pursue it further in this note. See O. Cullmann, *The Christology of the New Testament*, pp. 83–107; J. Baehr, *NIDNTT*, vol. 3, pp. 32–42. See A. J. B. Higgins, "The Priestly Messiah," *NTS* 13 (1967), pp. 211–39; J. R. Schaefer, "The Relationship Between Priestly and Servant Messianism in the Epistle to the Hebrews," CBQ 30 (1968) pp. 59–85.

Only here is **High Priest** modified by the adjectives **faithful** and **merciful**, although they are appropriate for the title and would suit other contexts admirably well. Only in one other instance is an adjective used: "great High Priest" (4:14). **Sins** is a very important word for our author, occurring more often in Hebrews than in any other NT book except Romans. The reason is plain: Hebrews is an extensive treatise on the work of Christ, our High Priest, in accomplishing atonement for sin. This was already announced in 1:3 and is the reason for the incarnation and death of Jesus, as we have seen from the present chapter. The author uses almost exclusively the word *hamartia*. See W. Günther, *NIDNTT*, vol. 3, pp. 577–83. The words **sins would be forgiven** represent what in the Greek text stands in the active (middle) rather than the passive voice, describing not so much the effect of the High Priest's work, as the work itself. The key Greek word (*hilaskesthai*) has been much debated by NT scholars. C. H. Dodd argues, on one hand, that its meaning in the NT is "expiation," i.e., reflecting action directed toward sins, in the sense of "to wipe away"; L. Morris argues, on the other hand, that it means "propitiation," i.e., reflecting action directed toward God in the "appeasement of wrath." RSV ("to make expiation") and NEB ("to expiate") reflect Dodd's perspective in our verse. KJV ("to make reconciliation") and NIV ("make atonement") sensibly reflect what can be called a neutral position, without specifying how reconciliation or atonement is accomplished, and yet retaining an active statement of the work of Jesus. See the full discussion of the debate in H.-G. Link and C. Brown, *NIDNTT*, vol. 3, pp. 148–66.

2:18 / The translation of *peirazō* by "test" rather than "tempt" (as in NEB) may be of some help in understanding this verse, although the distinction is not always easy to make (cf. James 1:13–15). See the discussion in C. L. Mitton, *The Epistle of James* (London: Marshall, Morgan and Scott, 1966), pp. 46–50. For the testing of Jesus, see Mark 3:21; 8:32; and esp. Matt. 4:1–11, material with which our author was familiar, if not from the written Gospels, at least from the oral tradition.

Christis Superior to Moses

My Christian brothers, who also have been called by God! Think of Jesus, whom God sent to be the High Priest of the faith we profess. ²He was faithful to God, who chose him to do this work, just as Moses was faithful in his work in God's house. ³A man who builds a house receives more honor than the house itself. In the same way Jesus is worthy of much greater honor than Moses. ⁴Every house, of course, is built by someone—and God is the one who has built all things. ⁵Moses was faithful in God's house as a servant, and he spoke of the things that God would say in the future. ⁶But Christ is faithful as the Son in charge of God's house. We are his house if we keep up our courage and our confidence in what we hope for.

Having established the superiority of Christ to the angels and having sustained the point by a lengthy discussion of the significance of the incarnation, the author now turns to the superiority of Jesus to Moses, and by implication the superiority of Jesus to the Law. Given the commitments of Jewish readers—for whom Moses and the Law are of central importance—the argument is astonishingly bold, and the conclusions to which it eventually leads in chapter 8 are not easy ones, even for Christian Jews. Again the specific background of the readers is in view and especially the strong temptation that they were apparently experiencing to return to the faith of their fathers.

3:1 / The author appeals to his readers, placing himself together with them, in the words **my Christian brothers** (lit., "holy brothers"), a common designation for the community of the faithful. They **have been called by God** (lit., "sharers of a heavenly calling"). The readers, affirmed in their identity, are to **think of Jesus**, that is, resolutely to focus their thoughts on his true significance. He is the one **whom God sent**, literally, "the Apostle." There are many apostles, but Jesus is the supreme Apostle, sent by God. Only here in the NT is Jesus so called. He is indeed both Apostle and **High Priest of the faith we profess**. That is, the objective truth that we profess as Christians has been delivered by Jesus as Apostle and accomplished by Jesus as High Priest. Jesus as the one sent by God represents God to mankind; Jesus as High Priest represents mankind to God. Jesus is therefore God's revelation and makes possible man's response. He is, as the author will describe him later, even if in a different connection (8:6; 9:15; 12:24), well qualified to be the "mediator" (cf. 1 Tim. 2:5).

3:2 / Jesus was **faithful to God** (cf. 2:17); he was obedient to the will of one **who chose him to do this work**, literally, "to the one who appointed him." This fact has already been demonstrated by the author. So far as faithfulness is concerned, however, Moses stands on a par with Jesus. **Moses was faithful . . . in God's house** is drawn from the LXX (Num. 12:7), in a passage where Moses is exalted as the only one with whom God speaks "mouth to mouth" and not indirectly. **God's house**, as we shall see in verse 6, is not to be understood in any literal sense—not even in the sense of the Temple itself. It refers instead to the purpose or work of God as it finds expression first in Israel and then the church.

3:3 / In addition to the similarity between Moses and Jesus, however, there is also an important difference between them, now brought to our attention by the analogy of a builder and the house he builds. It is regarded as self-evident that the builder **receives more honor than the house itself**. When the author proceeds to conclude that similarly **Jesus is worthy of much greater honor** (lit., "glory") **than Moses**, he in effect associates Jesus with the builder whereas Moses remains associated with the house. Jesus, as we have seen, has an all-important role in the very possibility that any house, in the sense just described, could come into being. The church depends upon the work of Jesus the Apostle and High Priest for its existence.

3:4 / And yet God of course is to be regarded finally as the builder of **all things** (cf. 1:2b; 2:10). Jesus in being faithful to his mission is being faithful to God and to God's purpose (v. 2). Compare Psalm 127:1: "If the Lord does not build the house, the work of the builders is useless."

3:5 / The true difference between Moses and Jesus emerges in this and the following verse. Moses' role was that of **servant**. Up to and including this word we again have a strong verbal allusion to the LXX of Numbers 12:7. Moses was the **servant** of something greater than himself—of God's purposes which were to have their realization only in time to come. **He spoke** (lit., "for a witness"), therefore, necessarily **of the things** that

38

God would **say in the future**. Those are the very things indeed of which our author writes "in these last days" (1:2). Moses, as important as he was, served in a role of preparation, not one of fulfillment (cf. 11:39 f.).

3:6 / Christ, on the other hand, functions faithfully **as the Son in charge of God's house**. To the Jews, Moses was the greatest person who had ever lived: it was through Moses that God delivered Israel from Egypt, constituted Israel as a nation, and brought Israel the Law. In all of this the magnificent Moses was faithful, but **as a servant**. In the era of fulfillment of which our author writes, Jesus is as far superior to Moses as a Son is to a servant. In the reference to Jesus as **the Son** (cf. 1:2, 5) and as the one who is over God's house we have an allusion to his deity. In Moses we have promise; in the Son we have fulfillment, for in him God has accomplished his saving purposes. In the words **we are his house** the author has in mind the church, that is, the people of God, the community of faith which is the recipient of the salvation brought by Christ.

The author adds a conditional clause that is pastorally motivated and again directed at the specific needs of the readers. Membership in **God's house** is not to be taken for granted. It is necessary **to keep up our courage and our confidence in what we hope for**. We have already had allusions to the danger in which the readers stand (2:1, 18) and more are to follow as this theme becomes one of increasing importance in the epistle. Faithfulness is required not only of God's special servants and his Son, but of his people as well (cf. Col. 1:23). It is with this primary concern that our author turns to an extended illustration-exhortation that occupies our attention until the end of chapter 4.

Additional Notes

3:1 / The word "sharers" is important for our author (five occurrences in Hebrews; only one elsewhere in the NT: Luke 5:7, "partners"). Christ "shared" (verb form of same root) our humanity, 2:14 (cf. 1:9); Christians are said to be sharers in Christ (3:14), in the Holy Spirit (6:4), and in discipline (12:8). For a further reference to Christians as "called by God," see 9:15. The adjective used to describe the calling of Christians as "heavenly" (*epouranios*) occurs more in Hebrews (six times) than in that other epistle famous for the same word, Ephesians (five times). Our author applies it not only to "calling," as here, but to the "gift" (6:4), the "sanctuary" and items related to it (8:5; 9:23), and to the eschatological "country" and city, Jerusalem (11:16; 12:22). It refers therefore to a perfection and reality associated with the fulfillment of God's purposes. Jesus is the Apostle and High Priest of **the faith we profess**, lit., "of our confession" (*homologia*). The word in this objective sense of faith which is believed is used absolutely in 4:14 and as "confession of our hope" in 10:23. Both of these references occur in exhortations. On Jesus as Apostle, see Rengstorf, *TDNT*, Vol. 1, pp 423 f. In the word order of the Greek text, "Jesus" stands climactically as the last word of the verse.

3:2 / "Appoint" here reflects *poieō* rather than the common *tithēmi* (as in 1:2). Some manuscripts include the objective "whole" (*holō*) modifying **house** in agreement with Num. 12:7. For **house** as God's people, see J. Goetzmann, *NIDNTT*, vol. 2, p. 249. Cf. Heb. 10:21.

3:3 / GNB reverses the order of the two sentences in this verse. The primary statement is that Jesus is worthy of much greater glory (*doxa*) than Moses. The Son indeed has already been described as "reflecting the brightness of God's glory" (1:3; cf. 2:7, 9). For a similar contrast, see 2 Cor. 3:7–11. The source of our author's analogy is probably in the first instance the material alluded to from Num. 12:7. Possibly, however, the idea of building a house is based on Zech. 6:12 f. (cf. 1 Chron. 17:11 f.). The metaphor of house or temple finds considerable expression in the NT (see e.g., Eph. 2:19–21; 1 Tim. 3:15; 1 Pet. 2:5).

3:4 / This verse is unnecessary to the argument; hence RSV's parentheses are justifiable. The author affirms that God is the builder of **all things**, without denying the role of subsidiary builders.

3:5 / The word for **servant** (*therapōn*, only occurrence in NT) is drawn from the LXX of Num. 12:7; *diakonos*, the common word for servant, especially in Paul's letters, does not occur in Hebrews. **That God would say in the future** translates a simple future passive participle (*tōn lalēthēsomenōn*). The passive voice is often used to indicate God's agency; the future tense describes what was future from Moses' perspective but what is past from the perspective of our author and his readers. It is possible that what is to be spoken in the future refers to the Law which Moses would deliver to his people, to which he was "a witness." It is more likely, however, that our author has in mind the contrast between preparation and fulfillment (cf. 10:1). From his perspective Moses was a witness to the fulfillment which has come (cf. John 5:46).

3:6 / The opening statement of this verse depends again on the passage about Moses in Num. 12:7. Christ is thus **faithful** (v. 2), like Moses—but the preposition "over" (*epi*), **in charge of**, as GNB appropriately translates, takes the place of the preposition *in* (see v. 2) God's house. Some Greek manuscripts include the words "firm unto the end" (KJV) at the close of the verse (probably by influence of 3:14; cf. 6:11). The word **courage** (*parrhēsia*) occurs four times in Hebrews; twice it is used in reference to the cultus (4:16; 10:19) and twice it refers to facing difficulty in life (here and 10:35). See W. S. Vorster, "The Meaning of *parrēsia* in the Epistle to the Hebrews," *Neotestamentica* 5 (1971), pp. 51–59. **What we hope for** translates the noun "hope" (*elpis*). This word expresses the author's future expectation, or eschatology proper in contrast to eschatology already realized in Christ (see above, p. 2).

7

An Exhortation Inspired
by the Exodus

HEBREWS 3:7–19

So then, as the Holy Spirit says,
"If you hear God's voice today,
[8]do not be stubborn, as your
ancestors were when they
rebelled against God,
as they were that day in the desert
when they put him to the test.
[9]There they put me to the test and
tried me, says God,
although they had seen what I did
for forty years.
[10]And so I was angry with those
people and said,
'They are always disloyal
and refuse to obey my commands.'
[11]I was angry and made a solemn
promise:
'They will never enter the land
where I would have given them
rest!' "
[12]My fellow believers, be careful
that no one among you has a heart so
evil and unbelieving that he will turn
away from the living God. [13]Instead,
in order that none of you be deceived
by sin and become stubborn, you
must help one another every day, as
long as the word "Today" in the
scripture applies to us. [14]For we are
all partners with Christ if we hold
firmly to the end the confidence we
had at the beginning.
[15]This is what the scripture says:
"If you hear God's voice today,
do not be stubborn, as your
ancestors were
when they rebelled against God."
[16]Who were the people who heard
God's voice and rebelled against him?
All those who were led out of Egypt
by Moses. [17]With whom was God
angry for forty years? With the people
who sinned, who fell down dead in
the desert. [18]When God made his
solemn promise, "They will never
enter the land where I would have
given them rest"—of whom was he
speaking? Of those who rebelled.
[19]We see, then, that they were not able
to enter the land, because they did
not believe.

The powerful exhortation offered by the author at this point depends upon an illustration drawn from Psalm 95:7–11 (cf. Num. 14:22 ff.), and in particular upon an analogy that is drawn between the experience of Israel and that of the church. We encounter in this passage, therefore, an example of exodus typology* that effectively directs

---

*Typology is the tracing of patterns of correspondence regarded as divinely intended between earlier and recent occurrences in history.

the readers' attention to the seriousness of rejection of Jesus. In the extended exegesis and application that follow the first quotation the author again reveals skillful midrashic exegesis wherein the phraseology of the quotation is used in elaborating the meaning that he has discovered for his readers in this passage of Scripture. The author also develops a unique concept of "rest" which he understands as the true position of the church in and through what Christ has done. He is convinced that the readers face a very serious danger and, therefore, that they must heed the warning that Israel's experience has to offer.

3:7-11 / **As the Holy Spirit says** serves as a further indication of the author's view of Scripture (the OT) as the word spoken by God (cf. 1:6, 7, 13). The Holy Spirit is similarly said to be the speaker in Scripture in 10:15 (cf. 9:8). The human authors are not denied, but they are not important to the author since in the last analysis it is God who is responsible for what they say. Again our author quotes from Psalms, his favorite OT book. The quotation, Psalm 95:7-11, is taken from the LXX and agrees verbatim, with only a few minor differences. Psalm 95 is divided into two parts: the first consists of praise and worship, the second of the warning that our author quotes in full. The psalmist's warning is based upon the narrative recorded in Exodus 17:1-7 (cf. Num. 20:1-13) and the judgment passage in Numbers 14:20-35. The psalmist appeals to his own generation not to fall into the unfortunate plight of the generation that perished in the wilderness. We know much less about the way in which the psalmist understood these sentences to apply to his generation than we know about how the author of Hebrews applied them to his readers. Presumably the psalmist associates entering the rest of the promised land with entering God's presence in the Temple: faithfulness is required in both instances. We may also have in the psalm, therefore, the beginning of an association between the rest promised by God, and God's own resting place, the Temple. The climax of the passage comes in the **solemn promise** of verse 11. The promise is, literally, "they will never enter my rest." GNB interprets this to mean **the land where I would have given them rest**. This interpretation is at this point, and in itself, correct, but has the effect of obscuring the double entendre that the author discerns in the words. For, as we will see, the **rest** announced in this psalm is seen finally by the author to refer to the rest that Christians are to enter—and that has nothing to do with the literal promised land.

In the verses that follow, the author presents a Christian commentary on the quotation. The exodus typology that underlies this interpretation is not only found at several places in the NT (e.g., 1 Cor. 5:7; 10:1–12), but is found even within the OT where, for example, Israel's return from the exile is deliberately described in language derived from the Exodus narrative. The complex of events associated with the Exodus are of such great importance that they become paradigmatic for later events in the history of redemption. In particular, the Exodus and the deliverance accomplished through the cross stand in special relationship. If the Jews were delivered from slavery in Egypt, God has through the cross delivered mankind from a greater slavery. God has acted gloriously and triumphantly in both instances, the earlier foreshadowing the later. And similarity exists not only in the redemptive events, but also in the aftermath of those events. Our author would be in perfect accord with Paul when he writes: "all these things happened to them as examples for others, and they were written down as a warning for us" (1 Cor. 10:11; cf. Rom. 15:4). The people that God led into the wilderness had experienced the great deliverance of the Exodus and yet they fell away. Those who have experienced the redemption of the cross may find themselves in a similar situation. The basis of all typology is analogy, the similarity in pattern between past and present. This method of warning the readers is far more powerful than any other the author could have employed.

3:12 / The author now begins his commentary, employing key words drawn from the preceding quotation in good midrashic form. The point of the quotation is immediately evident in the words **be careful**. What is to be avoided at all costs is a **heart** that is **evil and unbelieving**. **Heart** picks up the same word in verses 8 and 10, where it is described as "hardened" and "straying." This is the kind of heart that leads to apostasy, causing one to **turn away from the living God**. What is in view in this strong language (*tō apostēnai*, "to apostatize") is a deliberate rebellion against the truth and therefore against God. The adjective **living** adds to the perception of the dynamic character of God, who will in no way overlook such action on the part of his children.

3:13 / The readers must be careful lest they too, like the wilderness wanderers, **be deceived by sin** (lit., "the deceitfulness of sin") and **become stubborn**—which is purposely the word that is used in the quotation (v. 15). The readers are called to **help one another every day**. The importance of fellowship and mutual support is explicitly mentioned in 10:24–25. **Help** is needed **every day** because the call to faithful discipleship is a daily challenge. The Christian life can only be lived on a daily basis, and therefore every day is a new "today" when God calls and we must respond in obedience. **As long as**, therefore, suggests not that there will come a time in this life when the **"Today" in the Scripture** will no longer apply to us, but that faithfulness is required of us, as the next verse points out, **to the end**.

3:14 / By **partners with Christ** the author means those who share in the fulfillment he brings. Even as Christ became a sharer in our humanity, Christians become sharers of Christ by participation in the kingdom he has inaugurated, and by becoming heirs who "share his glory" (2:10). But this new status is not to be taken for granted because of a good **beginning**. Again our author's concern for the faltering faith of the readers is evident. Their beginning **confidence**, that is, that subjective assurance that produces faithful obedience, must be held **firmly to the end**, until Jesus returns or until the Christian through death goes to be with him.

3:15 / This verse presents the first of four occasions where in the ongoing exposition of the original quotation a portion of it is formally cited again (cf. 4:3, 5, 7). Here the opening two lines (Ps. 95:7) are repeated (cf. v. 7).

3:16–17 / Those who **heard** and **rebelled** (both words drawn from the preceding quotation) were the very Israelites who had experienced the exodus. The words **angry for forty years** (cf. vv. 9 f.) are also drawn from the original quotation (see Additional Notes). These people **sinned** (cf. v. 10) and **fell down dead in the desert** (lit., "whose bodies fell in the desert"), words quoted from Num. 14:29 (LXX), with the last three words also echoing the original quotation (v. 8). Our author's point is that those who **sinned** had been privileged to experience God's remarkable deliverance from Egypt. This wonderful beginning, however, did them no good in their later rebellion.

3:18 / The argument is repeated, this time by a further quotation of the **solemn promise** first cited in verse 11. The Greek text again has simply, "they shall never enter his rest" (see comment on v. 11). Those to whom these words were spoken were those who had **rebelled** (lit., "were disobedient").

3:19 / It is clear that the failure of the Israelites **to enter the land** (lit., "to enter in," with "rest" understood) was **because they did not believe**

(lit., "because of unbelief"). "Unbelief" here implies not intellectual doubting as much as deliberate unfaithfulness. From the author's perspective, unbelief and disobedience are inseparable. The unbelief and unfaithfulness of Israel were inexcusable because the Israelites had received abundant evidence of God's reality and love (cf. 4:2).

Additional Notes

3:7-11 / The Holy Spirit is regularly regarded in the NT as the one who inspires and thus who speaks through the writers of the OT. See e.g., Matt. 22:43; Acts 1:16; 28:25; 2 Pet. 1:20 f. See P. K. Jewett in *ZPEB*, vol. 3, pp. 194 f. The only important change made by the author in presenting the quotation is his addition of **and so** ("wherefore"), which causes the **forty years** to refer to the people's experience of God's provision rather than to the length of God's anger, as it stands in both Hebrew OT and LXX (cf. Ps. 95:10). Yet in v. 17 the forty years does refer to God's anger, so that the author regards both statements as true. The LXX is a careful translation of the Hebrew; the only significant change is the translation of the names Meribah ("contention": **when they rebelled against God**) and Massah ("testing": **when they put him to the test**). The initial **if** should not be taken to imply uncertainty as to whether or not **God's voice** is heard. In the original Hebrew it expresses a strong wish (as GNB of Ps. 95:7 suggests: "Listen today to what he says"). RSV accordingly translates the opening words: "Today, when you hear his voice." **Stubborn** translates the common metaphorical reference "to harden the hearts." See U. Becker in *NIDNTT*, vol. 2, pp. 153–55. **Your ancestors** (lit., "fathers") is brought forward from v. 9 to v. 8 in GNB.

Possibly the reference to forty years had special significance to the author and readers if it was about forty years since the exodus accomplished by Jesus (presuming the epistle was written just prior to A.D. 70). **Says God** (v. 9) is an addition by GNB to the original text. The special insertion of **and so** (*dio*) in v. 10, since it puts the **forty years** with what the Israelites had experienced, has the effect of intensifying their guilt. **Those people** (v. 10) is lit. "this generation," an alteration of the LXX text by our author that makes the present application more vivid. **Are always disloyal** is literally "go astray in their hearts" and is thus close to v. 8 in meaning. This language reflects the Hebrew view of the heart as the center of cognition and volition. **Refuse to obey my commands** is lit. "did not know my ways," but the issue, as GNB rightly reflects, is one of obedience, not knowledge. **I was angry** heightens the anthropomorphism of "as I swore in my wrath." This common formula adds a grave solemnity to the oath God makes (cf. 3:18, 4:3; for a positive use, see 6:13, 7:21). See H.-G. Link, *NIDNTT*, vol. 3, pp. 737–43.

3:12 / **My fellow believers** is lit. "brethren" and is similar to the address of 3:1. **Unbelieving** (*apistias*) is from the author's perspective the root problem leading to disobedience and eventually apostasy. In v. 19, the failure is directly linked to unbelief (*apistia*). This is the negative side of the "faith" or "belief" of the heroes catalogued in chap. 11. Can Jewish readers who revert back to their Judaism, as the recipients of this letter were apparently tempted to do, be described as turning away **from the living God**? Some have argued that this expression necessarily indicates a non-Jewish readership. But for our author, who sees Christianity as the fulfillment of the promises, and therefore as true Judaism and not as another religion, to apostatize from Christianity *is* to turn away from the living God. No room is given to the modern idea of the presence of God in, and therefore the legitimacy of, Judaism as a religion paralleling Christianity. Our author regards a relapse to Judaism on the part of his readers as most grievous and dangerous indeed. On the expression **living God**, see note to 9:12.

3:13 / Just as the Devil is the deceiver (2 Cor. 2:11), so his instrument, sin, is full of deceitfulness (Rom. 7:11). **Help** or "encouragement" (words used in GNB to translate *parakaleō* and *paraklēsis*) is sorely needed by the readers and is thus an important emphasis in the epistle. In addition to 10:25, see 13:22 ("this message of encouragement"); 6:18; and 12:5. In addition to its obvious meaning in the present context, the word **today** may also have had eschatological associations for the author (cf. 2 Cor. 6:2), but if so, he does not make use of them.

3:14 / For discussion of the word **confidence** (*hypostasis*), see comment on 11:1.

3:15 / See notes on v. 7.

3:16–17 / The structure of the two verses is parallel. Each contains two rhetorical questions, the second in both instances beginning with the negative *ou* that presupposes a positive answer. For this reason GNB turns these questions into positive statements. The word **rebelled**, as well as occurring as a noun in the quotation from Ps. 95, is also found in the narratives of Exod. 15:23; 17:7; and Num. 14; 20:2–5. Although the vocabulary is different, the same thought and the same motive for expressing it is found in 1 Cor. 10:10: "we must not complain, as some of them did—and they were destroyed by the Angel of Death." The words **angry for forty years**, unlike the way in which the author has presented the quotation in v. 9 f., correctly reflects the meaning of the OT text. Both the rebellion and the anger may be said to have characterized the forty-year period.

3:18 / The words **the land where I would have given them rest** are an interpretative paraphrase for the simple "rest." Here instead of "my rest," as in the original quotation (cf. v. 11), the text reads "his rest" (cf. also 4:10). The author uses the oaths or solemn promises of God much to the advantage of his argument in the epistle. Besides the references in this chapter, see also 4:3; 6:13; and 7:21. The disobedience referred to in this verse (in the verb underlying GNB's **rebelled**) is mentioned again by our author in 4:6, 11 with a noun of the same root (*apeitheia*, "disobedience"). For the root in the sense of unbelief, see BAGD, *apeitheō* (sec. 3).

3:19 / The word **enter** is drawn from the quotation in the preceding verse. The words **the land** are added again for clarity. It is correct to assume that entry into the land is the "rest" that is in view at this juncture. Those who died in the wilderness failed to arrive at the immediate goal of the possession of Canaan. Those who did enter did not enjoy the promised rest since the land was secure from enemies for only the briefest periods. Possession of the land was never the true rest that God had in mind for his people. That rest by its nature transcends all earthly prefigurations. As we shall see, the author is very creative in his use of the word "rest" in the verses that follow.

8

The Remaining Promise
of Rest

HEBREWS 4:1–13

Now, God has offered us the promise that we may receive that rest he spoke about. Let us take care, then, that none of you will be found to have failed to receive that promised rest. ²For we have heard the Good News, just as they did. They heard the message, but it did them no good, because when they heard it, they did not accept it with faith. ³We who believe, then, do receive that rest which God promised. It is just as he said,

"I was angry and made a solemn promise:
'They will never enter the land where I would have given them rest!' "

He said this even though his work had been finished from the time he created the world. ⁴For somewhere in the Scriptures this is said about the seventh day: "God rested on the seventh day from all his work." ⁵This same matter is spoken of again: "They will never enter that land where I would have given them rest." ⁶Those who first heard the Good News did not receive that rest, because they did not believe. There are, then, others who are allowed to receive it. ⁷This is shown by the fact that God sets another day, which is called "Today." Many years later he spoke of it through David in the scripture already quoted:

"If you hear God's voice today, do not be stubborn."

⁸If Joshua had given the people the rest that God had promised, God would not have spoken later about another day. ⁹As it is, however, there still remains for God's people a rest like God's resting on the seventh day. ¹⁰For whoever receives that rest which God promised will rest from his own work, just as God rested from his. ¹¹Let us, then, do our best to receive that rest, so that no one of us will fail as they did because of their lack of faith.

¹²The word of God is alive and active, sharper than any double-edged sword. It cuts all the way through, to where soul and spirit meet, to where joints and marrow come together. It judges the desires and thoughts of man's heart. ¹³There is nothing that can be hid from God; everything in all creation is exposed and lies open before his eyes. And it is to him that we must all give an account of ourselves.

4:1 / The first sentence in GNB is a considerable expansion of the Greek (which refers simply to "the remaining promise of entering his rest"), making explicit what is implicit. The rest offered to Israel was not entered into and God still offers the promise of that rest to his people (cf. vv. 3, 6, 11). It follows that **that rest he spoke about** cannot have been entry and possession of the land, but must have been a more fundamental kind of rest. The key word **rest** is drawn from the original quotation (3:11; cf. 3:18) and is the subject of the exposition that follows (cf. vv. 3–5, 8, 10, 11). **Let us take care** (cf. 1 Cor. 10:12) is perhaps a little weak for the strong warning "let us fear" (cf. KJV; RSV; NEB). **To have failed to receive that promised rest** is an expansion of "to have fallen short of it." The author applies the warning directly to his readers: **none of you**.

4:2 / As is evident through the teaching of the epistle, the **Good News** for the author and readers refers to the cross and its effects. For those in the wilderness it was the deliverance of the exodus (cf. 3:16) and the Sinai covenant. For both groups the **Good News** is God's redemptive love demonstrated in his saving acts. The difference between that generation of Israelites and the Christian readers of the epistle, who are the recipients of definitive fulfillment, is not alluded to here as it is elsewhere (e.g., 2:1–4). The Good News that the Israelites heard, however, **did them no good** because it was not received **with faith** (cf. 3:19). The implication for the readers is clear. Hearing must be accompanied by believing.

4:3 / By contrast, believers **do receive** (lit., "enter") **that rest**. These words again are drawn from the original quotation (3:11, 18). Here again we directly confront the ambiguity of our author's eschatology, which has both present (or realized) and future aspects. While the **rest** in its fullest sense remains a future expectation, there is also a sense in which we are already entering into that rest now, and therefore it is already ours (see comment on v. 10). In the second half of the verse we encounter a section of the original quotation presented again as a formal quotation (cf. 3:15; 4:5, 7). The point of the quotation here is not readily apparent despite the introductory words **it is just as he said**. The explanation is given in the following verses and rests on two important premises that our author is at pains to establish: (1) God's rest is in fact a reality (vv. 3b–4), and (2) the Israelites were prohibited from entering that rest (the quotations in vv. 3 and 5). It follows that the rest was not entered into and therefore remains for the people of the era of fulfillment (v. 6). What the Israelites failed to receive becomes available to those who believe in the Good News of Jesus Christ (cf. vv. 2 and 3). Thus the negative argument of the quotation serves ultimately as a support for the argument concerning the continuing availability of rest. God made the **solemn promise** prohibiting the Israelites from his rest **even though** that rest was already a reality. The implication is that he had others in mind who would indeed enter that rest. The reality of God's rest from his creative **work** (lit., "works," drawn from the quotation that follows) **from the time he created the world** (lit., "from the foundation of the world") is plainly evident.

4:4 / Again our author shows little concern with the human author of Scripture (**is said**, lit., "he [i.e., God] said") or even the location (**somewhere**) of the quotation. The quotation closely follows Genesis 2:2 according to the LXX and is used here to substantiate the argument of the preceding verse. **Seventh day** thus became in itself an expression for rest. This is more evident from the underlying Hebrew word for "seven," from which we get the word "Sabbath" (see comment on v. 9).

4:5 / Again a line from Psalm 95:11 is quoted to reiterate the failure of the Israelites to enter God's rest (cf. v. 3).

4:6 / This verse is a summary of the preceding argument and serves to pull together the various threads of the argument. The first sentence repeats the argument of v. 2b. Those who wandered in the wilderness **did not receive** (lit., "enter into," alluding to the original quotation) **that rest because they did not believe** (lit., "because of disobedience"). The result of this failure is that **others are allowed to receive it**. Literally, this sentence reads, "it remains for some to enter it" (RSV); again "enter" alludes to the original quotation. Phillips, however, catches the sense best: "it is clear that some were intended to experience this rest." God's rest does not exist in vain; it was always meant to be shared by his people, and now that intention is fulfilled. For in this rest God's ultimate purpose for the creation finds its realization.

4:7 / The words **this is shown by the fact that** are a justifiable expansion of the simple "and again" of the Greek text, since the author here adds further support to his argument. From the opening word of the original quotation (in 3:7) from Psalm 95—the word **today**—he deduces that **God sets another day** for his rest to be entered into. It is important that in the time of David, **many years later**, the same invitation to hear and obey could be given with the preface **today**. This suggests not only that the rest remains to be entered, but that the invitation extends to, and finds its true meaning in, the present. For every day is a new "today," and the word "today" applies pre-eminently to those who are "partners with

Christ" (cf. 3:13, 14). The quotation is the fourth and last time that material from the original quotation (3:7–11) is represented in smaller, formal quotations (cf. 3:15; 4:3, 5).

4:8 / **Joshua** did not lead the people to **the rest that God had promised** (the last four words are added by GNB). For if that had occurred, the offer would not have been repeated **later** "through David" and there would have been no mention of **another day**. Since in Greek the names Joshua and Jesus are identical, the readers could not have avoided the implicit contrast between the "Jesus" who failed to give rest and the Jesus who brings the true, promised rest to his people. Although it is not mentioned, it must be assumed that David's generation did not enter the promised rest—or at least that if they in some sense did, it was not in the definitive sense in which the OT rest is available to those who enjoy the fulfillment brought by Christ. Just as David contemporized the narrative of the wilderness rebellion by applying it to his readers, so the author in this passage has done for his readers. Yet the difference between David's time and that of the writer is clear from the argument of the entire epistle.

4:9 / The promised rest, therefore, **remains for God's people** to enjoy. Behind the words **a rest like God's resting on the seventh day** is a single word that occurs only here in the whole of the Greek Bible: "Sabbath-rest" (RSV, NEB, NIV). This word suggests God's own Sabbath-rest after creation (v. 4). God's gift of rest may thus be regarded as the gift of his own rest. To enjoy the blessings of the eschaton is to participate in the Sabbath-rest of God.

4:10 / By a skillful combination of language drawn from two of the OT passages that have already been quoted (Ps. 95:11 in 3:11, 18; 4:3, 5; and Gen. 2:2 in 4:4), the author indicates that the promised rest and God's rest are of the same kind. One who has entered God's rest thus "has rested from his own works" (cf. KJV). This is a literal rendering of the Greek underlying GNB's **will rest from his own work**. GNB chooses to focus upon the future aspect of the rest that shall be ours, thereby ignoring the past (aorist) tense of the verb. The ultimate realization of this rest must indeed lie in the future, but as has already been argued, there is also a present experience of this rest that the author is especially concerned to stress.

The way in which "works" is to be understood is not clear and commentators have differed in their interpretations of the word. Since the rest or cessation from works is something meant to be begun here and now it must not be thought of as a cessation of life or as that rest enjoyed only by the saints who through death have gone to be with Christ. If we look for something to be enjoyed in the present, it is unlikely that the works should be thought of as works-righteousness in the Pauline sense, so that the rest is one of justification by faith. This view is not articulated anywhere in the epistle and, more important, it is not appropriate to the context at this point. Faith for our author, furthermore, is not put over against works but is practically interchangeable with obedience. Possibly by "works" the author may have in mind the activity of the sacrificial ritual and the minutiae of ceremonial cleanness so important in the Judaism to which the readers were attracted. The most plausible interpretation, however, is that the author has in mind the ideal qualities of the Sabbath-rest, namely peace, well-being, and security—that is, a frame of mind that by virtue of its confidence and trust in God possesses these qualities in contradiction to the surrounding circumstances. In short, the author may well have in mind that peace and sense of ultimate security "which is far beyond human understanding" (Phil. 4:7). This interpretation has the further advantage of making the argument very pertinent to the needs of the readers—a concern never far from our author's mind.

4:11 / That the above interpretation is on the right track is confirmed by the exhortation now given to **do our best to receive** (lit., "enter") **that rest** (once again the allusion to the original quotation is plain). If this rest is entered into now, then none of the readers **will fail** (lit., "fall") as did the Israelites in the wilderness due to a **lack of faith** (lit., "disobedience"). Thus the rest, if entered into, will have the effect of producing obedience—here in the sense of faithfulness. The readers will thereby not take the road of apostasy, following the example (**as they did**) of the Israelites, but will, armed with the existential peace of God's Sabbath-rest, endure the hardships and persecution that they apparently face as Christians. It should be noted that in the argument of this chapter we encounter the tension between the indicative (we have entered the rest) and the imperative (we are to strive to enter the rest) which is often encountered in Paul's argumentation (e.g., Rom. 6:7, 12). This is in turn but a reflection of the tension between realized and future eschatology. The author's pastoral concerns for his readers are evident in this application, as well as in the following two verses.

4:12 / The close connection between this paragraph (vv. 12–13) and the preceding verses is indicated by the strong conjunction "for" (oddly omitted by GNB and NIV; contrast, for example, KJV, RSV). These two verses thus supply the ground or logical basis for the preceding exhortation, and this fact is important for correct interpretation. **The word of God** is neither a reference to Jesus nor even primarily to Scripture. It is instead what God speaks, and the idea was probably suggested to the author from the repeated reference to "hearing God's voice" in the preceding verses (3:7, 15, 16; 4:2, 7). The point is that God's voice, **the word of God**, by its very character demands authentic response. Before his penetrating word there can be no feigning of loyalty. Therefore the author's exhortation is to be taken with the utmost seriousness. What God speaks is **alive and active**. By his word he brought creation into existence and his word can never be rendered ineffective (cf. Isa. 55:11). The effectiveness of God's word is now expressed by the metaphor **sharper than any double-edged sword** (cf. Rev. 2:12). The sentences that follow are merely a development of this metaphor and are not meant to convey information extraneous to the point being made by the author. He does not here reveal his view of the nature of man (**where soul and spirit meet; the desires and thoughts of man's heart**). All of these details are concerned only to stress the utter effectiveness of God's word.

4:13 / Indeed, the point of the preceding is now made plain in the words **there is nothing** (lit., "no creature") **that can be hid from God**. All lies **exposed** and **open before his eyes** and the connotation of this language is that all are inescapably vulnerable not only to God's scrutiny but also his judgment. This aspect is made explicit in the final sentence: it is to God **that we must all give an account of ourselves** (cf. Rom. 14:12). Thus verses 12 and 13 are applied to the readers to remind them of the seriousness of their choice. It is worth wondering whether the readers contemplated some form of compromise that was meant to veil what was actually apostasy.

Additional Notes

4:1 / Héring offers an interesting interpretation of this verse that hinges on the meaning of the word "remaining" (*kataleipomenēs*), which he takes in the sense of "not being actualized." The point then becomes that failure to enter the rest might be attributed by some to the failure of eschatology (cf. 2 Pet. 3:4). Such a rendering is possible, but if it is what the author intended, he has expressed himself very obscurely.

The word **rest** (*katapausis*), which was introduced in the original quotation (3:11) and repeated in 3:18 occurs six times in chap. 4 (twice in repetitions of the first quotation). The word occurs in only one other place in the NT, Acts 7:49 (quoting Isa. 46:1). The cognate verb occurs in 4:4, 8, 10 (twice by quotation of Gen. 2:2). The background for the author's distinctive use of the concept *katapausis* probably is to be found in Jewish apocalyptic rather than Gnosticism. See G. von Rad, "There Remains Still a Rest for the People of God: An Investigation of a Biblical Conception," *The Problem of the Hexateuch and Other Essays* (Edinburgh & London: Oliver & Boyd, 1966), pp. 94–102; R. Hensel and C. Brown, *NIDNTT*, vol. 3, pp. 254–58. In understanding the present passage, it is important to realize that our author is speaking of three distinct, although related, kinds of rest: (1) literal rest in the land of Canaan (cf. Deut. 12:9), (2) God's own rest (v. 4), and (3) the rest that is meant to be the portion of Christians (this indeed may be subdivided into the rest available at present and the future rest of eschatology proper). It is clear that our author sees a typological relationship between rest in the land of Canaan and the rest that God intends for Christians. The blessings of the one foreshadow those of the other, just as the present rest Christians can enjoy is an anticipation of the final, eschatological rest. See H. A. Lombard, "*Katapausis* in the Letter to the Hebrews," *Neotestamentica* 5 (1971), pp. 60–71.

4:2 / **Heard the Good News** translates the verb *euangelizomai* (in Hebrews only here and in v. 6), a word which, particularly because of its use in the second half of Isaiah, is full of eschatological associations. Its appropriateness for what the readers have heard is evident; it can be used anachronistically to refer to the time of the wilderness wandering because of the theological continuity of their experience of deliverance and covenant relationship with that of the readers. Considerable textual difficulty exists concerning the Greek that underlies **they did not accept it with faith**, but no serious alteration of the meaning is involved. See Metzger, *TCGNT*, p. 665. NEB comes close to the literal meaning of the passage: "they brought no admixture of faith to the hearing of it." The language of the verse is similar to Pauline idiom in Rom. 10:16 (where Isa. 53:1 is quoted). For the necessity of adding faith to hearing, see, too, Gal. 3:2, 6. On the meaning of the word **faith**, see note on 11:1.

4:3 / Commentators are divided on whether the opening sentence in this verse should be taken to refer to a present entering into rest, as the present tense of the verb **do receive** (*eiserchometha*) suggests (Westcott, Spicq, Montefiore), or a future eschatological rest (Delitzsch, Héring; by implication, Bruce, Hughes). The former interpretation, which need not exclude an ultimate realization of rest in the future, is supported by implication in v. 1, explicitly in v. 10 (contrary to the future tense in GNB). This view alone makes sense of the exhortation in v. 11 and best supports the pastoral concern of the author. See also 12:22 ff. On the tension in Hebrews between realized and future eschatology, see G. Hughes, *Hebrews and Hermeneutics*, pp. 67–73. "Foundation of the world" is common phraseology in the NT to refer to the creation (cf. Heb. 9:26; Matt. 25:34; Luke 11:50; John 17:24; Eph. 1:4; 1 Pet. 1:20; Rev. 13:8).

4:4 / As in the preceding verse, GNB uses the singular **work** for the Greek plural (cf. v. 10). The word (*ergon*) is common in Hebrews, referring several times to God's creation, as here (1:10; 4:3). In 6:1, 10; 9:14; and 10:24 it refers to righteous deeds, but it is never used explicitly in a Pauline polemic against "works righteousness." See Bertram, *TDNT*, vol. 2, pp. 635–55. Unlike the description of the previous six days, the Genesis account of the seventh day makes no mention of evening. Jewish commentators concluded that God's Sabbath-rest, which began after creation, lasted indefinitely. The writer draws on this tradition when he argues that his readers may enjoy God's Sabbath-rest in the present. Again, an eschatological Sabbath, a thousand-year period following six thousand years of history, is also known in Jewish tradition. Our author, we have argued, knows of both a present Sabbath-rest and a future Sabbath-rest. See A. T. Lincoln, "Sabbath, Rest and Eschatology in the New Testament," in *From Sabbath to Lord's Day: A Biblical, Historical and Theological Investigation*, ed. D. A. Carson (Grand Rapids: Zondervan, 1982).

4:5 / **This same matter** more probably should be "in the same passage" (cf. RSV; NEB; NIV), referring to the requotation of the last line of Ps. 95.

4:6 / GNB reverses the order of the two sentences in this verse. The causal conjunction **then** (or "since") therefore immediately follows the preceding quotation and helps to indicate the way in which the author understands the quotation as supporting his argument. "Disobedience" (*apeitheia*) is a key word here and in v. 11; the verb form occurs in 3:18 and 11:31. See O. Becker, *NIDNTT*, vol. 1, pp. 588–93.

4:7 / **Sets** (*horizei*) alludes to a sovereign decree of God (cf. Acts 10:42; Rom. 1:4). The point of the reference to David is not a concern with authorship, since elsewhere, as we have seen, the author is oblivious to the human authorship of Scripture, regarding it simply as the word of God. David is referred to here in order to stress the chronological distance between the time of the wilderness wandering and the repetition of the promise with the word today. If the author understands his own day as the **today** spoken of in the time of David, then he may have understood Ps. 95:7 as prophetic, and it becomes possible to interpret **already quoted** (*proeirētai*) as "was foretold."

4:8 / The Greek name for Joshua, "Jesus," occurs in this form in the KJV of Acts 7:45, where the reference is to Joshua and not to some act of the preincarnate Jesus. In Josh. 22:4 (cf. 21:43–45), Joshua announced that God had in fact given the people rest (the verb is the same as the one in this verse). But this rest, like that brought by David (2 Sam. 7:1, 11) and Solomon (1 Kings 8:56), was at best a meager experience of the rest God intended for his people. The latter indeed must be regarded as being on a different level altogether. All former experience of rest is typological foreshadowing of the eschatological rest God intends and that is now beginning to be experienced by his people.

4:9 / The rare Greek word for "Sabbath-rest" in this verse (*sabbatismos*) is deliberately used by the author in place of the word for "rest" used previously in his argument (*katapausis*) in order to emphasize that the rest of which he has been speaking is of an eschatological order—indeed, of the order of God's own Sabbath-rest. God's Sabbath-rest thus becomes a symbol for our rest. For a similar perspective, wherein future heavenly blessings are conceived as realizable in the present, see 12:22–24. See A. T. Lincoln, "Sabbath, Rest and Eschatology in the New Testament," in *From Sabbath to Lord's Day,* ed. D. A. Carson. On *sabbatismos,* see Lohse, *TDNT,* vol. 7, pp. 34 f.

4:10 / **Receives that rest which God promised** interprets the simple "enters his rest" of the Greek, which in turn is drawn from the language of the original OT quotation. KJV, ASV, and NASB accurately render the Greek aorist tense with the past tense "has rested." Other versions (RSV, NEB, NIV) use the present tense, presumably regarding it as more consistent with the context (see v. 3) and understanding the aorist "has rested" as due to the influence of the same tense in the quotation of Gen. 2:2 in v. 4. In exegeting the meaning of "works," it is a mistake to put too much stress on the analogy of God's having rested from his works. The point of the analogy is the reality of the rest, not what one rests from. The rest, and therefore the cessation of works, is in principle eschatological, yet it is a rest to be entered into in the present. The interesting parallel in the language of Rev. 14:13 ("they will enjoy rest from their hard work") is therefore only partially pertinent here.

4:11 / **Do our best** translates *spoudazō* ("be diligent," or "zealous"), a common word in the ethical exhortation of the NT. The last half of the verse more literally reads: "lest anyone should fall in the same pattern of disobedience," alluding to the mention of disobedience as the cause of Israel's failure as mentioned in 4:6. See H. W. Attridge, " 'Let us strive to enter that rest': The Logic of Hebrews 4:1–11," *HTR* 73 (1980), pp. 279–88.

4:12 / Because in Philo the **word of God** (*logos tou theou*) is personified and said to divide different faculties within man, some have seen Alexandrian influence upon the author in the present passage. Although possible, such a conclusion is far from certain. The **word of God** is **alive** because God is "the living God" (3:12). Its dynamic and effective quality is thereby assured (cf. Jer. 23:29; see too 1 Pet. 1:23). Effective words are likened to a sharp sword (Isa. 49:2) and the word of God (but here *rhēma tou theou*) to the sword of the Spirit (Eph. 6:17). For "two-edged sword," see Rev. 2:12. "Wisdom" (*sophia*) has qualities that parallel those of the word of God in the present passage, especially with reference to powers of penetration (Wisd. of Sol. 7:23 ff.; 1:6). For the argument that the **word of God** refers to Jesus, see J. Swetnam, "Jesus as *Logos* in Hebrews 4:12–13," *Biblica* 62 (1981), pp. 214–24.

4:13 / The fact that at the time of judgment everything hidden will be revealed is stressed elsewhere in the NT (e.g., 1 Cor. 4:5). **Exposed** and **open before his eyes** indicates the precarious situation of every person at the time of judgment. For the connection between word and judgment, see John 12:48. See G. E. Trompf, "Conception of God in Hebrews 4:12–13," *StudTh* 25 (1971), pp. 123–132.

9

The High Priesthood of Jesus

HEBREWS 4:14–5:10

Let us, then, hold firmly to the faith we profess. For we have a great High Priest who has gone into the very presence of God—Jesus, the Son of God. [15]Our High Priest is not one who cannot feel sympathy for our weaknesses. On the contrary, we have a High Priest who was tempted in every way that we are, but did not sin. [16]Let us be brave, then, and approach God's throne, where there is grace. There we will receive mercy and find grace to help us just when we need it.

[1]Every high priest is chosen from his fellow-men and appointed to serve God on their behalf, to offer sacrifices and offerings for sins. [2]Since he himself is weak in many ways, he is able to be gentle with those who are ignorant and make mistakes. [3]And because he is himself weak, he must offer sacrifices not only for the sins of the people but also for his own sins. [4]No one chooses for himself the honor of being a high priest. It is only by God's call that a man is made a high priest—just as Aaron was.

[5]In the same way, Christ did not take upon himself the honor of being a high priest. Instead, God said to him,

"You are my Son;
today I have become your Father."

[6]He also said in another place,

"You will be a priest forever,
as the successor of Melchizedek."

[7]In his life on earth Jesus made his prayers and requests with loud cries and tears to God, who could save him from death. Because he was humble and devoted, God heard him. [8]But even though he was God's Son, he learned through his sufferings to be obedient. [9]When he was made perfect, he became the source of eternal salvation for all those who obey him, [10]and God declared him to be high priest, as the successor of Melchizedek.

In the last verses of chapter 4 the author again exhorts his readers to faithfulness, but this time on the basis of his argument concerning the high priesthood of Jesus. The connection has already been made between Jesus' high priesthood and his ability to help his people (see 2:17–18), but now it is elaborated and leads the author into the beginning of a discourse on how Jesus is qualified to be High Priest at all. First the author reviews the role and calling of high priests (5:1–4) and then he turns to the qualifications of Jesus as High Priest (5:5–10).

4:14 / The second sentence in GNB is a dependent clause in the Greek and precedes the first sentence. **The faith we profess** is literally "the confession" as in 3:1 (cf. 10:23); the exhortation implies the tendency of the readers to waver. What will enable them to remain true is the reality of **a great High Priest**. **Great** here suggests the uniqueness of this particular possessor of that exalted office. This indeed is no ordinary high priest. He is the man **Jesus**, but also the unique **Son of God**, the one **who has gone into the very presence of God** (lit., "who has passed through the heavens"). This last clause may be, as GNB seems to take it, an allusion to Christ's presence in the spiritual or "heavenly temple" where his priestly work is accomplished (cf. 6:20; 9:11–12). At the same time, there may also be a deliberate allusion to Psalm 110:1, so important a verse for our author, which is also associated with Christ's priestly work (see 8:1–2). Similar language is found in 7:26 where Jesus the High Priest is said to be "raised above the heavens," with which may be compared Paul's reference to Christ as the "one who went up, above and beyond the heavens, to fill the whole universe with his presence" (Eph. 4:10). Thus a number of themes concerning Jesus previously referred to by the author are now brought together again and associated with the title of High Priest: his humanity, his unique sonship, his exaltation, and as we are about to hear, his consequent ability to help Christians under testing.

4:15 / The author makes the same point negatively and positively. GNB draws attention to the contrast with the words **on the contrary** (lit., "but"). Our High Priest is not impassive, unable to share our feelings of weakness and vulnerability. He too lived as a human and thus as one **who was tempted in every way that we are**. The ambiguity of the Greek may justify the translation of NEB: "one who, because of his likeness to us, has been tested every way." The full humanity of Jesus means that he experienced the full range (rather than every specific manifestation) of human temptation, although to a much higher degree of intensity since, unlike all others, he never yielded to sin. Our author thus shares the NT view of the sinlessness of Jesus (e.g., 2 Cor. 5:21; 1 Pet. 2:22; 1 John 3:5). Whereas Jesus **feels sympathy** for us in our weakness, he is not, like other high priests, himself subject to sin (see 5:2 f.). Jesus became "like his brothers in every way," **but did not sin**; he therefore can now "help those who are tempted, because he himself was tempted and suffered" (2:17–18).

4:16 / If the readers are to "hold firmly to the faith" (v. 14), they will need to avail themselves of the help that comes from the very presence of God. Using imagery drawn from the temple cultus (e.g., **approach**), the author encourages boldness: **be brave** (cf. 10:19). It is no light matter to draw near to **God's throne, where there is grace** (lit., "the throne of grace"). But there the readers will find the **mercy** and **grace** they need, and **just when we need it**. In keeping with the language of the cultus, this "throne of grace" is probably analogous in the author's mind to the mercy-seat in the holy of holies (cf. 9:5). It is assumed rather than stated that the High Priest who is able to help is there at **God's throne** (cf. v. 14 and 1:3, etc.).

We have now reached that important stage in the author's argument where he must set forth the qualifications of Jesus as High Priest. This he does by first reviewing the role and the nature of the office according to the OT Scriptures, and then by showing how Jesus fulfills the same criteria.

5:1 / This verse is virtually a "dictionary definition" of "high priest." Representing mankind before God, a high priest is **chosen from his fellow-men** and it is **on their behalf** that he serves God, offering **sacrifices and offerings** (lit., "gifts and sacrifices") **for sins**. The language is deliberately general and comprehensive (for the same terminology, see 8:3). In view, as we shall see, is the special work of the high priest on the Day of Atonement, which will be the focus of attention in chapters 9 and 10.

5:2-3 / Since the high priest is human, he is **weak in many ways** (lit., "clothed in weakness," as Barclay translates). "The law appoints men in their weakness as high priests" (7:28 RSV). The high priest can therefore **be gentle** or patient with the **ignorant** and erring. GNB's **make mistakes** is perhaps too weak for the literal "go astray." Possibly in view are the unwitting sins for which the priest makes atonement according to Numbers 15:28 (cf. Lev. 5:17–19). Although Jesus satisfies the important criterion of humanness and thus qualifies to be a priest, he is not "clothed with weakness" as is the high priest, nor does he therefore need to offer sacrifices **for his own sins** (9:7; Lev. 16:6) as the high priest must (cf. 7:27). For although he suffered testing, and can help those who suffer testing, he himself "did not sin" (4:15). Thus Jesus is both similar and dissimilar to ordinary high priests. The key similarity, the atonement for the sins of the people, is left for later exposition (chaps. 9–10).

5:4 / The office of high priest is not entered into freely or by personal choice. God alone chooses a person for this **honor**. It is a matter of **God's**

call, as can be clearly seen in the case of Aaron (see Exod. 28:1) and his descendants (Num. 25:13).

5:5-6 / If Christ qualifies to be a high priest by virtue of his humanity, he also qualifies by virtue of divine appointment. He **did not take upon himself the honor** (lit., "glory") **of being a high priest**. This has been shown to be an impossibility in the preceding verse, apparently even for the Christ. The author now cites two OT passages to make his argument, and it is in seeing the connection between the two that he has achieved one of his most brilliant insights, unique in all the NT. The first quotation, Psalm 2:7, has already been utilized at the beginning of the book (1:5). Although the point of the unique sonship of Jesus has already been made by the author, at this point in the argument it must again be stressed from Psalm 2:7 that Jesus is the messianic King by divine decree. The second quotation, Psalm 110:4, refers to one who **will be a priest forever, as the successor of** (lit., "according to the order of") **Melchizedek**. The person addressed is the same as the one addressed in Psalm 110:1 with the words "Sit here at my right side until I put your enemies as a footstool under your feet." This important verse, although not quoted here, is elsewhere cited as referring to Jesus (1:13; and several allusions) and here may be understood as the bridge between Psalm 2:7 and Psalm 110:4. Jesus is the Son of God by divine decree and therefore the one who has been raised to the right hand of God. He is thus at the same time the one appointed by God to be **a priest forever** in the lineage of Melchizedek. As the author will explain later (chap. 7), Melchizedek was both a king and a priest (Gen. 14:18). Jesus is also king and priest, and thus corresponds to Melchizedek. There is for our author an important connection between the unique sonship of Jesus and his role as High Priest (cf. 1:2–3). He can be the ideal High Priest in the last analysis only because of his identity as the Son (see 7:28). Only as the Son can he perform the definitive atoning work which the author will describe in later chapters.

5:7 / This verse and the three verses that follow reveal briefly the essence of Christ's priestly work through the testing and suffering experienced by the divine Son in his humanity. The struggle referred to **in his life on earth** (lit., "in the days of his flesh") refers obviously to the experience of Jesus as he approached his imminent death. Almost certainly the author has in mind the agony of Jesus in the garden of Gethsemane (see Matt. 26:36 ff.), where Jesus prayed that if possible the cup (i.e., his death) might pass from him. The fact that the **prayers and requests** are said to have been directed to the one **who could save him from death** indicates almost certainly that the prayers in view were centered on the avoidance of death. But how then can the author continue by saying that **God heard him**? God always hears the prayers of those who suffer (see Ps. 22:24, a psalm that the early church understood as foreshadowing the passion of Jesus). Yet, it is clear that he does not always answer in the way that might be expected or desired. In this instance—although it is difficult to believe that this was Jesus' request—the answer came not in the avoidance of death, but in deliverance **from** (lit., "out of") **death** through the resurrection. Jesus was heard, according to our author, **because he was humble and devoted** (lit., "because of his piety"). This is the counterpart of the submission of Jesus to the will of his Father in the Gethsemane prayer, even where he prays to escape death. Because of his submission to God's will, the prayer of Jesus was heard in a much greater way than otherwise would have been possible.

5:8-9 / As **God's Son** Jesus was not exempt from suffering. His obedience was not accomplished in ideal circumstances, but was **learned** "in the school of suffering" (as NEB appropriately translates). In this sense Jesus serves as a model for the readers. This achievement of faithfulness to the will of God in adverse circumstances is a kind of learning insofar as it means arriving at a new stage of experience. The final stage of that experience is **when he was made perfect**, that is, when he accomplished the greatest obedience at the cost of the greatest suffering, his death (cf. 2:10). For, as our author will argue eloquently in later chapters, it is by his death that **he became the source of eternal salvation** (cf. 9:12) for those in turn **who obey him**. And as his obedience entailed suffering, so may the readers assume that obedience to him will mean the same.

5:10 / As "the source of eternal salvation" Jesus has been declared **High Priest** by God. The divine Son and yet fully human, Jesus possesses the qualifications needed to be High Priest: divine appointment (especially through Ps. 110:4) and ability to empathize with those whom he represents to God. He is thus a member of a unique priesthood—of the order of Melchizedek. At this point, however, the argument of the author is interrupted by a long parenthetical warning, and is not resumed until 7:1.

Additional Notes

4:14 / For further discussion of **High Priest**, see note on 2:17. The only other passage in Hebrews where High Priest is qualified by adjectives is 2:17, "faithful

62

and merciful High Priest." The literal words "who has passed through the heavens" should not be understood as either the three or seven heavens of popular Jewish cosmology (e.g., 2 Cor. 12:2), but probably simply as a general reference to Christ's ascension and exaltation. For the significance of this idea for the author, see the comment on the author's use of Ps. 110:1 in the note on 1:3. For the author's Son of God Christology, see note on 1:5.

4:15 / The Greek verb for **feel sympathy for** (*sympatheō*) occurs in only one other place in the entire NT, in 10:34, where the reference is to the readers' participation in the sufferings of those taken prisoner, apparently through religious persecution (RSV translates it "have compassion"). Behind GNB's **that we are** lies the ambiguous *kath' homoiotēta*, which can mean either "according to the likeness of our temptations" (as GNB takes it) or "according to his likeness to us" (as NEB takes it). **Tempted** (*peirazō*) in Hebrews ordinarily refers to the avoidance of suffering. See Seesemann, *TDNT* vol. 6, pp. 23–36. **Did not sin** is literally "without sin" and has been interpreted by some to mean that Jesus was tempted in every way that we are except by those temptations caused by previous sins. Others have insisted that the notion of the sinlessness of Jesus is incompatible with his full humanity as expressed in 2:17–19. Although humanness as we know it (i.e., since the fall) is inherently sinful, it does not follow that sin is intrinsic or essential to humanness. See J. K. S. Reid, "Tempted, yet without sin," *EQ* 21 (1949) pp. 161–67; R. A. Stewart, "The Sinless High Priest," *NTS* 14 (1967), pp. 126–35. For an opposing viewpoint, R. Williamson, "Hebrews 4:15 and the Sinlessness of Jesus," *ExT* 86 (1974), pp. 4–8.

4:16 / **Approach** (*proserchomai*), used in the imagery of the sacrificial cult elsewhere in Hebrews in 7:25; 10:1, 22; 11:6 (cf. 12:18, 22), is translated in GNB either as "come to" or "come near." This use of cultic language (that is, language having to do with the worship and ritual of the Temple) is also found in Paul: "In union with Christ and through our faith in him we have the boldness to go into God's presence with all confidence" (Eph. 3:12). "Throne of grace" here is unique in the NT. Grace (*charis*), however, is an important word in Hebrews (see 2:9; 10:29; 12:15; 13:9, 25). See H.-H. Esser, *NIDNTT*, vol. 2, pp. 115–24. **Mercy** (*eleos*) occurs only here in Hebrews, as does the expression for "timely help."

5:1 / In providing this "dictionary definition" of the qualifications and functions of the high priest, the author depends upon his knowledge of the OT and pays no heed to the contemporary perspectives on the high priesthood or its pathetic state. (The Qumranites, for example, had washed their hands of the high priesthood in Jerusalem.) The important verb **offer** (*prospherō*) is used far more in Hebrews (nineteen times) than in any other NT book. It is, of course, drawn from the language of the sacrificial ritual. See K. Weiss, *TDNT*, vol. 9, pp. 65–68. Since the Septuagint regularly uses the singular "sin" instead of **sins** when it refers to sacrifices, it may be that by using the plural the author hints at a communal setting such as on the Day of Atonement.

5:2 / The rare word **to be gentle** (*metriopatheō*) occurs only here in the entire Greek Bible and has the connotation of moderation when circumstances otherwise might well provoke severity.

5:4 / From the time of Antiochus IV and the cutting off of the Zadokite high priesthood, high priests had in fact been appointed by the whim of human rulers; legitimacy of descent and the call of God were no longer determinative. This is ignored by the author, who speaks idealistically of the high priesthood and continues to ascribe **honor** to it, although in the minds of the populace the office had long since been defiled.

5:5–6 / For further information on Ps. 2:7, see note under 1:5. GNB rightly supplies **God** as the speaker of the verse (although the subject is not specified in the original) not simply because of the content of the words, but also because for the author God is generally understood to be the speaker in the OT. The nuance of the somewhat unusual use of "glorify" (*doxazō*) behind GNB's **did not take upon himself the honor** is captured well by BAGD (p. 204): "he did not raise himself to the glory of the high priesthood."

At Qumran two Messiahs were expected in connection with the end of the age, a priestly Messiah of the line of Aaron and a royal Messiah of the line of David. From our author's perspective, Jesus as Messiah is both King and High Priest (although priest of an order other than the Aaronic). The two important offices had traditionally been kept separate in Israel until the unfortunate and unsatisfactory assumption of both offices by certain of the Hasmoneans in the second century B.C. For the very general introductory formula **he also said in another place**, see note on 2:6.

5:7 / Behind GNB's translation **made his prayers** is again the use of technical language from the sacrificial cultus (the worship and ritual of the Temple): "offered." Although there are no explicit references to **loud cries and tears** in any of the accounts of the Gethsemane experience according to the Synoptic Gospels, Matthew's description is the most similar to our author's words: "Grief and anguish came over him and he said to them, 'the sorrow in my heart is so great that it almost crushes me'" (Matt. 26:37 f.). No distinction need be made between **prayers and requests**. Although the latter (*hiketēria*) occurs only here in the NT, it is commonly linked with the former in contemporary literature.

The major difficulty of this verse, i.e., how the author can write that **God heard him** despite the fact that Jesus died on the cross, has been handled in a variety of ways. Perhaps the simplest way is to argue that Jesus prayed not that he would avoid death, but that he would be resurrected after his death, taking the "out of death" (*ek thanatou*, not *apo thanatou*, "from death") quite literally as a rescue from the clutches of death (cf. 13:20). Although we have argued above that this is a way in which we may understand God to have heard Jesus' prayer, it is unlikely that this was actually the prayer of Jesus. (It is certainly not the content of Jesus' prayer in the Garden of Gethsemane.)

Another solution to the problem, argued by some (e.g., Hewitt), is that in the Garden Jesus prayed that he might not die then and there under the great burden of anguish he was experiencing, i.e., that he might not die prematurely and thus fail to accomplish his intended death on the cross. If this was his prayer, it was of course heard by God. This, however, involves a difficult and unsatisfactory interpretation of the Gethsemane prayer. Yet another solution is to argue that Jesus prayed to be delivered not from death, but from the fear of death (cf. Calvin, Héring, Montefiore). It is possible to interpret the Greek underlying **because he was humble and devoted** (*apo tēs eulabeias*) as "from his fear," thus giving the sense of "God heard him [and delivered him] from his fear of death." This, however, is not only difficult syntactically, but also involves assigning a less common meaning to *eulabeia*, which normally means "godly fear" or "piety," implying obedience (the word for "fear" of death in 2:15 is *phobos*). Finally, we note the expedient of Harnack who, with no manuscript evidence whatsoever, conjectures that an original negative before **heard** has been inadvertently lost. The author had actually written that God did *not* hear the prayer of Jesus. On this verse see N. R. Lightfoot, "The Saving of the Savior: Hebrews 5:7 ff.," *RestQ* 16 (1973), pp. 166–73.

5:8–9 / This is the only occurrence of **learned** (*manthanō*) in the entire book and the only place in the NT where Jesus is the subject of the verb. In the Greek there is a play on words in the use of *emathen* ("learned") and *epathen* ("suffered"). "To learn" here means to arrive at a new level of experience in obedience **through his sufferings** (cf. Phil. 2:8). For the verb **made perfect** (*teleioō*), see note on 2:10. The idea is that in being obedient to God's will in his sufferings and death, Jesus brings God's saving purposes to fulfillment or completion (cf. 7:27 f.). Having accomplished God's will he himself has reached a state of completeness and fulfillment, thereby becoming **the source of eternal salvation** (cf. 2:10). **Source** (*aitios*) can also be translated as "cause," and is reminiscent of the word *archēgos* ("pioneer" or "leader") in 2:10 (cf. 12:2). **Eternal salvation** refers to the finality and definitive character of the saving work accomplished by Christ. Analogous to this expression are "eternal salvation" (lit., "redemption") in 9:12, "eternal blessings" in 9:15, and "eternal covenant" in 13:20. For an OT parallel, see Isa. 45:17. For **salvation** (*sōtēria*), see note on 2:3.

5:10 / **Declared** (*prosagoreuō*) occurs only here in the NT and corresponds in significance to "appointed" in 5:1. For further information on Melchizedek, see notes to 7:1–3.

The Importance of Christian Maturity

HEBREWS 5:11–6:3

There is much we have to say about this matter, but it is hard to explain to you, because you are so slow to understand. ¹²There has been enough time for you to be teachers—yet you still need someone to teach you the first lessons of God's message. Instead of eating solid food, you still have to drink milk. ¹³Anyone who has to drink milk is still a child, without any experience in the matter of right and wrong. ¹⁴Solid food, on the other hand, is for adults, who through practice are able to distinguish between good and evil.

¹Let us go forward, then, to mature teaching and leave behind us the first lessons of the Christian message. We should not lay again the foundation of turning away from useless works and believing in God; ²of the teaching about baptisms[d] and the laying on of hands; of the resurrection of the dead and the eternal judgment. ³Let us go forward! And this is what we will do, if God allows.

d. baptisms; *or* purification ceremonies.

Before continuing his argument concerning Melchizedek, the author pauses for an exhortation to maturity which is followed by remarks on the seriousness of apostasy. This digression is important particularly because of the information it provides concerning the character and situation of the addressees.

5:11-12 / The author apparently regards the argument concerning Jesus as High Priest according to the order of Melchizedek as too difficult for his readers in their present condition. It must be from some previous encounter or some report about them that he concludes they are **so slow to understand** (lit., "sluggish in hearing"). Their slowness in development is an exasperation to the author. The lapse of time, and perhaps something about the readers' background, is such that whereas they ought **to be teachers**, yet they need to be taught again **the first lessons of God's message**. NEB translates somewhat more literally: "the ABC of God's oracles." This probably refers to the basics of the Christian gospel, but as contained in the OT. If the readers still need elementary Christian exegesis of the OT, how shall they move to such exegesis at the more advanced level? They thus still have the need for **milk** and cannot digest **solid food**.

5:13–14 / The metaphor of milk for the immature and solid food for the mature is common and is found elsewhere in the NT in 1 Corinthians 3:2 and partially in 1 Peter 2:2. **Solid food** is what the author is presenting in this epistle, and in this particular context it is the argument about Melchizedek. His concern that they may not be ready for it suggests a degree of apprehensiveness as to how it will be received. **The matter of right and wrong** is literally "the word of righteousness" (so, RSV). GNB's translation takes its cue from the end of verse 14 and depends on the parallelism of the two verses. Possibly, however, the expression refers in a general way to the content of the gospel and is thus parallel to the "first lessons of God's message" in the preceding verse. The last phrase, **to distinguish between good and evil**, it must be admitted, is deliberately the language of the ethicists of our author's day. Although the language is drawn from secular writers, our author has primarily in mind the Christian immaturity of the readers, which may in turn be the cause of a more general ethical immaturity.

6:1 / The exhortation is essentially an appeal to accept the solid food the author offers in the argumentation of the present epistle. **Mature teaching** is literally "perfection" or "completeness." This perfection involves accepting the author's teaching, that is, the recognition of the absoluteness and finality of Christ and his atoning work as the true fulfillment of the OT promises. This recognition alone can keep the readers from lapsing finally into apostasy. The readers, therefore, cannot allow themselves to remain at the level of **the first lessons of the Christian message**. The **foundation** must not be repeatedly relaid while the superstructure is never built. But this appeared to be the danger for the readers. The author provides six examples of the kinds of things he has in mind when he refers to **the first lessons**. It is striking that the six items mentioned all find parallels within Judaism. This may suggest that the readers were attempting somehow to remain within Judaism by emphasizing items held in common between Judaism and Christianity. They may have been trying to survive with a minimal Christianity so as to avoid alienating their Jewish friends or relatives. **Turning away from useless works** (lit., "repentance from dead works") is certainly basic within Judaism. What is meant is repentance not from "works of the Law" (in a Pauline sense) but from sins. The second item, **believing** (lit., "faith") **in God** is of course also very important in Judaism. Thus, at the beginning of the list we encounter repentance and faith, two of the most central aspects of Jewish piety—both taken up by Christianity (cf. Acts 20:21).

6:2-3 / **Teaching about baptisms** refers to purification rites of Judaism (cf. marginal note in GNB), as the plural seems to indicate. Christian baptism may well be derived from just such Jewish ablutions, one of which—for the purifying of proselytes from paganism—seems a particularly suitable source for the practice of baptism by John and the disciples of Jesus. Christian baptism thus could well be classified as one such, if not indeed the culminating, rite of purification. **The laying on of hands** is yet another Jewish custom taken up by the Christian church, often as a symbol for the imparting of the Holy Spirit (see Acts 8:17; 9:17; 19:6), but also in connection with healing (Acts 9:12; 28:8) and, as in the OT and rabbinic Judaism, special commissionings (Acts 6:6; cf. 1 Tim. 5:22; 2 Tim. 1:6). The last two items, **the resurrection of the dead** and **the eternal judgment** were accepted by the Pharisees but not the Sadducees (cf. Acts 23:8). This suggests that the Jewish background of the readers was not Sadducean. For the readers, of course, the resurrection of the dead included the resurrection of Jesus. These items, then, could be held by the readers without necessarily departing very far from their Jewish origins. The author, on the other hand, chides them for not pressing on to the full doctrine of Christianity, such as contained in the content of his epistle, and the specific argument immediately before them.

The words **let us go forward** do not occur here in the text, but are effectively brought forward from 6:1 by GNB in order to define what **this** refers to in **this is what we will do**. The author and the readers will press on into the full comprehension and experience of the whole range of Christian doctrine. But this will occur only as and **if God allows**. That is, any arrival at maturity by readers or author depends in the last analysis upon the sovereign enabling of God (cf. Acts 18:21). Thus with the statement is an implied prayer to the same effect.

Additional Notes

5:11-12 / The single Greek word underlying **hard to explain** (*dysermēneutos*) occurs only here in the Greek Bible (Septuagint and NT). In Greek writers it has the connotation "difficult to describe." The word **slow** or "sluggish" (*nōthros*) occurs only here and in 6:12 (where it is translated by GNB as "lazy") in the Greek Bible. It is unlikely that the regular word used here for **teachers** (*didaskalos*) is to be taken in any special sense, such as that the readers were converted priests (see Acts 6:7) or former members of the Qumran sect and therefore under particular responsibility to become teachers. Probably **teachers** here is used not for the office in a formal sense (as in 1 Cor. 12:28) but simply refers to the ordinary sense in which all Christians should be teachers. **First lessons** translates the Greek word, *stoicheia*, a word whose meaning in Paul's epistles is disputed (Gal. 4:3, 9; Col. 2:8, 20) but which in the present context is quite clear and further supported by the statement of 6:1, where, however, GNB's *first lessons* is the translation of other Greek words than *stoicheia*. See H.-H. Esser in *NIDNTT*, vol. 2, pp. 451-53. **God's message** (lit., "the oracles of God," *logia tou theou*) almost always means the Law of the OT (cf. Acts 7:38; Rom. 3:2). Here, although it clearly refers to the Christian fundamentals, it may mean as they can be determined from the OT. The Greek expression for **solid food** (*sterea trophē*) is different from Paul's word for "solid food" (*brōma*) in 1 Cor. 3:2 and in the NT occurs only here.

5:13-14 / The word for **child**, understood figuratively, is used also in 1 Cor. 3:1, where, however, "children" stands for the fleshly ("belonged to this world") and stands in contrast to the spiritual ("who have the spirit"). In our passage **child** stands in contrast to **adults**, where the Greek word (*teleioi*) indicates perfection or completeness, involving maturity of understanding, as the context shows. The words **without any experience in** translate the single Greek word *apeiros*, which occurs only here in the NT and which BAGD translates "unacquainted with." The quasi-technical language of the ethicist in verse 14b is captured well (and quite literally) by Barclay: "it is for those whose faculties are disciplined by practice to distinguish between right and wrong." The author's Hellenism is readily apparent here. See H. P. Owen, "The 'Stages of Ascent' in Hebrews v. 11-vi.3," *NTS* 3 (1956-57), pp. 243-53.

6:1-3 / The six components of the **foundation** listed by the author have often been seen as consisting of three pairs; repentance and faith; purifying rites and laying on of hands; resurrection and judgment. The last four items are in turn governed by the words **teaching about**. This is true regardless of whether the word *didache* ("teaching") is in the genitive or the accusative case (as a few early and important witnesses have it). The sense of the Greek underlying **useless works** (*nekrōn ergōn*) is better given by NIV: "acts that lead to death." NIV appropriately gives the same translation of the same phrase when it occurs in 9:14, where GNB translates "useless rituals." These are the only two occurrences of the phrase in the NT. On the Jewish background of "baptisms," see G. R. Beasley-Murray, *NIDNTT*, vol. 1, pp. 144-50. On the Jewish background of "the laying on of hands," see H.-G. Schütz, *NIDNTT*, vol. 2, pp. 150-52. **This is what we will do** can hardly refer to laying again the foundation or teaching of the ABCs (as in 5:12) at some future time. Some important early manuscripts have the verb in the subjunctive mood resulting in the meaning "let us do this." The ordinary future tense, however, is well attested and more congruent with the final words of v. 3.

The Seriousness of Apostasy

HEBREWS 6:4–12

For how can those who abandon their faith be brought back to repent again? They were once in God's light; they tasted heaven's gift and received their share of the Holy Spirit; [5]they knew from experience that God's word is good, and they had felt the powers of the coming age. [6]And then they abandoned their faith! It is impossible to bring them back to repent again, because they are again crucifying the Son of God and exposing him to public shame.

[7]God blesses the soil which drinks in the rain that often falls on it and which grows plants that are useful to those for whom it is cultivated. [8]But if it grows thorns and weeds, it is worth nothing; it is in danger of being cursed by God and will be destroyed by fire.

[9]But even if we speak like this, dear friends, we feel sure about you. We know that you have the better blessings that belong to your salvation. [10]God is not unfair. He will not forget the work you did or the love you showed for him in the help you gave and are still giving to your fellow Christians. [11]Our great desire is that each one of you keep up his eagerness to the end, so that the things you hope for will come true. [12]We do not want you to become lazy, but to be like those who believe and are patient, and so receive what God has promised.

The manner in which this section is connected with the preceding material, with the logical connective **for**, suggests that if the readers do not "go forward" into the fullness of Christian doctrine, they will be in grave danger of falling away altogether, back into their prior Judaism, thereby committing apostasy. In their present state, indeed, even their grasp of the "first lessons of God's message" (5:12) is questionable. Thus, as further motivation for the readers to press on to a mature understanding of their Christian faith, the author points out the seriousness of apostasy. It is of the greatest importance that the readers give heed to the message of the author and receive the "solid food" he is offering them. Unless the readers "go forward," the author predicts disaster.

Before proceeding to our verse-by-verse commentary on this well-known and problematic passage, it is well worth noting that here especially the author is addressing a specific situation. He is not writing a calm, disinterested essay on the question of the perseverance of the saints, in which he carefully details the full range of possibilities that confront the readers. On the contrary, he is very anxious for the ultimate well-being of his readers. They must know the grave seriousness of falling away from their Christian faith and that there is no easy way back from apostasy. Again the author's strong pastoral concerns emerge.

6:4 / Because the Greek sentence that begins in this verse is long and complicated (not concluding until the end of v. 6), GNB has taken the liberty of re-expressing the thought in four sentences. The opening question in fact does not occur in the original, which begins with the statement **it is impossible** (cf. v. 6). The question, however, sets the stage for the following statement. The persons in view, who **abandoned their faith**, are described in five consecutive clauses. The first of these says that **they were once in God's light** (lit., "having been enlightened"). This language is especially appropriate in referring to conversion (cf. 10:32) and some have seen an allusion here to the initiatory rite of Christian baptism. The next two clauses also seem to refer to the reality of conversion. **They tasted heaven's gift** refers in a general sense to salvation (the expression "gift of God" is used similarly in John 4:10). The word **tasted** here (cf. v. 5) does not imply a less-than-complete experience of conversion. The word "taste" can elsewhere in Hebrews be used to indicate full experience of something, as for example in 2:9 where the same verb is used to refer to the death of Jesus (GNB translates: "the death he suffered"). **Received their share of the Holy Spirit** (lit., "having become partakers of the Holy Spirit") similarly refers to the event that marks conversion, the receiving of the Holy Spirit, not the special charismatic gifts received by Christians.

6:5 / **Knew from experience** is GNB's appropriate translation of "having tasted" which recurs in this verse. **That God's word is good** refers probably to the message of salvation which they had believed. The fifth descriptive clause notes that they had **felt the powers of the coming age**. The nouns of this clause are governed by the "having tasted" of the preceding clause; GNB adds the word **felt**, but could as easily have made the words dependent on the previous words **knew from experience**. What is in view is the realized eschatology presently enjoyed by the Christian church. The assertion is therefore in keeping with the perspective of the author set forth in such places as 1:2; 2:5; 4:3; and 12:18–24.

6:6 / In the first sentence GNB has turned a subordinate clause into an exclamatory sentence. **Abandoned their faith** is an apt translation of the participle "having fallen away," which in this context means to "commit apostasy" (so, RSV). The word **impossible** actually appears in verse 4 at the beginning of the long Greek sentence. The impossibility of repentance is attributed (by the strong **because** in GNB, which is implicit rather than explicit in the Greek) to the re-crucifying of **the Son of God** and the **exposing** of him **to public shame** (again the last three words are not explicit but are implicit in the meaning of the final participle).

Two major questions emerge from the statement in these three verses: (1) How is the word **impossible** to be understood? and (2) Can authentic Christians really apostatize? Complex answers are required in both instances and depend finally upon distinguishing what is actual from what is only apparent. In one sense the word **impossible** must be taken as absolute by the very nature of apostasy. This sin is not like any other sin: it is the unforgivable sin because it undercuts the very basis of salvation (cf. Mark 3:29; 1 John 5:16). Those guilty of true apostasy thus, as our author states, **are again crucifying the Son of God**. That is, they align themselves with the enemies of God who crucified Jesus and hence figuratively do so themselves. By using the title **the Son of God**, the author points out the full gravity of the offence, for it was just this view of Jesus that had once been believed and is now rejected by the apostate. Moreover, they are **exposing him to public shame**, for as others witness their disloyalty he becomes the object of ridicule. Apostasy, therefore, is the most serious of sins—a sin for which there is no remedy and from which there is no possibility of return. No other means of salvation is available other than that which is here finally rejected. It is impossible for true apostates to experience conversion anew. God will not force them into the kingdom.

On the other hand, although this is something our author understandably does not trouble himself to explain at this point, God's grace can, and often does, reach those who lapse into an apparent apostasy, but something that in fact is less than true and final apostasy. It will not serve the author's purpose, however, to speak of the possibility of a return from apostasy. The readers must be made to see the seriousness of what they are contemplating. The severity of his statement is to be explained by the situation and context of the readers. If they are to remain faithful to their confession in the face of persecution, they must understand the nature of apostasy. This is not a time for words concerning God's grace and the possibility of restoration. In any event, because it is both difficult and uncertain, a way back ought not to be counted upon.

Can Christians, then, fall away and lose their salvation? The answer again consists of a yes and a no. Certainly those described in verses 4 and 5 are Christians. If they can abandon their faith, then the warning is not merely hypothetical and empty, but real (cf. 10:26–31). Christians can apostatize (c. 2 Pet. 2:20–22). Yet paradoxically, if they become true apostates, they show that they were not authentic Christians (cf. 3:14). The writer of 1 John thus indicates that those who turned against their confession and left the Christian community did so "that it might be clear that none of them really belonged to us" (1 John 2:19). Concerning the readers of Hebrews, as of all Christians, it must be said that they are Christians thus far. In the last analysis only perseverance can demonstrate the reality of Christian faith. Our author is clearly not addressing the question of the perseverance of the saints. Yet the content of his epistle abundantly testifies to the incomparable resources his readers have in Christ for just such perseverance.

In sum, then, the authentic is revealed only at the end of the day. True apostasy is evident when repentance does not (i.e., cannot) occur. True Christian faith, on the other hand, is manifested when apostasy does not occur. True Christians do not (i.e., cannot) apostatize. This is the urgent message of the author for his readers.

6:7-8 / The preceding passage now finds an illustration in the metaphor concerning fruitful and unfruitful soil. In a way that must have reminded the readers of the parable of Israel as God's vineyard (Isa. 5:1–7), the author points to the judgment that may be expected to come upon the unproductive soil. To abandon one's faith is equivalent to producing only **thorns and weeds**, to being **worth nothing**, and hence leads to destruction by fire. The words **in danger of being cursed by God** (lit., "near to a curse") have the sense of "about to be cursed," that is, it is only a matter of time before judgment arrives.

6:9 / Despite the seriousness of the warning, the author assures the readers, whom he addresses as **dear friends** (lit., "beloved"), that he is confident that they will persevere in their faith. GNB emphasizes this confidence by adding the words **we know that**, not found in the original. **Better blessings** (lit., "better things") **that belong to your salvation** is a characteristic way our author has of describing Christianity in comparison with the old covenant.

6:10 / God remembers the readers' laudable performance in the past and is ready to sustain them in the midst of present difficulty. Later in the epistle (10:32–36) the author details some of that past performance and exhorts the readers to remember it themselves. As then, so now, God is on their side and will sustain them. Their good deeds in the past continue in the present (**are still giving**) and this itself bodes well for the future. **Your fellow Christians** is an appropriate translation of the original "the saints."

6:11–12 / Our author now expresses his exhortation in terms of his **great desire**. **Keep up his eagerness** is literally "show the same diligence" where the present tense of the verb could also be translated "keep on showing diligence." The readers are challenged to continue in the good path they are upon. **So that the things you hope for will come true** is a much stronger result clause and explicit statement than the original contains (cf. RSV: "in realizing the full assurance of hope until the end"). GNB substitutes **we do not want you to** for the simple "lest you," and **be like** for "be imitators of." **Believe** is literally "through faith," and constitutes an anticipation of the discourse on faith that appears in chapter 11. If the readers are diligent rather than sluggish, and if they exemplify the life of faith, they will inherit the promises made to their forefathers in the distant past (cf. 11:9).

Additional Notes

6:4 / The parallel passage in 10:26–32 supports the correctness of the conclusion that vv. 4 and 5 describe those who are indeed Christians. There it is explicitly "after receiving the knowledge of the truth" (RSV) that certain persons apostatize. (See below.) The metaphor of moving from darkness to light is frequently used in the NT for conversion and hence also came to have baptismal associations in the early church (e.g., Eph. 5:8–14; 1 Pet. 2:9). The verb "enlightened" (*phōtizō*) occurs again in 10:32 (cf. the similar use in John 1:9; Eph. 1:18; 2 Tim. 1:10). See Conzelmann, *TDNT*, vol. 9, pp. 310–58. Some have seen in the words **tasted heaven's gift** a reference to the Eucharist or Lord's Supper. This remains only a possibility, since in the present context the word "taste" refers to experiencing (not necessarily to eating) and **heaven's gift** is at best a very oblique way of referring to the sacrament. For the words "heavenly" and "partakers" see notes on 3:1. Correspondences sometimes seen between items mentioned in this verse and those in v. 2 (e.g., **in God's light**—"teaching about baptisms"; **received** their share **of the Holy Spirit**—"the laying on of hands") are debatable and of no significance.

6:5 / The underlying Greek for **God's word** employs *rhēma* and not *logos*, thereby ruling out a logos Christology (the identification of Christ as the *logos* or "Word" of God; cf. Jn. 1:1), which in any case is not found in Hebrews. On the notion of realized eschatology, see comments and notes on 1:2.

6:6 / The Greek verb *parapiptō*, translated **abandoned**, in the NT occurs only here. Outside the NT the verb can mean "to go astray," but here the stronger meaning is to be preferred (cf. 3:12; 10:29). **Bring them back** (*anakainizō*) again occurs only here in the NT and is to be understood in the sense of "restore" or "renew." It is, of course, impossible to repeat the experience of conversion or its accompaniment, baptism. Thus again the author points to the gravity of apostasy. It *is* possible to renew repentance generally, as the Jews well knew, from within a covenantal relationship with God. Repentance is a fixed pillar in Judaism. But to abandon one's faith makes such a renewal of repentance impossible. The sin of apostasy is thus like no other sin. This is the sense in which it is **impossible to bring them back to repent**. Despite the interpretation of the passage by certain groups in the early church, it is very unlikely that what is in view is the unforgivable character of any deliberate postbaptismal sin. In this view the reference to "restoration" means rebaptism. Although this passage was used by some to buttress such a perspective, the character of the sin referred to by the author is much greater than ordinary sin, however deliberate; it is the rejection of the very truth upon which salvation itself depends. The attempt to avoid the difficulty of the verse by assuming a transposition of words and different punctuation (associating the participle "crucifying" with "unto repentance") is a drastic and unconvincing expedient. For a convenient summary of this view, see M. Zerwick and M. Grosvenor, *A Grammatical Analysis of the Greek New Testament* (Rome, 1979), vol. 2, p. 664 f.

Again crucifying is a translation of *anastauroō*, which in extrabiblical Greek does not contain the idea of repetition. Here, however, the prefix *ana* probably is to be understood as "again" (see *BAGD*, p. 61). **Because**, although not actually in the Greek text, is a correct interpretation of the nuance of the participles, **crucifying** and **exposing**. The attempt to understand these participles as temporal— hence, "it is impossible to restore them to repentance *while* they are crucifying, etc."—is hardly convincing. It is **because** of what they have done that they cannot be brought back to repentance. **Exposing him to public shame** translates *paradeigmatizō*, a word that occurs only here in the NT and means "to make a public example of," and in the present context, "to expose to public disgrace." See R. P. Martin, *NIDNTT*, vol. 2, p. 291. See also, P. E. Hughes, "Hebrews 6:4–6 and the Peril of Apostasy," *WTJ* 35 (1978), pp. 137–55; J. C. McCullough, "The Impossibility of a Second Repentance in Hebrews," *BibTheo* 20 (1974), pp. 1–7.

6:7-8 / Such language as **plants, thorns, and weeds**, and **cursed** is similar to that of the creation narrative in Genesis (1:11; 3:17–18). Thorns and weeds become a common metaphor for the wrong kind of fruitfulness (e.g., Matt. 7:16;

13:7, 24–30), and in the same contexts, destruction by fire, as a symbol of eschatological judgment, is almost always present.

6:9 / **Feel sure** translates a common word (perfect passive of *peithō*) meaning to be "convinced" or "certain" (cf. same use in 13:18). "Beloved" occurs only here in Hebrews. For the importance of **better** in Hebrews, see note on 1:4.

6:10 / **For him** abbreviates the original "for his name," rightly reflecting the intimate relationship between name and person in Hebraic thinking. The Greek word behind **help you gave and are still giving** is *diakoneō*, an important technical term for "ministering" or "serving." See K. Hess, *NIDNTT*, vol. 3, pp. 544–49. **Work** and **love** are linked in a similar way in Paul's praise of the Thessalonian church (1 Thess. 1:3).

This verse should not be taken to imply salvation by works. The point is not that God is obligated or that the readers have some claim upon him for their past performance, but simply that God looks upon them favorably and is eagerly willing to sustain them in their time of need.

6:11–12 / For **eagerness** (*spoudē*), which occurs only here in Hebrews, see W. Bauder, *NIDNTT*, vol. 3, pp. 1168–70. The emphasis in the original is more on the full assurance (or possibly, fullness) of hope than on the actual experiencing of the things hoped for, although the latter is implied in the words **to the end**. On the word for "full assurance," (*plērophoria*), see R. Schippers, *NIDNTT*, vol. 1, p. 735. Similar emphases are evident in the book (for "hope" see 3:6; for "to the end" see 3:14). **Lazy** translates the same Greek word as "slow" in 5:11, which may also be translated as "sluggish. "Imitators" (cf. verb form in 13:7) and **patient** or "longsuffering," although in Hebrews they occur only here, are both important words in NT ethical exhortation. For "imitator," see W. Bauder, *NIDNTT*, vol. 1, pp. 490–92; for "patience," see U. Falkenroth and C. Brown, *NIDNTT*, vol. 2, pp. 768–72. Patience is also linked with receiving what God has promised in 10:36, where, however, a different Greek word for patience if used (*hypomonē*). For "promise" (*epangelia*), see note on v. 15. For "faith," see 11:1.

The Unchangeable Character
of God's Purpose

When God made his promise to Abraham, he made a vow to do what he had promised. Since there was no one greater than himself, he used his own name when he made his vow. ¹⁴He said, "I promise you that I will bless you and give you many descendants." ¹⁵Abraham was patient, and so he received what God had promised. ¹⁶When a person makes a vow, he uses the name of someone greater than himself, and the vow settles all arguments. ¹⁷To those who were to receive what he promised God wanted to make it very clear that he would never change his purpose; so he added his vow to the promise. ¹⁸There are these two things, then, that cannot change and about which God cannot lie. So we who have found safety with him are greatly encouraged to hold firmly to the hope placed before us. ¹⁹We have this hope as an anchor for our lives. It is safe and sure, and goes through the curtain of the heavenly temple into the inner sanctuary. ²⁰On our behalf Jesus has gone in there before us and has become a high priest forever, as the successor of Melchizedek.

As a new prelude to the argument our author is about to resume (in chap. 7), an argument of key importance in the book, he stresses God's complete fidelity to his promises to Abraham, and thus to Israel. Despite certain implications the author will draw from his argument about the priestly order of Melchizedek (see esp. 7:12), God has not changed course, nor have his purposes changed. In the definitive High Priest, Jesus, God is bringing to pass his promises to the fathers of Israel. This is an important point to affirm to Jewish Christians who are feeling the pressure of the arguments of nonbelieving Jews.

6:13–14 / GNB divides the single Greek sentence in these verses into three sentences, adding for clarity the words **he made a vow to do what he had promised**. The custom that underlay the taking of a vow in the ancient Hebrew culture is indicated in verse 16. God, having no one or nothing greater than himself to swear by, **used his own name** (lit., "swore by himself"). The promise referred to is, of course, the so-called Abrahamic covenant, not however in its first statement (Gen. 12:1–3) but in its re-statement to Abraham following the near sacrifice of Isaac in Genesis 22:16–17 ("I make a vow by my own name"). The covenant is itself now stated, utilizing an emphatic form (expressed in GNB's **I promise you**) not found in the initial formulation of the covenant. This brief statement is representative of the entire content of the covenant.

6:15 / **Abraham** (lit., "he") exhibits the relationship between patience and the receiving of the promises just referred to in verse 12. **He received what God had promised** must refer only to the initial signs of fulfillment experienced by Abraham (cf. Gen. 24:1), since from the author's Christian perspective Abraham and other heroes of the faith "did not receive the things God had promised" (11:13, 39). Only when joined by the saints of the NT era would they fully arrive at what God intended for them (11:39–40).

6:16 / The **someone greater** by whose name an oath or vow was taken was most often the Lord (cf. Exod. 22:11, "an oath by the LORD," RSV). When such an oath was taken by someone in the Lord's name, it was obviously of an absolutely binding character, and hence **the vow settles all arguments** (lit., "in all disputes is final for confirmation").

6:17 / Since God **wanted to make it very clear** that his purposes were finally fixed, he did something very unusual: **he added his vow to the promise** (cf. vv. 13–14). He wanted above all to make clear **that he would never change his promise** (lit., "the unchangeable character of his purpose," RSV). This strong statement, with its exceptional double affirmation, is meant to counter any Jewish suggestion that Christianity involves a departure from, rather than the fulfillment of, the promises upon which Israel based her hopes.

6:18 / The two unchangeable things are God's word (i.e., the promise itself) and the vow that he added to it. God's word, of course, is of absolute validity in itself; the vow, therefore, is superfluous, but exactly because of this, exceptionally impressive. It is impossible, then, that God could have lied; he is doubly bound to be faithful to his promises to Abraham. The result is that we may very courageously hold **the hope placed before us**. The implication is that the Christian hope consists of nothing other than what God promised to Abraham (cf. Rom. 15:8), and therefore that our realization of that hope is as finally certain as God's word and his oath. The unity between old and new is in view. **We . . . have found safety**

with him (lit., "we who have fled for refuge") refers metaphorically to the security believers have in Christ in contrast to the insecurity and uncertainty of the world.

6:19-20 / Because of the nature of the Christian hope as confident expectation, hope serves as **an anchor for our lives**, and therefore as that which can counteract the tendency of "drifting away" mentioned in 2:1. Our hope depends entirely on the priestly work of Jesus. This **safe and sure** hope is said metaphorically to go **into the inner sanctuary**, by which is meant that such hope involves our free access into the very presence of God. The language **goes through the curtain** (lit., "within the veil") alludes to Leviticus 16:2, 12 and refers to entering the holy of holies (**inner sanctuary**). GNB adds the words **of the heavenly temple**, not found in the original text, in order to indicate that the temple language is used metaphorically and is not to be understood literally. This is the first occurrence of imagery that will be vitally important in chapters 9 and 10. Our unrestricted entrance into God's presence is made possible only by the one who **on our behalf** has gone before us to prepare the way, who **has become a high priest forever**. Because of his work as high priest, we all can now go where only the high priest was privileged to go, and that, once a year. **The successor Melchizedek** is literally "according to the order of Melchizedek," another brief allusion to Psalm 110:4 which was first quoted in 5:6 (cf. 7:17). Having again mentioned Melchizedek, and Jesus' high priesthood, the author has come back to the argument he began in chapter 5 but broke off in 5:10.

Additional Notes

6:13-14 / The author utilizes the same kind of argument about God adding a vow to his word in 7:20-22 in the argument about the Melchizedekan priesthood. These passages together with the negative oath of the Lord referred to in the author's use of Ps. 95:11 in 3:11, 18 and 4:3 give Hebrews more occurrences of the verb "to swear" or "take an oath" than any NT book except Matthew. For this verb, see H.-G. Link, *NIDNTT*, vol. 3, pp. 737-43. The fact that God confirmed his promise to Abraham with an oath is noted elsewhere in the NT (Acts 2:30; Lk. 1:73) as well as in the Apocrypha (Sirach 44:21: "Therefore the Lord assured him by an oath"). The closest parallel, however, to the argument here is in Philo, *Allegorical Interpretation*, 3.203, 205 f. **I promise you** reflects the emphasis of the Hebrew infinitive absolute, often translated "surely I will," but involving a repetition of the word. Thus a literal translation of v. 14, which is drawn from the Septuagint, is "Blessing (or "with blessing") I will bless you." The Greek indeed further intensifies the promise with the addition of two small particles (*ei mēn*).

Although it is not stated here, almost certainly the author regards the Christian church as the fulfillment of the Abrahamic covenant, especially of the clause that in Abraham all the families of the earth would be blessed (cf. 3:6).

6:15 / The Greek word for **received** (*epitynchanō*) is different from that in 11:13 (*lambanō*) and 11:33 (*komizō*). It is more likely that our author regards Abraham as having received a degree of fulfillment in his own lifetime (note **was patient**) than that he received only the promises (as *epitynchanō* probably means in 11:33), even if in some new way. **What God had promised** (lit., "the promises") became a stereotyped expression synonymous with the hope of Israel. The noun "promise" (*epangelia*), occurring in both singular and plural forms, is found in Hebrews more than in any other NT book (thirteen times). See E. Hoffmann, *NIDNTT*, vol. 3, pp. 68–74.

6:16 / GNB appropriately avoids the unnecessary male-oriented language of the original ("men swear by a greater than themselves"). Oaths were taken by the name of an especially holy object (cf. Matt. 23:16, 18) or more commonly, by the name of the Lord. To violate such an oath was to take the Lord's name in vain. Oathtaking nevertheless suffered abuse and was condemned by Jesus (e.g., Matt. 5:34).

6:17 / **Those who were to receive what he promised** (lit., "the heirs of the promise") is again a very common expression for the descendants of Abraham, and subsequently those who belong to Christ (cf. Gal. 3:29). The word for "unchangeable" here and in the next verse (*ametathetos*) occurs only here in the NT. **Added** (*mesiteuō*, lit., "guaranteed") occurs only here in the NT.

6:18 / A fixed point in the Bible is that God does not lie (cf. Num. 23:19; 1 Sam. 15:29; John 7:18; Titus 1:2). Christian hope is by nature a confident expectation because it depends upon what God has done for us in Christ. This is why hope "does not disappoint us" (Rom. 5:5). The expression hope **placed before us** (*prokeimai*) is similar to Paul's words in Col. 1:5, hope "kept safe for you in heaven" (*apokeimai*). Only here in the NT do we have the phrase "strong encouragement" (**greatly encouraged**).

6:19–20 / The metaphorical use of **anchor** is found only here in the entire Bible, although it is so used by classical writers. See BAGD, p. 10. **Lives** is an appropriate translation of *psychē* (lit., "soul") since the word often means "life" rather than the immaterial part of our being. The words **safe and sure** are combined only here in the NT and are deliberately redundant to reinforce the author's point. **Before us** is GNB's translation for the noun "a forerunner" (*prodromos*), a word that occurs only here in the NT. The word is similar in meaning to *archēgos* (see 2:10 and 12:2, which RSV translates as "pioneer") and conveys the idea not merely of one who precedes, but one who prepares the way by the work he accomplishes, making it possible for others to follow (note: **on our behalf**). On **high priest**, see note on 2:17. The idea that Christ's high priesthood continues forever will be developed in 7:24 f.

The Enigma of Melchizedek and His Priestly Order

HEBREWS 7:1–14

This Melchizedek was king of Salem and a priest of the Most High God. As Abraham was coming back from the battle in which he defeated the four kings, Melchizedek met him and blessed him, ²and Abraham gave him one tenth of all he had taken. (The first meaning of Melchizedek's name is "King of Righteousness"; and because he was King of Salem, his name also means "King of Peace.") ³There is no record of Melchizedek's father or mother or of any of his ancestors; no record of his birth or of his death. He is like the Son of God; he remains a priest forever.

⁴You see, then, how great he was. Abraham, our famous ancestor, gave him one tenth of all he got in the battle. ⁵And those descendants of Levi who are priests are commanded by the Law to collect one tenth from the people of Israel, that is, from their own countrymen, even though their countrymen are also descendants of Abraham. ⁶Melchizedek was not descended from Levi, but he collected one tenth from Abraham and blessed him, the man who received God's promises. ⁷There is no doubt that the one who blesses is greater than the one who is blessed. ⁸In the case of the priests the tenth is collected by men who die; but as for Melchizedek the tenth was collected by one who lives, as the Scripture says. ⁹And, so to speak, when Abraham paid the tenth, Levi (whose descendants collect the tenth) also paid it. ¹⁰For Levi had not yet been born, but was, so to speak, in the body of his ancestor Abraham when Melchizedek met him.

¹¹It was on the basis of the levitical priesthood that the Law was given to the people of Israel. Now, if the work of the levitical priests had been perfect, there would have been no need for a different kind of priest to appear, one who is the successor of Melchizedek, not of Aaron. ¹²For when the priesthood is changed, there also has to be a change in the Law. ¹³And our Lord, of whom these things are said, belonged to a different tribe, and no member of his tribe ever served as a priest. ¹⁴It is well known that he was born a member of the tribe of Judah; and Moses did not mention this tribe when he spoke of priests.

I n order to make the argument about Christ's high priesthood as convincing as it can be, the author begins by establishing the great importance of Melchizedek, who resembles the Son of God in many respects and hence serves as a type of Christ. His superiority to Abraham and Levi is then made plain. This in turn leads to a discussion of the significance of his priestly order, which in recent history had found a new and definitive representative in fulfillment of the expectation in Psalm 110:4. Again the discussion is midrashic in character, utilizing at several points the actual phraseology of the original quotation of Genesis 14:18–20.

7:1-2a / The identification of Melchizedek given here, as well as the brief description of his encounter with Abraham, is drawn from Genesis 14:18–20. (The author's language is heavily dependent on the LXX version of this passage.) GNB brings additional definition in the words **the battle in which he defeated the four kings** (lit., "the defeat of the kings"). Melchizedek appears in the Genesis narrative as an extraordinary person, indeed, but not more than a human king and priest. The Salem, of which Melchizedek was king, is probably Canaanite Jerusalem. He is said to have been **priest of the Most High God**, that is, of El Elyon, the head of the Canaanite pantheon. This God is seen to be the same as the God of Israel, as is evident from his description as the one "who made heaven and earth" and who gave Abraham his victory (Gen. 14:19–20). It is remarkable in itself that the priesthood of a Canaanite king, outside the stream of salvation history, could be recognized as legitimate. The only other biblical reference is in Psalm 110:4, which of course our author uses most skillfully. Melchizedek blessed Abraham upon his return from a victorious battle, and Abraham gave a tithe of **all he had taken** to Melchizedek. The significance of these deeds is midrashically explored in the next paragraph (vv. 4–10).

7:2b-3 / The parenthetical explanation of the meaning of Melchizedek and Salem is important because of the appropriateness of the titles in describing Christ, who is pre-eminently King of Righteousness and Peace. This supports the conclusion that Melchizedek **is like the Son of God**. GNB's twofold addition of the words **no record of** interprets for us the otherwise terse and difficult original (lit., "fatherless, motherless, without genealogy, having neither beginning of days, nor end of life"). It is the literal reading of verse 3 that has led some to the conclusion that Melchizedek was actually an appearance of the pre-incarnate Christ. What actually is being pointed out by the author, however, is the surprising silence of Scripture about the lineage and the birth and death of Melchizedek. In a rabbinic way, the silence is seen to be significant rather than simply fortuitous, especially for a person of such great status, who was both a king and a priest. Because there is no record of Melchizedek's death, nor therefore of the termination of his priesthood (or of any succession to it), the conclusion can be drawn that **he remains a priest forever**. So far as what Scripture says and does not say about Melchizedek, then, it is evident, that **he is like the Son of God**, who also is without beginning of days or end of life and whose priesthood therefore is eternally valid (cf. v. 17 with its quotation of Ps. 110:4).

7:4-6 / The opening statement is best understood as an exclamation: "Look how great this one is!" Even **our famous ancestor** (lit., "the patriarch") gave him a tenth of **all he got in the battle** (lit., "the spoils"). The importance of the event already mentioned in verse 1 is now stressed. It was one no less than the **great** Abraham who tithed to Melchizedek. The author now proceeds to acknowledge the practice of tithing among the descendants of Abraham. The levitical priesthood, not having an inheritance in the land, received according to the Law a tithe **from the people** (GNB adds **of Israel** for clarity), that is, **their own countrymen** (lit., "their brethren"). This was in return for their service (Num. 18:21). Tithing thus involved the **descendants of Abraham** (lit., "those from the loins of Abraham") both on the receiving and giving end of the transaction. Melchizedek, on the other hand, **was not descended from Levi** (lit., "not genealogically from them") and therefore his right to receive a tithe from Abraham depended not on the Law but on his own superior worth (cf. v. 7). His priesthood accordingly is of an exceptional character. Thus Melchizedek received the tithe, from and **blessed** (the word is drawn from Gen. 14:19), the very one who was the recipient of **God's promises** (lit., "the promises") and from whom eventually would come the levitical priesthood itself (cf. v. 10). The remarkable significance of this is brought out in the verses that follow.

7:7-8 / Just as the one who receives the tithe is of higher position than the one who gives the tithe, so also the one who confers a blessing **is greater than the one who is blessed** (lit., "the lesser is blessed by the greater"). The great Abraham is thus subordinate to Melchizedek. Furthermore, the levitical priesthood is inferior to Melchizedek's because **in the case of the priests** (lit., "here") we have mortal recipients of the tithe. But **as for Melchizedek** (lit., "there"), the recipient is **one who lives**. The words **as the Scripture says** (lit., "it is testified") may be misleading since although the conclusion is indeed drawn from Scripture, it is an inference based on what Scripture does not say (i.e., its failure to record Melchizedek's death) rather than on what Scripture actually says (cf. v. 3).

7:9-10 / GNB adds some words for clarity: **when Abraham paid** (lit., "through Abraham"); **Levi (whose descendants collect . . .)**, (lit., "Levi who collects"); **for Levi had not yet been born**; and **but . . . so to speak**. The point is clear. Since Levi was an eventual descendant of Abraham, he was **in the body of** (lit., "in the loins of") **his ancestor Abraham** (lit., "his father") when Abraham was met by Melchizedek (the words again allude to Gen. 14) and gave him a tithe. Therefore Levi may also be said to have tithed to Melchizedek through Abraham, and it is implied that Levi and his descendants are thus also subordinate to Melchizedek.

7:11 / The first sentence is an expansion of a subordinate clause that in the Greek occurs in what is the middle of GNB's second sentence and that several translations put in parentheses (e.g., RSV; NEB; NIV). The sentence cannot be taken literally since the priesthood did not precede the Law. What seems to be meant is that the priestly system is basic to the entire superstructure of the Law. The two are inextricably related, as can be seen from the argument in verse 12. The words **if the work of the levitical priests had been perfect** (lit., "if perfection had been achieved through the levitical priesthood") point to the inability of that system to arrive at the goal of full salvation. Had the levitical system been sufficient to the task, what need (the original asks) is there to speak of **a different kind of** (lit., "another") **priest** to arise, one of the order of Melchizedek, and not Aaron? That is, if the levitical system were self-sufficient, why then does Psalm 110:4 speak of the one at the right hand of God, who waits for his enemies to become a footstool for his feet, as one who is a "priest forever according to the order of Melchizedek"? Psalm 110:4 thus points to the inadequacy of the Aaronic priesthood.

7:12 / This change in priesthood has important consequences for the Law: there **has to be** (lit., "is of necessity") **a change in the Law**. Thus for all our author's stress on the continuity between the old and the new and on the nature of Christianity as the fulfillment of the promises to Israel, he also is forced to acknowledge important discontinuity between the old and the new. It would have taken great courage on the author's part to say something so problematic and so contrary to the disposition of his Jewish readers, not to mention the Jewish critics of Christianity who apparently exercised some influence over the readers. In the immediate context the change of the Law involves one from the tribe of Judah—and not Levi—becoming a priest. The implications are wider, however, as will be seen below (see vv. 18–19, and 8:7, 13). But despite his insistence upon the necessity of a change in the Law, the author's basic perspective remains: Christianity stands in continuity with the past as the fulfillment of what God promised he would do.

7:13-14 / GNB moves forward the words **our Lord** (from v. 14) and adds **as a priest** (lit., "at the altar"). It was plain that Jesus, the Son of David, was of the tribe of Judah and thus, according to the Law, could not qualify to be a priest. Yet he is the one referred to in Psalm 110:4 (**of whom these things are said**), the priest of the order of Melchizedek. No precedent exists for this turn of events. The levitical priesthood is now replaced by another order altogether. **Moses** here, of course, refers to the Pentateuch.

Additional Notes

7:1-2a / Melchizedek held an important place in the Judaism of the first century. Because he is so remarkable in the Genesis narrative, he became associated with the eschatological events to come. Thus, at Qumran a scroll has been discovered (labeled *11Q Melchizedek*) that portrays Melchizedek as a heavenly deliverer of Israel and avenger against the enemies of God. In this role he functions in a way similar to the archangel Michael as portrayed in the scrolls. In Jewish writings of the Middle Ages the identification of the two is made explicit. It is unlikely, however, that the author of Hebrews viewed Melchizedek as an angel or archangel as some of his Jewish contemporaries may have. Certainly if this had been the case, the author would have been explicit about it, given his earlier preoccupation with angels. See M. de Jonge and A. S. van der Woude, "11Q Melchizedek and the New Testament," *NTS* 12 (1966), pp. 301–26; and J. A. Fitzmyer, "Further Light on Melchizedek from Qumran Cave 11," *JBL* 86 (1967), pp. 25–41.

Another example of a priesthood regarded as legitimate although not of the levitical line, is found in Jethro, the Midianite priest who became the father-in-law of Moses (Exod. 2:16; 18:12). Although this does not enter our author's argument, it does confirm the idea of a priesthood such as Melchizedek's being somehow acceptable to God. It is interesting to note our author's refusal to mention or to utilize the potential symbolism of the bread and wine offered by Melchizedek to Abraham in the Genesis account. The sacramental allusion proved irresistible to the early fathers of the church. The giving of a tenth of the spoils of war to a deity or deities is known in Greek culture but is nowhere stipulated for Israel in the OT, where tithing has to do solely with agricultural produce. Abraham's tithe is apparently a kind of thanksgiving offering to God (cf. Gen. 28:22) through Melchizedek's mediation, something that in itself emphasizes the importance of this priesthood.

7:2b-3 / Although Philo, the Hellenistic Jew of Alexandria, allegorizes the Genesis narrative concerning Melchizedek in a way quite foreign to our author, he does explain the names Melchizedek and Salem in the same way, relating Salem to the Hebrew *shalom* ("peace"). See Philo, *Allegorical Interpretation*, 3.79. Philo also describes Sarah as "without mother" (same word used by our author to describe Melchizedek) since no record of her mother is to be found (*On Drunkenness*, 59 ff.).

Jewish eschatological expectation (e.g., Qumran) looked for a priestly and a royal Messiah. In Christ the two are combined, and Melchizedek as king and high priest serves as a type or an anticipation of Christ. In time not too remote from our author, the two offices had been combined, viz., in Simon the Maccabee and other Hasmonean rulers of the second century B.C. But the high priesthood of Simon was not of the legitimate line, being conferred by human authority (and hence contradictory of Heb. 5:4). Thus Melchizedek **is like the Son of God**. As is usually true, the type resembles the antitype, or that which is prefigured (and hence normative). Yet the author can also say that Christ is "like Melchizedek" (7:15). For **Son of God**, see note on 1:5. The Greek words that underlie **forever** (*eis to diēnekes*) occur only in Hebrews in the NT and the LXX (the same phrase is found in 10:1, 12, 14). For an important study of Melchizedek and the present passage, see F. L. Horton, Jr., *The Melchizedek Tradition*, SNTSM 30 (Cambridge: Cambridge University Press, 1976); M. Delcor, "Melchizedek from Genesis to the Qumran texts and the Epistle to the Hebrews," *JSJ* 2 (1971), pp. 115–35; B. Demarest, "Heb. 7:3: A *Crux Interpretum* Historically Considered," *EQ* 49 (1977), pp. 141–62; *A History of the Interpretation of Hebrews 7, 1–10 from the Reformation to the Present* (Tübingen: Mohr, 1976); see too the excursus "The Significance of Melchizedek" in Hughes, pp. 237–45; A. J. Bandstra "*Heilsgeschichte* and Melchizedek in Hebrews" *CTJ* 3 (1968), pp. 36–41; J. W. Thompson, "The Conceptual Background and Purpose of the Midrash in Hebrews 7," *NovT* 19 (1977), pp. 209-23.

7:4-6 / **How great** translates *pēlikos* (the same word occurs only once again in the NT, in Gal. 6:11, where Paul uses it to describe his handwriting). The language of v. 4 is drawn from the LXX of Gen. 14:20. Josephus describes the tithe offered by Abraham as a "tithe of the plunder" (*Ant.* 1.181). The pervasiveness of the principle of tithing is seen in the fact that the tithe received by the Levites was further tithed to the priests (Num. 18:26; cf. Neh. 10:38 f.). The reference to "the patriarch," standing at the end of the Greek sentence, is emphatic. In v. 6 GNB appropriately restates the subject **Melchizedek**, which the Greek text leaves unexpressed. The Greek word underlying **not descended** in v. 6 (*genealogoumenos*) is found in the NT only here.

7:7-8 / The concept of "blessing" has a rich OT background that is taken up in Judaism and the NT. Here a special priest confers the divine power of God's blessing upon a central figure in the history of redemption. See Beyer, *TDNT*, vol. 2, pp. 754–65. The argument of v. 8 is rabbinic in character, drawing great significance from the silence of the text (cf. v. 3). The reference to **one who lives**, however, finds its parallel in the references to Christ in vv. 16 and 24, where the reference to endless life is literally true.

7:9-10 / The Hebraic use of the Greek word for "loins" in referring to the source of physical generation is found only in the LXX and NT (in dependence on the LXX). See Seesemann, *TDNT*, vol. 5, pp. 496 f.

7:11 / Since the argument assumes the importance of both the levitical priesthood and the Law, it seems obviously directed to Jewish rather than Gentile readers. The latter would have regarded the levitical priesthood as merely preparatory for what had come in Christ; but even in their eschatological expectations many Jews looked for the appearance of a high priest from the line of Levi. Indeed, Judaizing groups in the early church (represented, for example, in *The Testament of the Twelve Patriarchs*) continued to stress the importance of the tribe of Levi, as well as Judah, in eschatological expectation. Such groups either did not know of the argument of the author of Hebrews about the obsolescence of the levitical priesthood, or else they found it unacceptable. See the discussion in Hughes, pp. 260 ff.

"Perfection" here again refers to completeness in the sense of arriving at the intended goal. Although the root is very important and other forms of it occur frequently in Hebrews, this is the only occurrence of the noun form *teleiōsis*. See note on 2:10. The verb underlying **was given** (*nomotheteō*) occurs only here and in 8:6 (with a different subject) in the NT. See Gutbrod, *TDNT*, vol. 4, p. 1090.

Ps. 110:4, just quoted in 5:6 and about to be quoted again in vv. 17 and 21, is obviously the basis for the argument in this verse. See commentary on 5:6.

7:12 / The tension between continuity and discontinuity of the old and the new is common to all NT writers to some extent and is only to be expected because of the nature of the fulfillment brought by Christ. That the author of the Hebrews can express the discontinuity as sharply as he does, however, is surprising, given his readership. The word **change** (*metathesis*) means more than a slight modification (the same word occurs in 11:5 and 12:27, where it connotes removal). As we learn from v. 18 and 8:7, 13, what is meant is essentially an abrogation of the Law, paradoxically by its fulfillment in Christ—to whom it pointed all along. Thus, for our author, as for Paul, the significance of Christ and his work cannot be fully appreciated without at the same time realizing the temporary status of the Law. Unlike Paul, however, our author limits himself to the temporary character of the ceremonial legislation of the OT.

7:13-14 / Although the word is common in the NT, the word "altar" (*thysiastērion*) occurs only once again in Hebrews (13:10). Here to "officiate at the altar" is obviously a priestly function. Although David (and Solomon), of the line of Judah, did sacrifice animals to the Lord, this involved no sanctioning of the tribe of Judah as priests. The expression **our Lord** occurs in Hebrews only here and in 13:20, where it is "our Lord Jesus."

Was born is from the verb that means literally "to rise" (*anatellō*), and hence "to spring from." It is probably used deliberately to allude to Num. 24:17 where the same verb refers to the star of Jacob who is to rise in fulfillment of God's promises.

The Legitimacy and Superiority of Christ's Priesthood

HEBREWS 7:15–28

The matter becomes even plainer; a different priest has appeared, who is like Melchizedek. [16]He was made a priest, not by human rules and regulations, but through the power of a life which has no end. [17]For the scripture says, "You will be a priest forever, as the successor of Melchizedek." [18]The old rule, then, is set aside, because it was weak and useless. [19]For the Law of Moses could not make anything perfect. And now a better hope has been provided through which we come near to God.

[20]In addition, there is also God's vow. There was no such vow when the others were made priests. [21]But Jesus became a priest by means of a vow when God said to him,

"The Lord has made a vow
    and will not change his mind:
'you will be a priest forever.' "
[22]This difference, then, also makes Jesus the guarantee of a better covenant.

[23]There is another difference: there were many of those other priests, because they died and could not continue their work. [24]But Jesus lives on forever, and his work as priest does not pass on to someone else. [25]And so he is able, now and always, to save those who come to God through him, because he lives forever to plead with God for them.

[26]Jesus, then, is the High Priest that meets our needs. He is holy; he has no fault or sin in him; he has been set apart from sinners and raised above the heavens. [27]He is not like other high priests; he does not need to offer sacrifices every day for his own sins first and then for the sins of the people. He offered one sacrifice, once and for all, when he offered himself. [28]The Law of Moses appoints men who are imperfect to be high priests; but God's promise made with the vow, which came later than the Law, appoints the Son, who has been made perfect forever.

Extending the argument of the preceding section, the author now explores ways in which the priesthood of Christ, resembling that of Melchizedek, is superior to the levitical priesthood set forth in the Law of Moses.

7:15 / GNB adds the words **the matter** and changes the original "if" (RSV translates "when") into a semicolon, as well as the present tense "arises" to **has appeared**. The possibility of greater clarity, according to the author, is the result of the reality of another priest of this Melchizedekan order, **like Melchizedek**. That is, such a one exists, and from this fact the point of the argument can now be better understood.

7:16-17 / A relative clause is turned into an independent sentence by GNB. This priest "has become and remains" a priest (this is the sense of the Greek perfect tense) not on the basis of **human rules and regulations** (lit., "the law of a fleshly commandment")—that is, concerned with external matters such as bodily descent—but on the basis of **a life which has no end** (lit., "an indestructible life"). The reference to **power** in this context may be an allusion to the resurrection. Whether this is true or not, the point of the argument rests on the unique identity of the Son (cf. Ps. 110:1)—whose life continues on forever, and in whom alone, therefore, the promise of Psalm 110:4 ("a priest forever") can be understood to be fulfilled literally. Jesus is made the priest of Psalm 110:4 because he is the person described in Psalm 110:1. He who presently sits at the right hand of God alone can be the priest appointed forever. The anti-type is truly without beginning and without end, just as the type is apparently without beginning or end. The authority of Christ's priesthood depends on his identity as the Son of God. In the quotation of Psalm 110:4 (cf. the earlier use of this verse in 5:6; 6:20) again for GNB's future tense the original has a present "you are," and for **the successor of**, the original reads "according to the order of." The word **scripture** is added by GNB (and for **says** the original reads, "it is witnessed" [cf. RSV]).

7:18 / The statements in verses 18 and 19b are linked in the original (cf. RSV "on the one hand" . . . "on the other hand"). **The old rule** (lit., "a former commandment") refers to the Mosaic legislation concerning the levitical priesthood, which is now **set aside** (lit., "a setting aside occurs"). This stern note of discontinuity with the Law of Moses (anticipated in 7:12; cf. 8:13) is justified by noting that the Law **was weak and useless** (lit., "its weakness and uselessness"). The description of the commandment as **weak** or ineffective finds a parallel in Paul (Rom. 8:3; cf. Gal. 4:9). The strongest word of all, however, is "uselessness," which is used in the LXX of Isaiah 44:10 to describe idols (cf. RSV "profitable for nothing"). The author's point apparently is that although the Law had a proper role to play before the fulfillment brought by the Christ, once the latter has been realized, the Law is outmoded and hence useless. It should be noted, however, that it is the Law concerning the levitical priesthood and ritual that is particularly in view (cf. 10:9b). Our author does not draw further implications.

7:19 / The first sentence in this verse is parenthetical (RSV and NIV use parentheses), interrupting the contrast between 18 and 19b. **The law** (GNB adds **of Moses**) literally "made nothing perfect." That is, it was unable to bring anything to God's intended purpose of redemption (cf. 5:9). But in the new situation, which it is the major task of our author to expound, a **better hope** enters the picture, one which indeed makes it possible to **come near to God**, which is exactly what the Law of the cultus did not allow, and to realize the fullness of salvation that he promised. Again the language is that of the temple cult, but now transposed to a new key because of the very nature of God's definitive work in Christ.

7:20 / Verses 20–22 constitute one sentence in the Greek, with a comparison beginning in verse 20 ("to the degree that" there was a divine oath) that concludes in verse 22 ("by so much" is Jesus' guarantee of a better covenant). In the long sentence the name **Jesus** is the very last word and, because of this artistic placement, becomes emphatic. Verses 20b–21 thus amount to an insertion. The appeal to **God's vow** (lit., "it was not without an oath") is reminiscent of the argument concerning the covenant made with Abraham in 6:13 ff. The point again is that something already fixed becomes doubly sure, since to God's word is added an oath (cf. v. 28). In the case of the levitical priesthood, however, **there was no such vow** (lit., "without an oath"). GNB adds **the others** to indicate the levitical priesthood.

7:21-22 / In the case of the priesthood of Jesus, on the other hand, when in Psalm 110:4 it is said that he **will be** (lit., "you are") a priest forever according to the order of Melchizedek, that same verse says that **the Lord has made a vow and will not change his mind**. Thus the author uses the full content of Psalm 110:4 to the advantage of his argument. This is a confirmation of the superiority of the priesthood of Jesus to that of the Levites. The **difference** caused by this state of affairs is such that Jesus has become **the guarantee of a better covenant**. Thus a better promise (one confirmed with an oath) implies a **better covenant**—indeed, what will later be identified as the "new covenant" (cf. 8:8; 9:15). And Jesus is the ground or basis of the security of that covenant (cf. 9:15, and 12:24 where Jesus is described as "the mediator of a new covenant," RSV).

7:23-24 / For clarity, GNB adds **there is another difference; . . . other**; and **their work. Because they died** (lit., "by death") the levitical priests were unable to remain perpetually in office. It was necessary to have **many** priests in order that the work might continue. In contrast, **Jesus lives** (lit., "he continues") **forever** (cf. 13:8). The last word involves a Greek phrase (*eis ton aiōna*) that is a deliberate allusion to Psalm 110:4. The result is, as the text literally reads, that Jesus "has the priesthood permanently." It **does not pass on to someone else**.

7:25 / The fact that Jesus' priestly work is not hindered by death means that he is able **to save those who came to God through him**. GNB's words **now and always** could also be rendered "fully" (cf. NEB, "absolutely") or "for all time." The point, in any event, is not *when* Jesus is able to save but rather the *quality* of the salvation offered. By its very nature it is an "eternal salvation" (cf. 5:9; 9:12; 10:14; 13:20) and a perfect or "complete" salvation, unlike the temporary and the incomplete work of the levitical priests. **Because** is added by GNB, being inferred from the participial clause "always living." The priestly work of Christ depends directly on "the power of an indestructible life" (7:16, RSV) and it is that same kind of permanence that determines the character of the salvation experienced by its recipients. They are sustained by the continual intercession of Jesus on their behalf. On this point the author is in agreement with Paul (Rom. 8:34; cf. 1 John 2:1).

7:26 / GNB adds the name **Jesus** in this verse, and in the second half of the verse changes the list of adjectives into sentences. The words **that meets our needs** are an interpretation of the literal "it was fitting." The inference that Jesus is able to meet our needs is a correct one, but the emphasis here falls rather upon the superior character of Jesus and hence the superior character of his work, as the following verses show. That he is **holy** by itself affirms the separateness of Jesus from the rest of humanity, as do the accompanying words, literally, "blameless" and "unstained." Not only by virtue of his character is Jesus incomparably superior, but also because of the fact of his ascension whereby he has been **set apart from sinners and raised above the heavens** (cf. 4:14; Eph. 4:10). In these last words we again encounter an allusion to Psalm 110:1 (cf. 1:3 and the note on 1:13). Thus, despite the full humanity of Jesus—that he became "like his brothers in every way" (2:17)—the author strongly reaffirms (cf. 4:14) the sinlessness of Jesus.

7:27 / The result is plain: Jesus has no daily need **to offer sacrifices . . . for his own sins**, as do the priests (cf. 5:3). These last few words are apparently the source for GNB's opening statement in this verse, for which there is no counterpart in the original. Over against the necessarily repetitive sacrifices of the levitical priests, which for our author represents a self-confessed inadequacy (cf. 10:11), Jesus **offered one sacrifice once and for all** (lit., "this he did once for all"). This he accomplished when **he offered himself**. This shocking fact—that this high priest offers *himself* in sacrifice—here mentioned directly for the first time (but cf. 2:9, 14; 5:8), becomes a central argument in 9:11–28. The definite, once-and-for-all, character of the work of Christ is of course a hallmark of the Epistle to the Hebrews.

7:28 / This verse serves as a summary of the argument thus far by again contrasting what is true according to the Law with the greater truth found in the one to whom the Melchizedek passage in Psalm 110:4 points. **The Law** (GNB adds **of Moses** for clarity) appoints as high priests **men who are imperfect** (lit., "having weakness"), but **God's promise made with the vow** (lit., "the word of the oath") appoints **the** (lit., "a") **Son** (cf. Ps. 2:7) . . . **forever**. These words, which occur together in the Greek text, constitute an allusion to Psalm 110:4, but with the word "Son" from Psalm 2:7 being substituted for "priest." This conflation is reminiscent of the utilization of the two quotations successively in 5:5–6. The author's observation that this oath-confirmed word **came later than the Law** reflects a Jewish conclusion that new revelation is more authoritative than the older revelation (although by no means is this conclusion always accepted!). The notion of having **been made perfect** is again best understood as the state of having accomplished God's saving purposes (cf. 5:9) and being raised to God's right hand. As we have seen, "perfection" in Hebrews generally has this teleological connotation and therefore is well-suited to express the sense of fulfillment that is so prominent in the epistle.

Additional Notes

7:15 / The actual Greek words used here, "according to the likeness of Melchizedek," are again a deliberate allusion to Ps. 110:4. **Has appeared** (lit., "arises"), although representing a different verb (*anistēmi*), may also allude to the coming of the promised Messiah (see note on v. 14 above). The present tense of "arises" emphasizes the present reality of his existence. **Different** (*heteros*) may also be translated "another," although, to be sure, it is evident from the context that Jesus' priesthood is unique.

7:16–17 / The word "fleshly" (*sarkinos*; GNB: **human**) is used here because it is the earthly (and hence transitory) sphere to which the commandment applies. See Schweizer, *TDNT*, vol. 7, pp. 143 f. The **power** (*dynamis*) of "an indestructible life" (cf. Acts 2:24) is such that it is self-validating. The power of God is regularly linked in the NT with the resurrection of Christ (cf. 1 Cor. 6:14; 2 Cor. 13:4; Rom. 1:4). The quotation in v. 17 again reminds us of the importance of Ps. 110 for the argument of the book. On the significance of Ps. 110:4 see commentary on 5:6.

7:18 / The word used for "setting aside" (*athetēsis*) means "to declare invalid" and is used in the papyri for official, legal annulment (cf. the verb form of the same root in Gal. 3:15). The author's courage to say that the Law concerning the levitical priesthood is **set aside** is especially notable given such a reference as in Exod. 40:15 to "a perpetual priesthood throughout their generations" (cf. Jer. 33:18). Only the author's perception of the fulfillment and the concomitant newness brought by Christ can account for this. "Weakness" is twice ascribed to the levitical priests in Hebrews (5:2; 7:28). The Greek word for **useless** (*anōpheles*) occurs elsewhere in the NT only in Titus 3:9, where it describes futile controversies.

7:19 / Whereas in the preceding verse the word "commandment" (*entolē*) is used, now the author uses the broader word, "law" (*nomos*). Again the author stresses the importance of arriving at the intended goal (using the verb *teleioō*), but this time negatively by pointing out the inadequacy of the Law (cf. 7:11). See note on 2:10 (cf. 5:9). The positive use of the same verb can be seen below in v. 28. One of the author's favorite words to describe Christianity is the word **better**. (See note on 1:4.) Here it modifies **hope**, an important word in our epistle (3:6; 6:11, 18; 10:23). As in 6:18, here the word refers to a present rather than a future reality. Or, to put it another way, our confidence concerning the future (because it rests on the finished work of Christ) is such that it transforms the present. Eschatology is not only future, but also realized. On "hope," see E. Hoffmann, *NIDNTT*, vol. 2; pp. 238–44.

7:20 / In this verse we encounter again the rabbinic argument from the silence of the text (cf. 7:3). That is, since no vow is mentioned in connection with the establishment of the levitical priesthood, it is taken as inferior to the priestly order of Melchizedek which *was* established with a vow. Although the argument is very similar to that in 6:13–18, the rare word for vow here and in the next verse is *horkomosia* rather than the more common *horkos*.

7:21–22 / Again, the important prooftext of the argument in this section of the epistle, Ps. 110:4, is quoted (cf. 5:6, 10; 7:17), but now in its entirety for the first time. And again the new is contrasted with the old by being called **better** (cf. note on 1:4). In this instance a **better covenant** is in view–the first occurrence of the word "covenant" (*diathēkē*), which will become very important in the next few chapters (see 8:6, 8–10; 9:15–20; 10:16, 29; 12:24; 13:20). The word indeed occurs far more often in Hebrews (seventeen times) than in any other NT book. Like Paul, the author can use *diathēkē* in the legal sense of "testament" or "will" (9:16; cf. Gal. 3:15 ff.). The primary sense of the word, however, is religious, referring to the arrangement whereby God's saving purpose becomes a reality. There was an old arrangement or covenant (at Sinai) whereby Israel experienced redemption. From our author's perspective, this has now given way to a new state of affairs to which, indeed, it pointed. The "new covenant" (as it will be called in 9:15 and 12:24) is defined over against the old (note especially the great dependence on the Jeremiah passage [31:31–34] quoted initially in chap. 8) and of course depends absolutely on the saving work of Christ in fulfillment of the promises (cf. 8:6; 9:15; 10:29; 13:20). See Behm, *TDNT*, vol. 2, pp. 124–34; G. Vos, "The Epistle's Conception of the *Diathēkē*" in *The Teaching of the Epistle to the Hebrews* (Grand Rapids: Eerdmans, 1956), pp. 27–45; E. A. C. Pretorius, "Diathēkē in the Epistle to the Hebrews," *Neotestamentica* 5 (1971), pp. 37–50. The word **guarantee** (*engyos*) occurs only here in the NT. Through his priestly work, Jesus has become the solid assurance that God's saving purpose has become a reality, fully sufficient for both the present and the future. See Preisker, *TDNT*, vol. 2, p. 329.

7:23–24 / GNB's **were** in the first sentence does not adequately reflect the periphrastic construction in the Greek, where the finite verb is in the present tense. The implication of this (which also occurs in v. 20) is that there *are* many priests at the time of writing. The concept of "continuing on forever" as well as the allusion to Ps. 110:4 recall the statement made about Melchizedek's priesthood in 7:3. But that it is the life of Jesus that is primarily in view (and only then the priesthood) is indicated by the statement in v. 16. The Greek word underlying **does not pass on** (*aparabatos*) occurs only here in the NT and LXX; it means "permanent," "unchangeable." See J. Schneider, *TDNT*, vol. 5, pp. 742 f. Josephus provides the graphic statistic that there were eighty-three high priests from Aaron to the destruction of the temple in A.D. 70 (*Ant.* 20.227).

7:25 / The verb "be able" (*dynamai*) and the negative "be unable" occur often in Hebrews, especially in explicating the contrast between the new and the old. The new is always able to do what the old could not do. In the present instance the object is **to save**, and although not made explicit, a contrast with the old is implied. The phrase translated **now and always** by GNB (*eis to panteles*) may be taken to mean "forever" in that the location spoken of is permanent, or it may be understood to connote totality. Since the full adequacy of the salvation is in view, and since totality includes the idea of permanence, the latter seems preferable. See Delling, *TDNT*, vol. 8, pp. 66 f. The idea of permanence is of course implied in the fact that Jesus **lives forever** (*pantote*, only occurrence in Hebrews) to intercede. The fact of this intercession again points to the sufficiency of the salvation. GNB's **plead** should not be taken literally, for as F. F. Bruce (p. 155) notes, Jesus intercedes "as a *throned* Priest-King, asking what He will from a Father who always hears and grants His request." On "intercede," see C. Brown, *NIDNTT,* vol. 2, pp. 882–6. The language **to come to God** has overtones of the Temple worship (cf. 11:6).

7:26 / The verb "it was fitting" (*prepō*) occurs also in 2:10. What is "right" and "appropriate" comes very close to, and may imply, "what God wills"—that is, the working out of his perfect providence. Jesus as **High Priest** is of course a central motif in Hebrews (cf. note on 2:17). Only here in Hebrews is Jesus called **holy** (*hosios,* cf. Acts 2:27; 13:25; Rev. 15:4; 16:5). The words "blameless" (*akakos*) and "unstained" (*amiantos*) remind us of the total innocence of the sacrificial victim (cf. the next verse).

7:27 / The language of this verse is obviously that of the Temple cultus. Aaron is explicitly directed to make a sin offering for himself first and then for his house and the people (Lev. 16:6 ff.). The reference here to **high priests** offering sacrifices **daily** is unusual, since the high priest's work is generally associated with the annual sacrifice of the Day of Atonement and not the daily sacrifices of the ordinary priests (see 9:7, 25). The argument about the **once and for all** character of Christ's sacrifice is repeatedly stressed by the author in the next two chapters, using two almost identical words (*ephapax*: here, 9:12; 10:10; *hapax*: 9:26, 28). The completeness and finality of this one act is bound up with who it is that sacrifices and is sacrificed, and the fact that this is the consummation of God's provision of salvation. The contrast with the repetitive futility of the levitical cultus is immediately evident and telling. See Stählin, *TDNT,* vol. 1, pp. 381–4.

7:28 / The "weakness" of the levitical priests is again stressed, as it was in 5:2. By contrast, Jesus is able to "feel sympathy for our weaknesses" because of his full humanity. Yet he did not know the weakness that stems from imperfection and sin. The "word of the oath" (a literal rendering of what GNB translates **God's promise made with the vow**), a unique expression in the NT, refers of course to the argument that begins in v. 20 which is based on Ps. 110:4. The final verb, **has been made perfect** (*teleioō*) is in the perfect tense, suggesting action completed in the past with results lasting into the present. Thus **the Son**, having accomplished his once-and-for-all sacrifice, has brought God's saving purposes, as well as his own personal calling, to their goal, all of which produces a state of completion and permanence—this in contrast to the Law (7:19), which could bring nothing to this stage of completeness and fulfillment.

15

The True High Priest
and His Ministry

HEBREWS 8:1–6

The whole point of what we are saying is that we have such a High Priest, who sits at the right of the throne of the Divine Majesty in heaven. ²He serves as high priest in the Most Holy Place, that is, in the real tent which was put up by the Lord, not by man.

³Every high priest is appointed to present offerings and animal sacrifices to God, and so our High Priest must also have something to offer. ⁴If he were on earth, he would not be a priest at all, since there are priests who offer the gifts required by the Jewish Law. ⁵The work they do as priests is really only a copy and a shadow of what is in heaven. It is the same as it was with Moses. When he was about to build the Covenant Tent, God told him, "Be sure to make everything according to the pattern you were shown on the mountain." ⁶But now, Jesus has been given priestly work which is superior to theirs, just as the covenant which he arranged between God and his people is a better one, because it is based on promises of better things.

In this passage the author sums up his argument thus far but also brings it to a new stage. He continues to expound the definitive character of Christ's work, now drawing the contrast in a new and fascinating manner by using the language of shadow and reality.

8:1 / The **whole point** of the argument centers on the actual reality and sufficiency of our **High Priest**. He has been able definitively to accomplish what the levitical priesthood pointed toward in anticipation. He now has assumed his rightful place at the right hand of the **Divine Majesty in heaven** (this is a circumlocution for "God"; cf. 1:3). Once again the wording alludes to Psalm 110:1. Jesus is where he is because of who he is—both Son (cf. 4:14) and high priest (cf. Ps. 110:4).

8:2 / GNB begins a new sentence here with the words **he serves as high priest** in place of the word "servant" or "minister" (*leitourgos*). We have a high priest who ministers **in the Most Holy Place**, that is, in the Temple

(GNB adds the word **Most**). This our author now proceeds to describe as **the real** (or "true") tent (the words **that is** are correctly added by GNB), one "which the Lord set up, not man" (GNB changes the active voice to a passive construction). The same point is made in verse 5, where the levitical priests are said to have been concerned with only a copy or shadow of "heavenly" realities. There has been considerable discussion of the possible influence of Greek dualism upon the author in his argumentation here and in succeeding passages (e.g., 9:23 f.; 10:1; see note on 8:2).

Does the author believe in the existence of an actual sanctuary somewhere "in heaven" of which the earthly sanctuary is a copy? Although the language indeed sounds like that of the Greek philosophers, it is much more probable that our author takes his idea from the OT where Moses is instructed about building the tabernacle and its furniture by being shown patterns or models. (In addition to Exod. 25:40, which our author quotes in v. 5, see Exod. 25:9; 26:30; 27:8.) The issue here is not the existence of a heavenly tabernacle but rather Moses' faithfulness to God's intended purpose. In our passage the point being made is that true and finally efficacious atonement transcends the tabernacle and its ritual because now God's purpose has been realized. What took place in that ritual of the historical tabernacle only through pictures and symbols actually takes place in the sacrificial work of Christ. The work of our High Priest, therefore, concerns not pictures or symbols, but ultimate reality—the reality of God himself. What preoccupies our author is not a vertical dualism, but a historical progression from promise to fulfillment. The final and definitive character of the fulfillment is underlined by the fact that our High Priest sits at the right hand of God, now fulfilling his ministry of intercession (7:25). The words "which the Lord set up" are possibly an allusion to the LXX of Numbers 24:6, where the tents of Israel (cf. Num. 24:5) are said to have been pitched by the Lord. The language is figurative and poetical.

8:3-4 / The opening words, **every high priest**, are exactly the same as in 5:1 where the high priests are described as "appointed for the offering of gifts and sacrifices" (GNB adds **to God**). Since it has been already established by our author that Jesus is the High Priest spoken of in Psalm 110:4, it is obvious that **our High Priest** (lit., "this one") **must also have something to offer**. Although the author has already indicated what that "something" is ("himself " in 7:27), he also here anticipates what he will argue in chapters 9 and 10. But the priesthood of Jesus is categorically superior to that of earthly priests: his distinctive offering is not made **on**

earth, "according to the Law" (GNB adds **required** and **Jewish**). This is no denial of the death of Christ in history, but rather a way of saying that his work of atonement is of eschatological or ultimate meaning and hence "heavenly" in contrast to the "earthly" work of the levitical priesthood. This is forcefully pointed out in the following verses.

8:5 / GNB restates this verse expansively. The inferiority of the work of the levitical priesthood is now stressed by noting that it concerns but **a copy and a shadow** of the heavenly realities. This is but another way of saying that their work only prefigured the definitive atoning work of Jesus, which alone is of ultimate significance. The point is further substantiated by reference to the words spoken to Moses as he was about to build **the Covenant Tent** (lit., "the tent"). He was told to follow **the pattern you were shown on the mountain** (Exod. 25:40). This alone indicates that the tabernacle (and it successor, the Temple) with its sacrificial ritual (stipulated through Moses) was not itself the ultimate reality, but only a reflection of it. The contrasting of the earthly and temporal with the heavenly and ultimate occurs again in 9:23 and 10:1. Paul can use very similar language, as in Colossians 2:17 where, speaking of certain items of the Mosaic legislation such as dietary and Sabbath rules, he writes: "All such things are only a shadow of things in the future; the reality is Christ."

8:6 / **But now,** in the new situation, **Jesus** (lit., "he") has obtained a **superior** priestly ministry (GNB adds **to theirs**). This is the first of three comparatives used in this verse. The second occurs in the statement that Jesus "is the mediator of a better covenant" (cf. 7:22). GNB paraphrases the word "mediator" with the words **which he arranged between God and his people.** Here and in other occurrences of "mediator" (9:15; 12:24) the word "arrange" is ineffective in conveying the meaning intended, that is, that the sacrifice of Jesus is itself the means or agency by which the new covenant (the word "new" is added in 9:15 and 12:24) becomes a reality. More than something he "arranges," the new covenant is something he effects, since it is absolutely dependent on his person and work. GNB's **because it** is literally "which." The third comparative refers literally to "better promises" upon which the new covenant **is based** (lit., "[legally] enacted," cf. NEB "legally secured"). These promises will be the focus of attention in the quotation from Jeremiah 31 which will take up the remainder of chapter 8. Thus our High Priest is concerned with matters altogether superior to the old covenant. His priestly work itself, the new covenant resulting from it, and the promises to which that new covenant points—in all of this the old pales in comparison to the greater excellence of the new.

Additional Notes

8:1 / **Whole point** (*kephalaion*) can be understood to refer to a summary or to a new main point. Both aspects seem present in the opening verses of this chapter. **Majesty** (*megalosynē*) occurs in the NT only here, in 1:3, and in Jude 25. The expression **such a High Priest** is found also in 7:26. For High Priest, see note on 2:17. **In heaven** is, in Hebraic fashion, literally a plural, "in the heavens."

8:2 / **The Most Holy Place** is literally "the holies" (*tōn hagiōn*) and can have three possible meanings: "holy things," "holy ones," or "sanctuary." The last is preferable because this is the meaning of the same words in 9:2, 8, 24; 10:19; 13:11. GNB leads us to think of the Holy of Holies, the innermost sanctuary (where indeed the work of the high priest took place on the Day of Atonement) by adding **Most**, which, however, is not in the original text. "Holy place" can, according to context, indicate the "Holy of Holies" (as in 9:12, 25; for the full expression see 9:3). The word "servant" or "minister" occurs elsewhere in Hebrews only in 1:7 in reference to angels and in the NT in Rom. 13:6 (referring to authorities of the state), Rom. 15:16 (Paul), and Phil. 2:25 (Epaphroditus). The cognate verb (*leitourgeō*) is used frequently in the LXX referring to the priestly work of the Levites. For the cognate noun "ministry" (*leitourgia*), see 8:6 and 9:21.

The word **tent** (*skēnē*) here and in 9:11 has been taken to refer to the humanity of Christ (Calvin), to the church (Westcott), and to the heavenly regions through which Christ passed on the way to the Holy of Holies (Spicq, Héring). Despite John 1:14 (where the cognate verb [*skēnoō*] occurs), and other NT references to the body as a "tent" (e.g., 2 Cor. 5:1, 4), the suggestion that the humanity of Christ is in view is hardly compatible with the statement in 9:11 that the tent "is not a part of this created world." The same must be said concerning the view that "tent" refers to the heavens. The argument that the church is in view depends on being able to equate "church" and "tent" (an equation found nowhere in the NT) on the basis of a third term, "body," common to both—a rather tenuous connection at best. "Sanctuary" and "true tent" are best taken as referring to the same thing, the very presence of God (see 9:24). For a full discussion of this problem, see the excursus in Hughes, pp. 283–90. The word "tent" (*skēnē*) is used in Hebrews far more than in any other NT book. It almost always refers to the tabernacle, the predecessor of the permanent Temple (see 8:5; chap. 9; 13:10), and invariably is shown to be inferior to the reality it foreshadowed. For a discussion of the use of this word in Hebrews, see Michaelis, *TDNT*, vol. 7, pp. 375–77.

The Greek dualism often mentioned as the background to this passage derives from the philosophy of Plato wherein every earthly object is said to be the manifestation of a corresponding archetypal "idea" or "form" that can only be known through the intellect. This dualism between earthly and "heavenly" reality was influential in the Hellenistic world, especially in such a center as Alexandria, where it can be detected in Philo, the Hellenistic Jew (who was active just prior to the time of Christ). Some indeed have seen considerable influence from Philo upon the author of Hebrews, and this has given rise to the speculation that the book was written from Alexandria, and even that Apollos, with his Alexandrian background (Acts 18:24) was the author. Although the debate concerning the influence of Philo upon our author has not ended, R. Williamson has presented a very convincing case that the author of Hebrews is not at all influenced by Philo. See *Philo and the Epistle to the Hebrews*. Williamson also denies the influence of Platonism upon our author, arguing that the stress on the importance of history, as well as the temporal sequence of promise and fulfillment, is quite alien to Plato. See "Platonism and Hebrews." The "dualism" in Hebrews is not of a metaphysical kind but of an eschatological kind, and our author's background is more Jewish than Hellenistic.

8:3-4 / The expression "gifts and sacrifices" (cf. Lev. 21:6), which occurs also in 5:1 and 9:9, is unique to this epistle in the NT. The phrase is a general reference to a variety of sacrifices offered by the priests. In describing this work of the priests the author uses the present tense (*prosphero*, the regular word for "offer"), implying the necessary repetition (and also possibly the existence of the sacrificial ritual at the time the author writes); but in referring to the offering **our High Priest** must offer he uses the aorist tense, implying the once-and-for-all character of his high-priestly work. The argument that if Jesus were an earthly priest (in contrast to one whose work is "heavenly" or ultimate) he would not have anything to offer harks back to the admission that Jesus was not a member of the tribe of Levi—of which alone Moses spoke when he instituted the sacrificial ritual (7:14). If then he is a high priest, his offering must be of an entirely different order.

8:5 / The word for **copy** (*hypodeigma*) and the word for **shadow** (*skia*) sound like the language of Hellenistic philosophy, but the ultimate reality to which they point is not something perceived only by the intellect, but something which occurred in the historical process: the cross of Christ. **Copy** occurs in the same sense in 9:23. See Schlier, *TDNT*, vol. 2, pp. 32 f. *Shadow* is used similarly in 10:1 (and in Col. 2:17). See H.-C. Hahn, *NIDNTT*, vol. 3, pp. 553–56. Related to these two words is another key word in this verse, which occurs in the quotation: **pattern** (*typos*). Although this is the only occurrence in Hebrews, the counterpart "antitype" (*antitypos*) is found in 9:24 (see note on this verse), where the earthly sanctuary is described as "a copy of the real one." On *typos* see Goppelt, *Typos*, translation of 1939 German original (Grand Rapids: Eerdmans, 1982); *TDNT*, vol. 8, pp. 246–59.

What is in heaven is lit. "the heavenlies," which can mean the "heavenly things" (cf. ASV), as it is translated in 9:23, or the "heavenly sanctuary" (on the analogy of "the holies" as in 8:2). The difference is of little consequence. The earthly ritual is but a pointer to the definitive and ultimate atoning work of Christ. "Above all, the vertical typology, which is all-important in Philo, is in Hb. merely an aid to the presentation and characterisation of the horizontal" (Goppelt, *TDNT*, vol. 8, p. 258). **God told him** is literally "Moses was warned by God." The verb (*chrēmatizō*) occurs also in 11:7 and in 12:25 where it also refers to matters of especially serious importance. After the words **be sure** in the quotation, the Greek contains a common formula used to indicate the quotation of Scripture: *phēsin*, "He says" or "it says" (cf. 1 Cor. 6:16). For "tent" (*skēnē*), see note on v. 2. Exod. 25:40 is also utilized in Stephen's speech (Acts 7:44).

8:6 / The word for **priestly work** (*leitourgia*), which is common in the LXX, occurs again in 9:21. The word is generally spiritualized in the NT to refer to Christian ministry (see 2 Cor. 9:12; Phil. 2:17, 30), but in Luke 1:23 the original sense is retained. See K. Hess, *NIDNTT*, vol. 3, pp. 551–53. GNB's **just as** does not quite capture the comparison as it stands in the Greek, where comparison of degree is in view. (Cf. JB: "he has been given a ministry of a far higher order, and to the same degree it is a better covenant of which he is the mediator.") On the importance of the word **better** (*kreittōn*) for our author, see note on 1:4. In the Greek that lies behind **he arranged** is the first occurrence of the word "mediator" (*mesitēs*), found also in 9:15 and 12:24 (cf. 1 Tim. 2:5). The word involves more than the idea of a "middleman." It connotes the accomplishment of salvation and is close to the meaning of "guarantee" in the parallel phrase of 7:22, "the guarantee of a better covenant." See Oepke, *TDNT*, vol. 4, pp. 598–624. On **covenant** (*diathēkē*), see note on 7:22. See also J. Schildenberger, "Covenant," in *EBT*, pp. 140–46. The Greek word underlying **based** (or "legally enacted") is *nomotheteō*, which occurs also in 7:11, where it refers to the Mosaic legislation (see note on 7:11). The new covenant thus possesses the same authoritative and binding character in God's will as did the old. "Better promises" anticipates not only the content of the quotation from Jer. 31, which follows, but also alludes to such eschatological realities as true Sabbath rest (4:3, 9), an unshakable kingdom (12:28), and the heavenly Jerusalem (12:22). See E. Hoffmann, *NIDNTT*, vol. 3, pp. 68–74.

16

The Promise of
a New Covenant

HEBREWS 8:7–13

If there had been nothing wrong with the first covenant, there would have been no need for a second one. ⁸But God finds fault with his people when he says,
"The days are coming, says the Lord,
when I will draw up a new covenant with the people of Israel and with the people of Judah,
⁹It will not be like the covenant that I made with their ancestors
on the day I took them by the hand and led them out of Egypt.
They were not faithful to the covenant I made with them
and so I paid no attention to them.
¹⁰Now, this is the covenant that I will make with the people of Israel
in the days to come, says the Lord:
I will put my laws in their minds and write them on their hearts
I will be their God, and they will be my people.
¹¹None of them will have to teach his fellow citizen
or tell his fellow countryman, 'Know the Lord,'
For they will all know me, from the least to the greatest.
¹²I will forgive their sins, and will no longer remember their wrongs."
¹³By speaking of a new covenant, God has made the first one old; and anything that becomes old and worn out will soon disappear.

The author now cites one of the major prooftexts of the entire epistle, Jeremiah 31:31–34. The explicit reference to the new covenant in this text makes it ideal for his purpose. The internalizing of the law and the reality of the forgiveness of sins in particular are significant for our author's argumentation, and sections of this same passage are quoted again in 10:16–18. The quotation enables the author to stress the discontinuity between Christianity and the Mosaic Law while at the same time indicating an underlying continuity in God's purposes. What the author has been describing so well is now shown to have been anticipated within the prophetic Scriptures themselves.

8:7-8a / Implicit in the present existence of a new and better covenant with its better promises, which has been the subject of the preceding passage, is the intrinsic inadequacy of **the** (lit., "that") **first covenant**. Had the latter been sufficient, **there would have been no need for a second one** (lit., "no occasion for a second would have been sought"). And yet the hope of a new covenant is precisely what we read about in the prophet Jeremiah. But the problem lies not simply in the first covenant (which by its nature was only preparatory), but more fundamentally in the people themselves. Thus "he [GNB correctly defines the pronoun, **God**], having found fault with them [GNB specifies **his people**], says," whereupon the words of the prophet follow. This assignment of the real blame to the people rather than to the first covenant is somewhat reminiscent of Paul's vindication of the Law in Romans 7:7–12.

8:8b-12 / God speaks through the prophet about a future time when a new covenant will be established with his people. The prophet Jeremiah writes in a time of trouble and disillusionment; Judah and Jerusalem have fallen to the invading Babylonians and have been carried off into exile, all this by way of judgment upon the people for their disobedience. The root problem, and the reason why the new covenant will be unlike the old (for the old, see Exod. 19:5), is "because" (omitted by GNB) **they were not faithful to the covenant I made with them** (lit., "they did not continue in my covenant"). The old covenant was unable to produce obedience, and hence judgment came upon the nation (**and so I paid no attention to them**). The new covenant, however, will accomplish what the old could not do: it will produce true righteousness (**I will put my laws in their minds and write them on their hearts**), the personal knowledge of the Lord, and effective forgiveness of sins. Our author does not exegete these fruits of the new covenant, but it is nevertheless clear that they are the "better promises" referred to in verse 6 and now realized in the people of God, the Church. For from his perspective we have arrived at that new level of existence spoken of by the prophet. Fulfillment has come. This is the meaning of Jesus Christ and his finished work of atonement, for he is "the guarantee of a better covenant" (7:22), "the mediator of a new covenant" (9:15).

Although Jeremiah is the only OT writer to refer explicitly to a *new* covenant in the future, Ezekiel apparently had a similar expectation. He speaks of an "everlasting covenant" (cf. Heb. 13:20) which the Lord will establish and which will involve transformation, knowledge of the Lord, and the forgiveness of sins (Ezek. 11:19–20; 16:60–63; 36:26–29; 37:26–

28, including the words "I will be their God and they shall be my people"). Other prophets foresee similar circumstances in the future (e.g., Isa. 54:13; cf. reference to the "covenant of peace" in 54:10; 27:9, quoted in Rom. 11:27).

The idea of the "new covenant" is of course found elsewhere in the NT. In the eucharistic words of Jesus the new covenant is referred to both in Luke 22:20 and 1 Corinthians 11:25. Paul refers to it in 2 Corinthians 3:6 (cf. his explicit reference to the "old covenant" in 3:14). A similar contrast between two covenants is found in Galatians 4:24–26. Nowhere, outside of Hebrews, however, do we encounter the quotation of this passage or the argument based upon it that we have here (cf. too 9:15; 10:16–18; 12:24). Our author capitalizes upon Jeremiah's reference to the new covenant. A new situation is in view within the Scriptures of the old covenant itself, a situation that envisages a new kind of living, a new spiritual possibility, and a new experience of a definitive forgiveness of sins. The law is internalized and a new intimacy of relationship between God and his people becomes possible. Knowledge of the Lord becomes the possession of all, and the cleansing of sin becomes a reality at the deepest level. It is this that Jeremiah looked for, and it is this that has come to the readers in Christ (see the application of the passage to the readers in 10:15–18). But if the latter statement is true, the implications for the old covenant are startling.

8:13 / Indeed, by virtue of the reality of the new covenant, **God** (lit., "he") **has made the first one old** (or "obsolete," cf. RSV, NIV). The same God who brought the old covenant into existence in anticipation of the new has now brought the fulfillment of the new. But the new, in turn, is so much better than the old that the old must give way to it. The purpose of the old has been accomplished and hence it **will soon disappear**. This statement that the old covenant is near to disappearing is probably a reference to the continuance of the cultic ritual of the levitical priesthood at the time the author writes. From his perspective that ritual is outmoded and pointless, and therefore cannot last long. If the author writes in the early sixties, he may well be thinking of the prophecy of Jesus about the fall of Jerusalem (Mark 13:2). In any event, had he written after the fall of Jerusalem and the destruction of the Temple in A.D. 70, he could hardly have avoided referring explicitly to the historical confirmation of his theological argument. The author's courage in expressing to Jewish readers the transitory nature of the Mosaic covenant is notable. It is possible only because the discontinuity is counterbalanced by the underlying continuity of promise and fulfillment stressed by the author throughout the book. The new, the better, has come, but it was nothing other than this to which the old pointed and for which the old prepared the way.

Additional Notes

8:7–8a / By **first covenant** the author means the Sinai covenant (see v. 9) and not chronologically the first covenant of the Bible (whether with Noah or Abraham), just as by **second** he means in context that referred to by Jeremiah. **Nothing wrong** translates the word "faultless" or "blameless" (*amēmptos*), which occurs only here in Hebrews. The argument of v. 7 is similar to that of 7:11, i.e., if the old is sufficient, then why is a further reality mentioned in the text of Scripture? The perfect tense of the Greek participle in 8a, "having found fault with them" (*memphomenos*) implies that he not only did so in the past, but continues to do so. The pronoun "them," which underlies GNB's **the people** is in the dative case (*autois*) in some important manuscripts rather than the accusative case (*autous*). This has led some commentators (e.g., Hughes) to construe the pronoun with "he says," i.e., "to them he says." Despite the advantage of such a hypothesis—it avoids the complexity of the author faulting both the old covenant *and* the people—the most natural reading even with the dative case is that the people are held blameworthy.

8:8b–12 / The author cites the LXX very closely, making only the slightest changes. The most significant lies behind GNB's **will draw up** in v. 8, where the verb *synteleō* ("accomplish" or "fulfill") is used in place of the ordinary "establish" of the LXX. This befits the author's teleological perspective. The LXX (Jer. 38:31–34) closely follows the Hebrew text (Jer. 31:31–34) except for the following: in v. 32 the words "although I was like a husband to them" are omitted by the LXX; and in v. 33 for "within them" LXX has "in their minds." The author of Hebrews quotes the LXX very accurately, making what appear to be only stylistic changes.

Although the **new covenant** is to be made with Israel and Judah, the ultimate recipients are the people of Christ. To be sure, our Jewish readers were **the people** (lit., "the house," as also in v. 10; cf. 3:6) of Israel and Judah. But Jewish nationalism and political aspirations find no place in our epistle. In v. 9 GNB adds **it will . . . be**, in keeping with the opening words of the quotation, and the Hebraic term "fathers" is translated **ancestors**. The words **took them by the hand and led them out of Egypt** (lit., "took them by their hand to lead them out of the land of Egypt") is of course a reference to the exodus and is expressed in language that had much earlier become formulaic. At the end of v. 9 GNB omits the words "says the Lord." This explanation of Israel's plight as the result of her failure to abide by the covenant is widespread in the prophets (e.g., Isa. 24:5; Ezek. 16:59; Hos. 8:1; Mal. 2:10). In v. 10 GNB's **now** is "because," i.e., the new covenant is not like the old for the reasons about to be stipulated. The expression "after those days," which is language referring to an eschatological era (cf. the opening words of Acts 15:16; quoting the LXX of Amos 9:11), GNB appropriately translates **in the days to come**. The possibility of an internalizing of the Law (cf. the notion of "circumcision of the heart," Deut. 10:16; Jer. 4:4), although intimated in the OT (cf. Deut. 30:11–14) was never achieved. The affirmation **I will be their God and they will be my people** is common OT language describing the basic aspect of covenant relationship, which though repeatedly promised had not become a full reality until the new covenant became effective (cf. Exod. 6:7; Lev. 26:12; Ezek. 37:27; Jer. 7:23). Knowledge of the Lord is a very common eschatological expectation among the OT prophets. GNB renders "brother" in v. 11 **fellow countryman**, probably by influence of the parallel **fellow citizen** in the preceding clause. For **fellow citizen** (*politēn*) some manuscripts of lesser importance read "neighbor" (*plēsion*). Two further changes in v. 11 involve GNB's omission of "saying" before **know the Lord** and "of them" after **greatest**. In v. 12 GNB's **I will forgive their sins** is lit. "I will be merciful to their iniquities" (cf. RSV); **wrongs** is lit. "sins." This last assertion of the quotation is climactic within Jeremiah, whose contemporaries had experienced judgment for their sins, but also for our author, who sets forth Christ's death as the true remedy for the sinfulness of humanity.

8:13 / This verse is a midrashic commentary on the significance of the single word **new** (*kainē*) which occurs at the beginning of the quotation (GNB adds the word **covenant**). When God speaks in this way through the prophet, he has in effect declared **the first** covenant transitory and outmoded. The word "first" is used repeatedly in the argument that follows in such a way as to imply being outmoded (cf. 9:1, 15, 18; 10:9). The verb underlying **made . . . old** and **becomes old** (*palaioō*) occurs elsewhere in Hebrews in the quotation of Ps. 102:26 in 1:11, where it is said that the heavens will "wear out like clothes" (the only other NT occurrence of the word is in Luke 12:33). **Worn out** translates a synonym for "grow old" (*geraskō*). It is worth noting that the contemporary Jewish sect at Qumran explicitly referred to themselves as the people of the new covenant. But whereas they understood their community as about to experience the fulfillment of the prophecy in Jer. 31, they looked for the future reformation rather than the abrogation of the Temple cultus. Only the eschatological event of Christ's cross and exaltation enable the author to draw his radical conclusion concerning discontinuity. See D. Peterson, "The Prophecy of the New Covenant in the Argument of Hebrews," *RefThR* 38 (1979) pp. 74–81.

17

The Old Testament Ritual Described

The first covenant had rules for worship and a man-made place for worship as well. ²A tent was put up, the outer one, which was called the Holy Place. In it were the lampstand and the table with the bread offered to God. ³Behind the second curtain was the tent called the Most Holy Place. ⁴In it were the gold altar for the burning of incense and the Covenant Box all covered with gold and containing the gold jar with the manna in it, Aaron's stick that had sprouted leaves, and the two stone tablets with the commandments written on them. ⁵Above the Box were the winged animals representing God's presence, with their wings spread over the place where sins were forgiven. But now is not the time to explain everything in detail.

⁶This is how those things have been arranged. The priests go into the outer tent every day to perform their duties, ⁷but only the High Priest goes into the inner tent, and he does so only once a year. He takes with him blood which he offers to God on behalf of himself and for the sins which the people have committed without knowing they were sinning. ⁸The Holy Spirit clearly teaches from all these arrangements that the way into the Most Holy Place has not yet been opened as long as the outer tent still stands. ⁹This is a symbol which points to the present time. It means that the offerings and animal sacrifices presented to God cannot make the worshiper's heart perfect, ¹⁰since they have to do only with food, drink, and various purification ceremonies. These are all outward rules, which apply only until the time when God will establish the new order.

We are now at the beginning of a lengthy section (9:1–10:18) that many regard as the heart of the epistle's argument. In this section the author draws out parallels and contrasts between the old levitical ritual and the priestly work of Christ in considerable detail. Much of the argumentation up to this point has had just this goal in view. Indeed, the argument of this major section has already been anticipated (e.g., 7:23–27).

The first task the author undertakes is to describe the physical setting of the tabernacle (vv. 1–5) and the sacrificial ritual associated with it (vv. 6–10). This he does by drawing upon the descriptions provided in the books of Exodus and Leviticus. Only after providing this historical picture does he turn to the corresponding and final work of Christ.

9:1 / In order to comprehend the importance of the work of Christ, it is all important to understand that which pointed to him. **The first** (GNB rightly adds **covenant**) was ordained by God both so far as **rules** and **place** were concerned. The author turns his attention first to the latter, which GNB describes as **a man-made place for worship as well** (lit., "the earthly sanctuary").

9:2 / The author's guided tour begins with the **outer** (lit., "first") tent, traditionally called **the Holy Place**. In this part of the sanctuary were to be found **the lampstand** (the seven-branched menorah) and **the table** which had upon it **the bread offered to God** (lit., "the presentation of the loaves"), better known as "the bread of the Presence." Directions for the construction of the tabernacle are given in Exodus 26. For the table and the lampstand, see Exodus 25:23–40.

9:3-5 / More space is given by our author to describing the Holy of Holies (translated **the Most Holy Place** by GNB) because of its importance as the place of atonement. It lay **behind the second curtain** (Exod. 26:33), a curtain meant to restrict access to the innermost chamber that could only be entered once a year (see v. 7). A minor problem exists with regard to the first item said to be in the Holy of Holies, **the gold altar for the burning of incense**. According to the account in Exodus 30:1–6 (cf. Exod. 40:26 f.) this altar was placed "before" or "outside" (so GNB) the curtain, and thus it was located in the Holy Place, not the Most Holy Place. Yet so vital was the burning of incense on the Day of Atonement (cf. "lest he die," Lev. 16:13; cf. Num. 16:40) that the author automatically associates the altar of incense with the Holy of Holies. It is after all the Day of Atonement that is his real concern as we see from verses 6–10.

The second item in the Holy of Holies is the **Covenant Box all covered with gold** (see Exod. 25:10–16, 21) more traditionally known as "the ark of the covenant." In this container were three special objects that recalled the experience of Israel at Sinai in the wilderness: **the gold jar** containing **the manna** (see Exod. 16:13–33), Aaron's rod that had miraculously budded (GNB adds **leaves**; see Num. 17:8–10) and **the two stone tablets with the commandments written on them** (lit., "the tables of the covenant"; see Deut. 10:3–5; 1 Kings 8:9). **Above the Box** (lit., "it") were **the winged animals representing God's presence**, which is GNB's free rendering of "cherubim of glory." Although of course we cannot know what these cherubim looked like, it is better to speak of winged "beings" or "creatures" rather than "animals" so as not to exclude the possibility of a human likeness, as ascribed to the cherubim in the rabbinic tradition, for example. The "glory" is indeed the *shekinah* (i.e., "dwelling") glory that hovered over the ark of the covenant (cf. Lev. 16:2; Exod. 40:34 f.) symbolizing the presence of God. With their wings, these beings overshadowed **the place where sins were forgiven** (see Exod. 25:18–20). This is GNB's appropriate translation of a single technical term (*hilastērion*) indicating the lid of the ark (as it does regularly in the LXX). This cover to the ark was the place where the high priest sprinkled the blood of the sacrificed bull and then of the goat on the Day of Atonement (see Lev. 16:14 f.). In this way the word came to signify the taking away of sin (as indeed an alternate rendering of the consonants of the Hebrew word *kpr* allows, that is, not only "to cover," but "to wipe away") and hence came to be translated "mercy seat" (Exod. 26:34; cf. RSV). In Romans 3:25, the only other occurrence of this noun in the NT, Jesus is described as an "expiation" (RSV) or "propitiation" (KJV, NASB) for our sins, or as GNB paraphrases it, "the means by which people's sins are forgiven."

It is apparent that the author draws his knowledge of the furniture of the tabernacle from a literary source, almost certainly the Greek translation of the OT (LXX). This is the more certain since the Holy of Holies in the Second Temple could hardly have contained the enumerated items, which must have been destroyed or lost in connection with the destruction of the Temple in 587 B.C. (cf. Pompey's surprise at the empty Holy of Holies, Josephus *War* 1.152 f.; *Ant.* 14.71 f.). The author contents himself with this brief description of the physical setting of the levitical ritual, wherein he points to his competence in these matters, and now turns to the more important matter of the accomplishment of atonement in that setting. It is proper to note that here and in what follows the author avoids the kind of irresponsible allegorical exegesis of these details that is found in certain contemporary or near-contemporary writers such as Philo and Josephus (see Montefiore).

9:6–7 / GNB's first sentence refers not to what follows but to what has been described in the preceding five verses—that is, it is in that setting that the priests do their work. The daily duties of ordinary priests are first in view. They go **into the outer** (lit., "first") **tent every day** in order to accomplish their priestly duties (see Num. 18:2–6). These involved the burning of incense morning and evening, the maintenance of the lamps of the lampstand, and the removal of the old and placement of the new loaves upon the table every Sabbath. The contrasting clause contains three major points of difference: **only the High Priest** can perform the vital work of atonement; he does so by entering **the inner tent** (lit., " the second"), and **only once a year**, on the Day of Atonement (Lev. 16:2–15; Exod. 30:10). **He takes with him** (lit., "not without") the **blood** prescribed by the Law which is offered **on behalf of himself** (the contrast here has already been made in 5:3 and 7:27) and for the "sins of ignorance" committed by the people. This technical phrase, paraphrased by GNB, alludes to the fact that only unintentional sinning could be atoned for (see Lev. 4:1, 13, 22, 27; 5:15, 17–19), not that done "with a high hand" (see Num. 15:30; Deut. 17:12).

9:8 / The author now draws a lesson **from all these arrangements** (words added by GNB), that is, the physical setup and the continuing cultic practice. As the **Holy Spirit clearly teaches** (lit., "makes clear"), through the Scriptures from which the information in the preceding verses has been gleaned, **the way into the Most Holy Place has not yet been opened** (lit., "made visible"). That is, the situation under the old covenant with its elaborate protection of the Holy of Holies, is self-confessedly one that excludes the people of God from his presence and hence the fulfillment of God's promises remains to be experienced. The continued existence, therefore, of **the outer tent** (lit., "the first tent"), which together with the curtain before the Holy of Holies barred the way to the very presence of God, showed the futility of the old covenant and at the same time pointed inescapably to the future. That future has now come for the author and his readers.

9:9-10 / The continuing necessity of an "outer tent," itself symptomatic of the problem of the old covenant, serves as **a symbol** (lit., "parable") **which points to the present time**. By this the author means, as he will begin to show beginning in verse 11, that the significance of Christ's work, as now known and proclaimed, is that the way has been made clear for us to draw near to God (cf. 10:19–22). Just as light is shed upon the work of Christ by its anticipation in the old covenant, so a knowledge of the fulfillment brought by Christ illuminates the significance of the tabernacle and the levitical sacrifices. By its very nature the old covenant points to what can now be seen to be its fulfillment. According to the old situation (this is a more literal rendition of GNB's **it means that**), the "rules for worship" (mentioned in 9:1) mandated various sacrificial offerings by their nature unable to bring the worshiper to the intended goal of full salvation. **Cannot make the worshiper's heart** (lit., "conscience") **perfect** is to be understood as "unable to bring the true, inner person to the intended goal of full salvation." The nagging, unconvinced conscience of the worshiper in this circumstance is evidence of this failure of the old system. The reason for the inability of the arrangements under the old covenant is that they had to do only with **outward** (lit., "fleshly") **rules**, involving **food, drink, and various purification ceremonies** (lit., "ablutions"). Thus Bruce writes, "The really effective barrier to a man's free access to God is an inward and not a material one; it exists in his conscience" (p. 196). It is finally to be stressed that these regulations are only temporary and **apply** (lit., "being imposed") only until "the time of the new order" (GNB adds **when God will establish**). It is clear from what he has already written that our author regards that **new order** as already existing. The time of fulfillment has already come in and through the work of Christ (see comment on 1:2). If this is true, then the whole levitical system and the Mosaic legislation upon which it rests has come to an end. This conclusion is indeed inescapable given the conclusions drawn in 8:13. The author's argument here is reminiscent of Paul's perspective in Colossians 2:16–17: "So let no one make rules about what you eat or drink or about holy days or the New Moon Festival or the Sabbath. All such things are only a shadow of things in the future; the reality is Christ." The old covenant stipulations are displaced when the new covenant with its new order comes into existence. This analysis is borne out in the verses that immediately follow the present passage. Christ fulfills the anticipations of the old covenant and brings his people to the realization of the salvation God has intended from the beginning. The new era, the time of reformation and fulfillment, has arrived.

Additional Notes

9:1 / The past tenses of this and the following four verses do not imply that the situation here described no longer exists. They are due instead to the fact that the historical origin of the tabernacle, and its successor the Temple, is being set forth. Confirmation of this is found in the use of the present tenses in vv. 6–10 (see especially v. 9). The **rules** (*dikaiōmata*), which become the center of attention in vv. 6–10, are referred to as "outward" (or "fleshly") and temporary in v. 10. The word underlying **worship** (*latreia*) refers specifically to service in the Temple cultus (cf. the use of the cognate verb in 8:5 and 9:9). The Greek word for "the sanctuary" (*to hagion*, "the holy place") is translated by GNB as a **place for**

worship. The adjective underlying **man-made** is *kosmikon*, by which is meant of the "created" or "earthly" order. (Barclay translates "a this-worldly one.") The intended contrast, of course, is to the "heavenly" sanctuary already mentioned (8:5; cf. 9:11, 24).

9:2 / Whereas in Exod. 26:33 one tent is divided into two compartments, our author speaks apparently of two tents (cf. "first" here and in vv. 6 and 8; and "second" in v. 7). It is unlikely, however, that he means us to understand the first as the earthly and the second as the heavenly, as did some in Hellenistic Judaism, since for him the entire Mosaic setting represents the earthly copy of a greater reality. He may mean nothing more than "outer" and "inner" in the way that GNB understands the words. Elsewhere the author refers to the entire tabernacle as a single "tent" (8:5; 9:21). For "tent" see note on 8:2. The Greek word underlying **was put up** (*kataskeuazō*) is the same word translated "build" in 3:3 f. For **the Holy Place** (*hagia*) and **the Most Holy Place**, "the Holy of Holies" (*hagia hagiōn*) of v. 3, the author uses the literal translation of the underlying Hebrew words for the tabernacle found in the LXX (where, however, the definite article is regularly included). For the former expression, see also 9:12, 25; 10:19; 13:12 (with the definite article) and 9:24 (without the article). **The bread offered to God**, sometimes called "the showbread," refers to the twelve newly baked loaves or cakes placed upon the table in the Holy Place every Sabbath (see Lev. 24:5–9). On this and the following verses, see the extensive discussion in Strack-Billerbeck, vol. 3, pp. 704-41.

9:3-5 / **The second curtain** separated the Holy of Holies from the Holy Place; a "first curtain" separated the Holy Place from the tabernacle court. The word for **curtain** (*katapetasma*) occurs in Hebrews only here and in 6:19 and 10:20. Although the Greek word used here for **altar** (*thymiatērion*) was not used to refer to the incense altar in the LXX, it is so used by contemporary authorities such as Philo and Josephus, who also explicitly note (together with the Babylonian Talmud) that in the Second Temple the incense altar was in the Holy Place with the lampstand and the table. The reference to Aaron's rod may be seen to have special importance, given the argument of chap. 7. The budding rod demonstrated the sole legitimacy of Aaron and the tribe of Levi in priestly service at the altar (cf. Num. 18:7). But that uniqueness has now been displaced—indeed, canceled—by the High Priest of the order of Melchizedek. Technically the jar with the manna and the rod of Aaron were put alongside the ark rather than in it (cf. 1 Kings 8:9). The **commandments** were given in the context of the covenant and thus may appropriately be designated the "tables of the covenant." Faithfulness to the covenant involved keeping the commandments. The only other NT occurrence of the word tables (*plax*) is in 2 Cor. 3:3 where the adjective "stone" is included (cf. Exod. 32:16). On "cherubim" see Lohse, *TDNT*, vol. 9, pp. 438 f. Although the noun "mercy seat" (*hilastērion*) occurs only here and in Rom. 3:25 in the NT, the cognate verb "expiate" or "propitiate" (*hilaskomai*) occurs in 2:17

and in Luke 18:13. The related noun *hilasmos* is found in 1 John 2:2 and 4:10. On these words see H.-G. Link and C. Brown, *NIDNTT*, vol. 3, pp. 148–66.

9:6-7 / The "first" or **outer tent** is that introduced in v. 2. The Greek word behind **duties** (*latreia*) is the same word that is translated "worship" in v. 1, referring in both places to the priestly service. The cognate verb (*latreuō*) has already been encountered in 8:5 ("work") and occurs again in vv. 9 and 14. The "second" or **inner tent**, although not explicitly mentioned earlier, is implied in v. 3. The word **once** is very important to the author in describing the work of Christ. The high priestly work of the old covenant has its "once" too, but it refers to **once a year**, unlike the definitive "once-and-for-all" character of Christ's work as High Priest (see vv. 12, 20–28).

This is the first of many references to the **blood** of sacrifices in this and the remaining chapters of the book. The sanctity of life, and hence of blood, together with the necessity of sacrifice, indicates the great costliness of atonement (cf. 9:22; Lev. 17:11). The mention of blood in the context of offering for atonement always presupposes the death of the sacrificial victim. The central importance of the blood of Christ first comes into view in vv. 12 and 14 below (although it is implied in 2:9, 14, and 17). For the significance of blood in the Bible, see Behm, *TDNT*, vol. 1, pp. 172–77.

The Greek word underlying **offers** (*prosphero*) is very frequently used by our author. See note under its first occurrence in 5:1. The description of the work of the high priest, in which he offers first for his own sin and then for the people, follows closely the account in Lev. 16:11–15. The word for "sins of ignorance" (*agnoēma*, lit., "ignorances") is used only here in the NT. The present tenses that begin in v. 6 do not necessarily demonstrate that the cultus was in operation in our author's day, although they are consistent with such a possibility (so, e.g., Hughes). Nevertheless, when the Temple ritual is in view the present tense is often used simply as reflecting the normative character of the Law. Thus many writers who clearly wrote after the destruction of the Temple continue to use the present tense in describing the Temple ritual (e.g., Clement of Rome, Justin Martyr, the rabbinic literature).

9:8 / In two other places the Holy Spirit is explicitly referred to as the speaker in OT material (3:7; 10:15). The Greek underlying **the Most Holy Place** is not "Holy of Holies" (*hagia hagiōn*) as it is in 9:2, but simply "the Holy Place" (*hagia*). The context, with its reference to **the outer tent** ("first tent"), suggests that the innermost chamber, the Holy of Holies, is meant. In several references to follow (vv. 12, 24, and 25; 10:19; 13:11), the single word is similarly used to refer to the Holy of Holies (as is the case frequently in the LXX, e.g., Lev. 16). It is also to be noted, however, that a different exegesis of "first tent" is possible. Thus some (e.g., Bruce) argue that "first tent" here refers to the entire sanctuary of the old or "first" covenant (so NIV, NEB) and that this is more appropriately what the author regards as the "symbol" referred to in the next verse. Yet the passage makes good sense if we regard the author's use of "first tent" as consistent and understand here the Holy Place, the outer compartment of the sanctuary (so RSV, JB, NASB). The "first tent" itself implies the lack of access to the Holy of Holies and hence is representative of the whole sacrificial system. See Michaelis, *TDNT*, vol. 7, pp. 375 ff.

9:9–10 / The antecedent of the relative clause "which is a parable" is not totally clear. The most natural reading understands the antecedent to be "the first tent." This is a suitable antecedent and yields good sense. It is, however, also possible to understand the totality of vv. 6–8 as the antecedent (and to explain the feminine gender of the relative by attraction to *parabolē*). The **present time** is clearly to be understood as the day of the author and readers. And yet this does not necessarily mean or imply that the sacrificial ritual was still in progress at the time of the writing of this epistle. In this case it is the past that has a message for the present. **Offerings and animal sacrifices presented to God** is (in the Greek) language that occurs in nearly verbatim agreement in two other passages: 5:1 and 8:3. **Makes . . . perfect** translates a favorite verb of our author (*teleioō*). See note on 2:10. The word **conscience** (*syneidēsis*) is important for our author, occurring five times (see 9:14; 10:2, 22; 13:18). It reflects the inner or true person and makes judgments upon the ultimate well-being or lack of well-being of the person. See C. Spicq, "conscience" in *EBT*, pp. 131–34. The **worshiper**, the one who does this priestly service, very probably includes in addition to the priests those ordinary believers who accomplish this service through the agency of the priests. **Food** and **drink** refer to the stipulations of the dietary legislation (e.g., Lev. 11); "ablutions" to various purifying rites (e.g., Lev. 14; 15). **Outward** ("of flesh") **rules** stand in deliberate contrast to the root problem of the inner man as represented by conscience. The word for **new order** (*diorthōsis*) occurs only here in the NT, and not at all in the LXX. On these verses, see J. Swetnam, "On the Imagery and Significance of Hebrews 9, 9–10," *CBQ* 28 (1966), pp. 155–73. On the significance of chap. 9 as a whole, see N. H. Young, "The Gospel According to Hebrews 9," *NTS* 27 (1981), pp. 198–210.

18

The Definitive Nature
of Christ's Work

But Christ has already come as the High Priest of the good things that are already here.ᵉ The tent in which he serves is greater and more perfect; it is not a man-made tent, that is, it is not a part of this created world. ¹²When Christ went through the tent and entered once and for all into the Most Holy Place, he did not take the blood of goats and bulls to offer as a sacrifice; rather, he took his own blood and obtained eternal salvation for us. ¹³The blood of goats and bulls and the ashes of a burnt calf are sprinkled on the people who are ritually unclean, and this purifies them by taking away their ritual impurity. ¹⁴Since this is true, how much more is accomplished by the blood of Christ! Through the eternal Spirit he offered himself as a perfect sacrifice to God. His blood will purify our consciences from useless rituals, so that we may serve the living God.

e. already here. *some manuscripts have* coming.

We now come to the first detailed statement of the definitive nature of Christ's work—an argument that will be restated in several forms before we reach the end of this major section of the epistle in 10:18. It is now convincingly shown that, although the work of Christ corresponds in considerable detail to that of the levitical priesthood, it stands in contrast to the work of the latter as its ultimate counterpart. It is what truth is to shadow, what pattern is to copy. The work of Christ is final, absolute, definitive, complete, and perfect. Only such words are appropriate to describe what the author expounds.

9:11 / Although the word **already**, which appears twice in GNB's first sentence, is not found in the underlying Greek, it is an appropriate inference from the tense of the participles. The focus is clearly on what has been accomplished through the work of Christ on the cross. **The good things** that have come refers to the degree of eschatological fulfillment that has already come to those who through Christ have become partici-

pants in the new covenant. This note of "realized eschatology"* encountered at the very beginning of the book (in the reference to "last days" of
1:2), as well as in other sections (see especially 12:18–24), is to be kept in
tension with affirmations of "future eschatology" that are found in the
book (e.g., 6:11, 18; 9:28; 10:25). The orientation of the writer is clearly
toward the present experience of the good things made possible through
Christ's work as High Priest. The long Greek sentence that composes
verses 11–12 is turned into several independent sentences in GNB (involving the addition of the words **in which he serves** and **it is**). The **greater
and more perfect** tent, not **man-made** (lit., "made with hands"), **not a
part of this created world** (lit., "not of this creation"), refers of course to
the truth of which the copy was but a shadow (cf. 8:2–5), namely, the
"heavenly sanctuary" or the very presence of God Himself (see 9:24).

9:12 / The words **when Christ went through the tent** are added by GNB,
but are likely to give the false impression that the **tent** here refers to the
outer sanctuary through which Christ passed in approaching **the Most
Holy Place**. The **tent** referred to in the preceding verse, however, is not
something through which Christ passed to get to the Holy of Holies (as,
for example, he passed through the heavens, 4:14). It is itself the heavenly
reality, not made by hands, the place of "the presence of God" (9:24). GNB
transforms prepositional phrases into sentences with the words **he did
not have** and **he took**, thereby adding what may at first appear to be a
suitable emphasis to these statements. Thus Christ entered **the Most
Holy Place** not with **the blood of goats and bulls** (GNB adds the ex-
planatory words **to offer as a sacrifice**), but with **his own blood**. But as
F. F. Bruce notes, the author refrains from actually saying that Christ
took his blood into the Holy of Holies. This is to press the analogy too far,
with the result that the atonement is made to depend upon something
subsequent to the cross, that is, the appearance of Christ and the offering
of his blood in the heavenly sanctuary. The text of the original says simply
that it was "through his own blood" that Christ entered once and for all
into the Holy of Holies. The necessity for the offering of blood is underlined in verses 18 and 22. So superior is the offering of **his own blood** that
it procured **eternal salvation** (GNB adds **for us**), by which language the
author intends a sharp contrast to the provisional character of what was

*"Realized eschatology" is a term used by theologians to represent the NT conviction that the bless-
ings of the messianic age have already become a reality, at least to a degree, through the First Coming
of Christ, especially by means of his death and resurrection. The emphasis is associated with the work
of C. H. Dodd.

accomplished by the offering of the blood of animals. Stress on the salvation accomplished by Christ as eternal is also found in 5:9 (cf. 13:20). Since his work is **once and for all**, its consequence is an **eternal salvation**. The superiority of Christ's accomplishment is thus both qualitative (intrinsic) and temporal (time-transcending).

9:13 / Verses 13 and 14 form one long sentence in the Greek text, with verse 13 providing an "if" clause, and verse 14 a "how much more" clause. The OT rituals, involving **the blood of goats and bulls** (cf. Lev. 16:15–16) and the sprinkling of the transgressors with **the ashes of a burnt calf** (lit., "heifer")—which were mixed with water to make "the water for removing ritual uncleanness . . . to remove sin" (Num. 19:9, 17–19)—cleansed the Israelites at only the external level. GNB brings this out in the words **by taking away their ritual impurity** (lit., "the purifying of the flesh"). This interpretation is supported by the Greek word for "defiled," translated by GNB **ritually unclean**. These ceremonies, therefore, were effective only for one kind of cleansing, that is, from ceremonial contamination.

9:14 / But the incomparably superior **blood of Christ** brings about the reality of a far more significant cleansing (GNB adds **since this is true**, to bridge between vv. 13 and 14). Christ gave himself **as a perfect** (lit., "blameless") **sacrifice to God** and this was done **through the eternal Spirit**—a further indication of the categorical difference between the offering of Christ and those of the levitical priesthood. Although the interpretation of the phrase is exceptionally difficult, **the eternal Spirit** probably means the Holy Spirit, being perhaps an allusion to the great importance of the Spirit throughout the actual ministry of Jesus, but perhaps also due to the importance of the Spirit to Israel's "Servant of the Lord" who ends up giving his life for the sins of the people (Isa. 42:1; 53:5–6, 10, 12). The Spirit is the agency par excellence of the accomplishment of God's saving will. It is only to be expected then that our "eternal salvation" (v. 12) be accomplished by Christ's offering through the **eternal Spirit**. The new kind of cleansing made possible by this offering of Christ is described as the purifying of our **consciences**. That is, this cleansing penetrates to the inner recesses of our personhood and so involves far more than the cleansing of the flesh from ceremonial defilement.

From useless rituals is GNB's interpretation of what is literally "from dead works." It is very unlikely, however, that it is useless rituals that pollute the conscience and from which it needs to be cleansed. Almost certainly the expression means here what it meant in 6:1 (where GNB translates "useless works"), namely, sinful deeds that properly produce repentance. Despite the author's minimizing of the levitical ritual he never regards it as sinful, nor does he connect it with repentance. Those who have experienced this new cleansing—the cleansing of the conscience—are now able truly to **serve the living God**. The word **serve** here (*latreuō*) is intentionally the same word earlier used for specifically priestly service (e.g., 8:5; 9:9). Only with the fulfillment brought by Christ's "once and for all" sacrifice, is it possible to arrive at the goal of serving God. The language of the cultus has been spiritualized here, as it is elsewhere in the NT (e.g., Rom. 12:1; 1 Pet. 2:5).

So significant is the contrast being drawn in this passage and so basic is it for the material that follows (which really only elaborates what has now been stated) that it is worth displaying the various elements in two contrasting columns:

New	Old
the good things already here, v. 11 (9:23–24; 10:1)	shadows, copies, 8:5; 10:1
greater and more perfect tent, v. 11 (9:24)	man-made ("earthly") place for worship, 9:1
entered once and for all the Most Holy Place, v. 12 (9:25–28; 10:1–3, 10–14)	every day, 7:27; once a year, 9:7
he took his own blood, v. 12 (9:18–22; 10:4–10)	blood of goats and bulls, 9:12
obtained eternal salvation, v. 12	outward rules until the new order, 9:10
purifies the conscience, v. 14 (9:15)	takes away ritual impurity, 9:13

That the content of the new elements corresponds to Jeremiah's promises concerning the new covenant is confirmed by the explicit statement of the next verse. Note too the use of the quotation from Jeremiah again at the end of this major section of the book (10:16–18).

Additional Notes

9:11 / Some manuscripts read "the good things to come," thereby orienting the verse to the future rather than to present fulfillment. On the basis of both antiquity and diversity of witnesses the reading of GNB's text is to be preferred. The reading "the good things to come" is probably caused by the influence of the same words in 10:1. On the importance for our author of the title "High Priest," see note on 2:7. The adjective "made with hands" (*cheiropoiētos*) occurs only once again in Hebrews, in this same chapter (v. 24), where it is used in exactly the same sense. Several other occurrences of this word in the NT touch upon an antitemple motif, a viewpoint that was probably also shared by our author (Mark 14:58; Acts 7:48; 17:24). Some have regarded the reference to a **greater and more perfect** tent as a reference to the incarnation (cf. note on 8:2). But this is most unlikely since Christ's humanity would then be **not a part of this created world** (contrast the view of the incarnation expressed in 2:14, 17). See J. Swetnam, "The Greater and More Perfect Tent. A Contribution to the Discussion of Hebrews 9.11," *Biblica* 47 (1966), pp. 91–106, who argues that "the greater and more perfect tent" refers to the Eucharistic Body of Christ.

9:12 / Beginning in v. 11 ("through the tent") and continuing in the present verse ("not through the blood of goats and bulls," but "through his own blood") is a series of phrases governed by the repeated preposition "through" (*dia*) which may also be translated "in virtue of" or "on the grounds of." The expression **the blood of goats and bulls** is also found in vv. 13, 19, and 10:4 (where, however, a different word for "bull" is used). For the importance of "blood" in this and succeeding chapters, see note on 9:7. The reference to **his own blood** (cf. 13:12 for the only other occurrence of this phrase) may be contrasted with 9:25 where an ordinary high priest necessarily depends on "blood belonging to another." Elsewhere we read of Christ having "offered himself" (7:27) and "the offering that he made of his own body" (10:10). **Once and for all** is very important for our author's argument (see note on 7:27). **Most Holy Place** is GNB's correct interpretation of the underlying *ta hagia* (lit., "the holies"). KJV, RSV, and NASB all retain the literal reading, "the Holy Place." It is clear that our author does not mean the Holy Place described in 9:2, but rather what he has described in 9:3. The same Greek expression is also used for the Holy of Holies in 9:8 (see too 9:24, 25; 10:19; 13:11).

This word for **salvation** (*lytrōsis*) occurs in Hebrews only here (the only other NT occurrences are Luke 1:68 and 2:38; for the verb, however, see 1 Pet. 1:18). It can equally well be translated "redemption." The meaning, however, is not greatly different from the ordinary word our author uses for "salvation" (*sōtēria*, for which see note on 2:3). On *lytrōsis* and related words, see Büschel, *TDNT*, vol. 4, pp. 340–56. The fact that **obtained** in the Greek text is an aorist tense participle indicates that salvation was already obtained (on the cross) and thus any idea of a subsequent presentation of Christ's blood in the heavenly sanctuary is ruled out. Only after our salvation had been secured did Christ ascend to heaven. On this and related questions, see the lengthy excursus, "The Blood of Jesus and His Heavenly Priesthood," in Hughes, pp. 329–54.

9:13 / This is the only reference in the NT to the ashes of the red heifer used for purifying purposes according to Num. 19. Our author finds the illustration to his liking since the sin removed by this rite was that of ceremonial defilement. This typifies the limited efficacy of the OT cultus. **Ritually unclean** translates *koinoō* (lit., "to make common"), a word used only here in Hebrews, but which is used with the same connotation of ceremonial defilement in other places in the NT (Mark 7:15–23; Acts 10:15; 11:9; 15:11–20; 21:28). The particular defilement that was to be remedied by "the water for impurity," as it was called, was that of having touched a dead body (Num. 19:11 ff.), but it was also applied to booty taken from an enemy (Num. 31:23). On the subject of cultic defilement, see Hauck, *TDNT*, vol. 3, pp. 789–809. On sprinkling and ceremonial cleansing, see Hunzinger, *TDNT*, vol. 6, pp. 976–84. The word underlying **purifies** (*hagiazō*), although it has a cultic sense here, elsewhere in Hebrews is used to refer to the sanctifying (the "setting apart," but now in a moral sense) of Christians (cf. 2:11; 10:10, 14, 29; 13:12). For the use of "flesh" (*sarx*) in Hebrews, see Schweizer, *TDNT*, vol. 7, pp. 141 f.

9:14 / Many commentators (e.g., Hughes, Montefiore, Delitzsch) prefer to understand **eternal Spirit**, not as the Holy Spirit (as a few manuscripts actually read), but as Christ's own personal spirit, which is eternal in nature. The reference thus is to Christ's unique personal nature, which enables him to accomplish this perfect sacrifice. On the other hand, a reference to the Spirit (which although it has no definite article, is still definite because of the modifier "eternal") would most naturally have been taken by the readers to be the Holy Spirit. Had the author intended Jesus' own spirit, he would have indicated it in no uncertain terms (e.g., by adding "his"), especially given the fact that no mention has hitherto been made of an eternal, personal spirit of Jesus. For the importance of the verb **offered** (*prospherō*), see note on 5:1. The word **perfect** means literally "blameless" (*amōmos*) and is a deliberate allusion to the necessity in the OT cultus that the sacrificial animal be "without blemish" (e.g., Lev. 14:10; cf. 1 Pet. 1:19). What could not be accomplished by the old sacrificial system—the cleansing of the conscience (see v. 9)—is now accomplished through Christ. For "conscience," see note on 9:9. An equal number of important manuscripts read "your consciences," but since the author reserves the second person for his exhortation sections, the reading **our consciences** is to be preferred. "Dead works" stands in stark contrast to the service of **the living God**. The latter is a common Hebraic manner of speaking of God (e.g., Matt. 16:16; 26:63; 2 Cor. 3:3; 1 Tim. 3:15; 4:10; Rev. 15:7; cf. Heb. 3:12; 10:31; 12:22).

19

Christ's Sacrifice: The Foundation of the New Covenant

HEBREWS 9:15–22

For this reason Christ is the one who arranges a new covenant, so that those who have been called by God may receive the eternal blessings that God has promised. This can be done because there has been a death which sets people free from the wrongs they did while the first covenant was in effect. ¹⁶In the case of a will it is necessary to prove that the person who made it has died, ¹⁷for a will means nothing while the person who made it is alive; it goes into effect only after his death. ¹⁸That is why even the first covenant[f] went into effect only with the use of blood. ¹⁹First, Moses proclaimed to the people all the commandments as set forth in the Law. Then he took the blood of bulls and goats, mixed it with water, and sprinkled it on the book of the Law and all the people, using a sprig of hyssop and some red wool. ²⁰He said, "This is the blood which seals the covenant that God has commanded you to obey." ²¹In the same way Moses also sprinkled the blood on the Covenant Tent and over all the things used in worship. ²²Indeed, according to the Law almost everything is purified by blood, and sins are forgiven only if blood is poured out.

f. covenant: *In Greek the same word means will and covenant.*

The author now turns to the relationship between the sacrificial death of Christ and the establishment of the new covenant. The existence of the latter, and the experience of it by Christians, depends squarely upon the former. The shedding of blood is thus essential to both old and new covenants.

9:15 / **For this reason**—that is, because of his death—**Christ** (lit., "he") is the "mediator" of **a new covenant**. Here, as in 8:6 (see discussion there), GNB's translation **the one who arranges** for "mediator" is less than adequate, for Christ through his death has become the actual means whereby the new covenant is made a reality (cf. 7:22, where Jesus is described as "the guarantee of a better covenant"). It is clear that the author has in mind the new covenant spoken of by Jeremiah (cf. the quotation in 8:8–12 and 10:16–17). The result of the inauguration of the new covenant is that **those who have been called** (GNB adds **by God**) become recipients of "the promise of the eternal inheritance" (a literal rendering of the Greek underlying GNB's **the eternal blessings that God has promised**). The author has already spoken of a special calling received by Christians, through the preaching of the gospel in 3:1. It is significant that he uses particularly Jewish concepts of "promise" and "inheritance" here (cf. 6:17). This strengthens the motif of the fulfillment of the OT promises in the church (cf. 13:20). The ground of this new covenant and its reception by the **called** is now set forth. (In the original text, the ground is explicated before the result, whereas GNB places the ground last, adding the words **this can be done because**.) The ground or basis of the new situation is the occurrence of **a death** which has as its result that it **sets people free** (cf. the reference to "an eternal redemption" in v. 12). It redeems them **from the wrongs** (lit., "transgressions") committed **while the first covenant was in effect** (GNB paraphrases the original, lit., "upon the first covenant"). The real answer to sins against the commandments of the Mosaic Law is found not in the sacrifice of animals, but in the sacrifice of Christ. The new covenant thus contains within it the answer to the failure to abide by the requirements of the old covenant (cf. 8:12; 10:17–18). And, forgiveness experienced during the OT period depended finally—although this was hardly understood at the time—upon an event that was to take place in the future. The sacrifice of Christ is the answer to sin in every era, past and present, since it alone is the means of forgiveness.

9:16–18 / At this point the author takes advantage of the dual meaning of the Greek word *diathēkē*. Having understood it as "covenant," he now shifts to the meaning "will." This is the same thing that Paul does in Galatians 3:15–17, where, however, the argument is a little different. GNB re-expresses the terse language of our passage with effective clarity (reversing the clauses in v. 17, adding the words **means nothing**, along with a few other minor alterations). The argument is transparent: a person's will is not valid until his death has occurred. But just as the death of a testator is necessary for his will to become effective, so in the case of a "covenant" a death is also necessary for it to become valid. Thus even **the first** (GNB rightly adds the word **covenant**) was inaugurated with the blood of a sacrificial victim. (GNB re-expresses v. 18 positively so as to avoid the negative form "not without blood.") The next three verses demonstrate this point in some detail.

9:19-21 / Our author first shows the close connection between the giving of the Law by Moses and the actual sealing of the covenant through the sprinkling of blood. (At the beginning of v. 19, GNB adds **first** and omits "all" before **the people**.) The ceremony described by the author is apparently that mentioned in Exodus 24:3–8, although several items in our passage are not found there, namely the **water** (GNB adds the words **mixed with**), **red wool**, and **hyssop** (GNB adds **using a sprig of**). Further differences between our passage and Exodus 24 are the absence of any mention of sprinkling **the book** (GNB adds **of the Law**) and any reference to **the blood of . . . goats**. If the author is not using a special source no longer available to us, then he must be bringing together material from different parts of the OT (e.g., Num. 19:18–19; Exod. 12:22; Lev. 8:15, 19; 14:4). An argument in favor of the latter suggestion is the association of Exodus 24 and Leviticus 19 in the synagogue lectionary. In Numbers 19:18, we also find reference to sprinkling the tent and its furnishings, just as in our passage it is **on the Covenant Tent and over all the things used in worship** that the blood is also sprinkled (GNB adds **Covenant**, as well as specifying that it was **Moses** who sprinkled the blood). But in Numbers 19:18, although hyssop is used, it is water rather than blood that is sprinkled.

In any event, the point of all this is clear: the sacrifice of animals and the ritualistic sprinkling of special objects with blood is important in the establishment of the covenant between God and Israel. This is made explicit through the citation of Exodus 24:8 in verse 20. GNB interprets the meaning of the quotation in the words **the blood which seals the covenant** (lit., "the blood of the covenant;" cf. Matt. 26:28). The blood of the covenant indeed serves a ratifying function whereby both parties obligate themselves to be faithful (hence GNB's added words **to obey**) to the stipulations of the covenant. Any unfaithful party was subject to the fate of the sacrificial animal. Thus the "blood of the covenant" confirmed the reality of the covenant in such a way as to emphasize the importance of faithfulness to it.

9:22 / Although it is generally true that the shedding of blood is required for ceremonial cleansing in the OT, some exceptions were allowed, and it is apparently these that our author has in mind. Thus, for example, for those unable to afford animal sacrifices, or even turtledoves or pigeons, the offering of fine flour was permitted (Lev. 5:11–13). The central importance of blood to the forgiveness of sins, however, is stressed in Leviticus 17:11, "The life of every living thing is in the blood, and that is why the LORD has commanded that all blood be poured out on the altar to take away the people's sins. Blood, which is life, takes away sins." It is probably this perspective that enables the author to write that **sins are forgiven only if blood is poured out** (lit., "without the shedding of blood there is no forgiveness"). Blood is necessary for the ratification of a covenant, and particularly in the case of the new covenant with its promise of a definitive forgiveness of sins (cf. 9:15, 26; 10:18).

Additional Notes

9:15 / For **new covenant**, see note on 8:8. The same expression, "mediator of a new covenant," occurs again in 12:24 (where, however, the word "new" is *neos* rather than *kainos*). The word "mediator" has already been used by our author in 8:6 ("mediator of a better covenant"). Elsewhere in the NT the word describes Christ only in 1 Tim. 2:5, where there is no mention of the new covenant: "there is one mediator between God and mankind, the man Christ Jesus." On the atoning significance of Christ's death, see also 2:9, 14–15. **Sets people free** is a translation of the Greek word *apolytrōsis*. This is the only occurrence of the word in referring to redemption from sin in Hebrews (for parallels to this usage, see Rom. 3:24; Eph. 1:7; Col. 1:14). But the related word *lytrōsis* occurs in 9:12 (see note there). The word translated **wrongs** (*parabasis*) is found in only one other place in Hebrews (2:2), where it refers to the sins committed under the Mosaic dispensation, for which due punishment was received. Only in Hebrews is the Mosaic covenant referred to as **the first covenant** (see note on 8:7). Surprisingly, the first covenant is never called the "old covenant" as it is in 2 Cor. 3:14, although this of course is implied by the reference to the "new covenant" (but cf. 8:13). The retroactive effect of Christ's death, whereby those in the earlier dispensation are ultimately redeemed, may also be alluded to in Rom. 3:25 (see RSV). **Those who have been called** refers to Christians who have heard the call and have responded in faith and obedience (see note on 3:1). The words "the promise of an eternal inheritance" are reminiscent of Paul's Christian application of the concept of the inheritance in Rom. 8:17: "Since we are his children, we will possess the blessings he keeps for his people, and we will also possess with Christ what God has kept for him." For the importance of what **God has promised** in Hebrews, see note on 6:12. The word "inheritance" (*klēronomia*) occurs only here and in 11:8 in Hebrews. The word "heir," however, and the verb "to inherit" are also found several times (1:14; 6:17). See note on 1:14.

9:16–18 / A few commentators, notably Westcott and Nairne, have argued that the word *diathēkē* is to be understood throughout the epistle as meaning "covenant," including the present passage. See also J. J. Hughes, "Hebrews ix 15ff. and Galatians iii 15ff. A Study in Covenant Practice and Procedure," *NovT* 21 (1979), pp. 27–96. This view understands the death referred to in v. 16 to be that of a sacrificial animal rather than that of the covenant-maker. The latter is thus understood "to die" only in a symbolic way, and this is the "establishment" or "proof" upon which the covenant becomes effective. But since the natural reading of v. 17 requires the death (apparently literal, not symbolic) of the one who makes the *diathēkē*, and since *diathēkē* can mean "will," it makes better sense to allow for a shift in the meaning of the word in vv. 16–17. Supportive of this conclusion is the fact that the language of v. 16 is careful and accurate legal language used in certifying the death of a testator. Thus, behind GNB's **to prove** is the Greek word *pherō*, lit., "to be brought," in the technical sense of being "registered." See K. Weiss, *TNDT*, vol. 9, p. 58; and the note of Hughes, pp. 371-73. We are still left in the present passage, however, with the unusual fact that the testator, upon whose death the will takes effect, is also the executor of the will—that is, "the mediator of a new covenant." The uniqueness of Christ and his work is such that while it is expressed in the categories of both covenant and will, it transcends the ordinary stipulations of both. The word *diatithēmi*, which underlies GNB's **person who made it**, is used both of wills, as in vv. 16 and 17, and of covenants, as in the quotation from Jer. 31:33 in 8:10 and 10:16. On this see Behm, *TDNT*, vol. 2, pp. 104–6; for the view that "covenant" and "testament" are not to be distinguished in the present passage, see K. M. Campbell, "Covenant or Testament? Heb. 9:16, 17 Reconsidered," *EQ* (1972), pp. 107–111; G. D. Kilpatrick, "Diathēkē in Hebrews," *ZNW* (1977), pp. 263–65. GNB's **went into effect** (v. 18) translates the Greek verb *enkainizō*, a verb found only here and in 10:20 in the NT. In the present passage the word is to be understood as "to inaugurate" or "to dedicate" in the sense of a consecration. See Behm *TDNT*, vol. 3, pp. 453 f.

9:19-21 / Many important Greek manuscripts do not contain the words **and goats**. It is difficult to decide whether these words were omitted by a copyist (either accidentally or, perhaps, intentionally in order to harmonize the text with Exod. 24:5) or whether they were added, perhaps in imitation of v. 12. Probably the words were omitted from the original, but the possibility remains that the shorter reading was expanded by a copyist. Hence the United Bible Society puts the words in brackets. See Metzger, *TCGNT*, pp. 668 f. **Water** was probably added to the blood to increase the quantity and to prevent coagulation. On the other hand, the water in view may be that mixed with the ashes of a heifer and used for purification according to Num. 19:17–18. The **red wool** was apparently used to fasten the **hyssop** sprig to a stick of cedar wood, thus making a utensil for ritual cleansing (cf. Lev. 14:4–7; Num. 19:6). In the citation of Exod. 24:8 (v. 20) our author departs only slightly from the LXX (which agrees exactly with the Hebrew text), substituting **this** for "behold," **God** for "the Lord," and employing a different main verb, **commanded**, for LXX's "made with you." In the NT the shed blood of Jesus is explicitly associated with the new covenant (Mark 14:24; Matt. 26:28; Luke 22:20; 1 Cor. 11:25). Even the ritual of the sprinkling of blood can be alluded to in reference to Christ's blood in 1 Pet. 1:2—but this, of course, is to be understood in a figurative rather than a literal sense. Like our author, Josephus (*Ant.* 3.206) refers to the sprinkling of the tent and its vessels. **The things used in worship** may be more literally translated "the vessels of the sacrificial ritual." Again the word *leitourgia* is used (see note on 8:6).

9:22 / Also among possible exceptions in our author's mind may be cleansing by water, incense, and fire, all of which can be found in the OT. But these exceptions serve only to prove the rule stressed in this verse. Behind GNB's **blood is poured out** lies a Greek noun (*haimatekchysia*) that does not occur in the LXX and that is found in the NT only here. It is possible, as many commentators contend, but not necessary, that our author coined the word. The saying "without the shedding of blood there is no forgiveness of sins" may have been a proverbial saying and appears to have been a perspective shared by the rabbis.

20

Christ and His Work:
The Final Answer to Sin

HEBREWS 9:23–28

Those things, which are copies of the heavenly originals, had to be purified in that way. But the heavenly things themselves require much better sacrifices. ²⁴For Christ did not go into a man-made Holy Place, which was a copy of the real one. He went into heaven itself, where he now appears on our behalf in the presence of God. ²⁵The Jewish High Priest goes into the Most Holy Place every year with the blood of an animal. But Christ did not go in to offer himself many times, ²⁶for then he would have had to suffer many times ever since the creation of the world. Instead, now when all ages of time are nearing the end, he has appeared once and for all, to remove sin through the sacrifice of himself. ²⁷Everyone must die once, and after that be judged by God. ²⁸In the same manner Christ also was offered in sacrifice once to take away the sins of many. He will appear a second time, not to deal with sin, but to save those who are waiting for him.

This section summarizes the argument of the preceding sections in a succinct and climactic manner. The repetition of the main points is deliberate (compare v. 24 with v. 11, and vv. 25–26 with v. 12) and indicates their importance to the author. Here, indeed, we are at the very heart of the Epistle to the Hebrews. The stress is on what Christ has already done, once-and-for-all, rather than on what remains to occur. And yet the author can affirm the second advent of Christ as the event that will round out the salvation experienced by those who have received the good news.

9:23-24 / It was necessary for the **copies of the heavenly originals** (lit., "things") to be cleansed **in that way** (lit., "by these things"), namely, the rites described in the preceding section (vv. 19–22; cf. v. 13). This was God's will for the Mosaic dispensation. And it was his intention that the levitical sacrifices foreshadow the sacrifice of Christ. For the **heavenly things**, the ultimate reality wherein final and complete atonement is accomplished, **much** (a word added by GNB) **better sacrifices** "than these" (words omitted by GNB) are necessary. The plural **sacrifices** here is caused by the generic contrast with the sacrifices of the old covenant. But from the present passage, as well as many others, we know that our author could easily have used the singular "sacrifice." It is the "once and for all" sacrifice of Christ that is the new covenant's counterpart to the sacrifices of the old covenant. Christ himself is the reality to which the copies pointed. His sacrificial work thus was presented, so to speak, in **heaven itself**, and there he now continues in his high priestly ministry of intercession in the very **presence of God** (cf. 6:20; 7:25; Rom. 8:34). This is what is meant by the statement that Christ did not enter **a man-made** (lit., "hand-made") **Holy Place**. This was but **a copy** ("anti-type") **of the real one** (lit., "of the true things"). But in Christ the anticipated reality has come.

9:25-26 / By its very nature the work of the **High Priest** (GNB adds **Jewish**) involves the annually repeated sacrifice and entry into the Holy of Holies to make atonement (GNB correctly adds the word **Most** to the simple **Holy Place** of the text). On the Day of Atonement, the high priest accomplished his duties using **the blood of an animal** (lit., "of another"). But since in the supreme act of atonement Jesus took his own blood, and not that "of another," it is impossible for him to repeat the act of atonement. For this would entail his repeated dying, and one might say even from **the creation of the world**, since atonement was needed from the time of the entry of sin into the world. But the central fact of Christianity is that in the already inaugurated eschatological era, **now when all ages of time are nearing the end** (lit., "at the consummation of the ages"; Barclay: "the consummation of history"), Christ **has appeared once and for all** for the final removal of sin **through the sacrifice of himself.** It is just here that the contrast between Christ's high priestly work and that of the levitical high priest is most startling and revealing. It is important to note the close connection that exists between the once-and-for-all character of Christ's sacrifice and the fact that Christ's sacrificial work depends upon his own blood (cf. 7:27; 9:12). Where sin has been definitively canceled, as it has in Christ, the aeons have reached a turning point (cf. 1:2; 1 Cor. 10:11).

9:27-28 / GNB makes verse 27 into an independent sentence, omitting the opening words, "just as." The author here draws a parallel between the experience of **everyone** (lit., "men") and that of Christ. In both instances, death can only occur once but is not the end of the story. After death mankind faces judgment (GNB adds **by God**); after his death, Christ will return **to save** (lit., "for salvation") his people from judgment. Whereas on the one hand judgment is a threat facing all, on the other, those who depend upon Christ's atoning work receive deliverance from judgment with the result that salvation is finally and fully experienced by those who **are waiting for him** (cf. Phil. 3:20; 2 Tim. 4:8). Thus, in keeping with the finality of Christ's sacrifice, the purpose of the second appearance of Christ does not have to do with the problem of sin but with the wrapping up of eschatological fulfillment begun in his first advent. The possibility of eschatological salvation depends squarely upon the reality of Christ's atonement for sin. Thus Christ **was offered** (GNB adds **in sacrifice**) **once to take away the sins of many**. This last clause probably constitutes a conscious allusion to Isaiah 53:12, whence the expression **many** derives (see note). Christ was offered **once** and with that sacrificial work now accomplished, his future work will involve only the salvation and vindication of his people.

Additional Notes

9:23-24 / The Greek word translated **copies** (*hypodeigmata*) occurs in a similar way in 8:5 (see note there). The same word, however, does not underlie **copy** in v. 24, where the Greek word is *antitypos* (which occurs in the rest of the NT only in 1 Pet. 3:21). "Anti-type" here refers to that which corresponds to the original as an impression to the die. The "anti-type" is thus contrasted with the "true things." Elsewhere (as in 1 Pet. 3:21) the opposite is the case, namely, that "anti-type" is the reality to which a "type" points. For **heavenly things**, the author uses the word *epouranios* (see note on 3:1). Again, the "things" referred to here are not to be understood literally but as a way the author uses to speak of spiritual realities. (See discussion on 8:2, 5.) For this reason the "heavenly things" are here synonymous with the "true things" (cf. 8:2). The description of the earthly sanctuary as **man-made** stands in deliberate contrast to the description of the heavenly sanctuary as "not man-made" in v. 11. The verb for "purify" or "cleanse" (*katharizō*) is applied both to the conscience (in 9:14 and 10:2) and to ceremonial purification (as in 9:22 and here). See Hauck, *TDNT*, vol. 3, pp. 423-31. But do the **heavenly things themselves** need to be purified? Again, there is no need to understand this literally. Our author is drawing a contrast between the old and new that involves the use of parallel language for things that are similar but not equivalent. The point in the present passage is that just as sacrifices were necessary in the old covenant context (the **copies**), so also the reality of the new covenant ("the true things") demands a superior—indeed, a definitive—sacrifice. And this is what Christ has accomplished **on our behalf**. The verb for **appears** (*emphanizō*) occurs in Hebrews only here and in 11:14.

9:25-6 / Since it is into the Holy of Holies that the high priest enters yearly to make atonement for the sins of the people, GNB is correct in specifying **the Most Holy Place**, although the Greek word (*hagia*) is the same as in the preceding verse, where GNB translates simply **Holy Place**. KJV, ASV, and RSV, however, retain the translation "the Holy Place." The use of the present tense **goes into** may well reflect the existence of the Temple and its cultus at the time of the writing of the letter. The verb **offer** (*prosphero*) is used repeatedly by our author. See note on 5:1. For **blood**, see note on 9:7. The word for "of another" occurs elsewhere in Hebrews only in 11:9, 34, where it has the connotation of "foreign." The same contrast between the **once and for all** character of Christ's priestly work and the repeated (**many times**) sacrifices of the levitical priesthood is found in 10:11 f. (cf. 7:27). The word **suffer** (*pascho*) here, as in 13:12 (where GNB translates "died"), is to be understood as "die," as the context clearly indicates. It would have been possible for Christ to suffer repeatedly, but not to die repeatedly (everyone dies only "once," v. 27). See Michaelis, *TDNT*, vol. 5 pp. 916–19.

The phrase **since the creation** (lit., "foundation") **of the world** occurs also in 4:3 and is common in the NT. According to 1 Pet. 1:20, in a context that refers to the redeeming blood of Christ, "he had been chosen by God before the creation of the world and was revealed in these last days for your sake." See Hauck, *TDNT*, vol. 3, pp. 620 f. For the very great importance of the concept of **once and for all**, see note on 7:27 (cf. 9:12). **To remove sin** may connote the "annulment" or "cancellation" of sin. *Athetesis* is the same word used in 7:18 (GNB "set aside"). (See note on 7:18.) The word for **sacrifice** (*thysia*) occurs frequently in Hebrews in describing the sacrificial ritual of the old covenant, but only here and in 10:12 is it used to refer to the sacrifice of Christ (cf. 9:23). See J. Swetnam, "Sacrifice and Revelation in the Epistle to the Hebrews: Observations and Surmises on Hebrews 9, 26," *CBQ* 30 (1968), pp. 227–34.

9:27-28 / For **must die**, see Gen. 3:19. The noun "judgment" (*krisis*) is found only here and in 10:27 in Hebrews (the verb is found in 10:30 and 13:4; cf. 6:2), although the idea is often present (e.g., 2:3; 4:1, 13). See W. Schneider, *NIDNTT*, vol. 2, pp. 362–67. Yet again we encounter the important words **once** (*hapax*) and **offered** (*prosphero*). For the former, see, in the immediate context, vv. 12, 26, 27, 28; 10:10; for the latter, see vv. 14, 25, 28 (cf. 10:14). The verb that GNB translates **take away** (*anaphero*) also means "to bear," as does the Hebrew verb in Isa. 53:12. Cf. BAGD, p. 63: "he took upon himself the sins of many." In a very similar passage, 1 Peter also makes use of the language of Isaiah: "Christ himself carried our sins in his body to the cross" (1 Pet. 2:24; cf. 3:18). **Many** is explained by the language of Isa. 53:12 and is probably to be understood as a Hebraic way of referring to all. Earlier in this epistle we have read that he died "for everyone" (2:9). Thus the "many" of Mark 10:45 is probably also to be explained in an inclusive sense as referring to all (see 2 Cor. 5:14 f. and 1 Tim. 2:6). Compare too the "many" of Rom. 5:15 and 19 with the "all" of 5:18. See Jeremias, *TDNT*, vol. 6, pp. 540–45. GNB's **not to deal with sin** is an expansive translation of the literal "without sin" (*chōris hamartias*). The same expression occurs in 4:15, where it refers to Christ's sinlessness. Here, however, the sense is different. Thus BAGD, p. 891: "without any relation to sin, i.e., not with the purpose of atoning for it." **Waiting** (*apekdechomai*) occurs only here in Hebrews. For "salvation" (*sōtēria*), see note on 2:3. The idea of appearing **a second time**, after the accomplishment of atonement in the presence of God, is reminiscent of the reappearance of the high priest after he had accomplished his task in the Holy of Holies. The apprehensiveness of the crowd while the high priest was out of sight, followed by their great joy at his reappearance, receives eloquent witness in contemporary sources (e.g., Sirach 50:5–10). Only by means of an acceptable offering was salvation assured.

21

The Ineffectiveness of the Law

The Jewish Law is not a full and faithful model of the real things; it is only a faint outline of the good things to come. The same sacrifices are offered forever, year after year. How can the Law, then, by means of these sacrifices make perfect the people who come to God? ²If the people worshiping God had really been purified from their sins, they would not feel guilty of sin any more, and all sacrifices would stop. ³As it is, however, the sacrifices serve year after year to remind people of their sins. ⁴For the blood of bulls and goats can never take away sins.

The argument of the preceding two chapters is restated in this section (10:1–18), bringing the central argument of the epistle, namely, the imperfection of the old order and the perfection of the new, to a conclusion. The only new material in this section is found in verses 5–10 where the author's thesis finds further support in his exegesis of Psalm 40:6–8. All the other material is in fact the restatement of points earlier made. The entire central section is then effectively rounded out by the requotation of Jeremiah 31:33–34. First, however, the author focuses on the repetitious character of the levitical sacrifices, using this to further his argument by pointing to the intrinsic inadequacy implied by the necessity of repetition.

10:1 / Since the **Law** (GNB adds **Jewish**) was only anticipatory of **the good things to come**, in itself it possesses no enduring or final significance. It is therefore but a **faint outline** (lit., "shadow"; cf. 8:5) and **not a full and faithful model of the real things**. In this last phrase GNB paraphrases what is literally "not the very image of the things." The **Law** involves copies and not the realities themselves (cf. 8:5; 9:23–24). Since the author stresses the fulfillment that has already come in Christ and earlier refers to "the good things that are already here" (9:11), the future aspect in the words **to come** is to be understood from the perspective of the OT (thus NEB: "the good things which were to come"). GNB's **forever** is to be understood in the sense of "continually." **Year after year** corresponds to "every day" in 7:27 (cf. 9:25). By **the same sacrifices** of course is meant the same kind of sacrifices. GNB makes shorter sentences out of the involved syntax of the Greek text and turns the last of these into a rhetorical question. The Greek text strongly asserts the impossibility (lit., "it is impossible") that the Law can make perfect those who draw near to offer sacrifices. Those **who come** (GNB adds **to God**) refers to those who participate in the sacrifices. Our author has already stated that "the Law of Moses could make nothing perfect" (7:19). Here, as throughout the book, "perfection" entails arrival at the goal of God's saving purposes. By their very nature, the sacrifices of the old covenant were unable to bring humanity to the full salvation God intended. This fulfillment depends upon that toward which those sacrifices pointed.

10:2-3 / The rhetorical question in the Greek of verse 2 is altered to a declarative statement by GNB. The author asks the logical question: Would not the sacrifices have ceased if the people had been cleansed in a final and complete way? Does not the repetition of the sacrifices itself point to their inadequacy? GNB's **really** is literally "once and for all," which echoes the once-and-for-all character of Christ's sacrifice, repeatedly stressed in the epistle. **Purified from their sins** is literally "cleansed," but with the removal of sins from the conscience (expressed by GNB in the words **not feel guilty**). For similar statements about the perfecting or cleansing of the conscience, see 9:9, 14. What is in view here, in contrast to the external cleansing of the old covenant, is the new, inner level of cleansing made possible by the era of fulfillment brought by Christ. Where that occurs no further need for the offering of sacrifices exists (cf. 10:17–18). (GNB adds the words **all sacrifices** at the end of v. 2.) Indeed, the continuing of the sacrifices **year after year** (cf. v. 1) itself serves as a reminder of the continuing problem of **their sins**. GNB sharpens the contrast in verse 3 with the words **as it is, however** (lit., "but").

10:4 / The author returns here to a fundamental point in his argument and the ground for his assertions in the preceding two verses. The Greek text is even more emphatic than GNB's **can never**: "for it is impossible . . . " Cleansing of a kind can be accomplished by the blood of animals (9:13, 22), but cleansing that results in the taking away of sins is beyond the power of such blood. Only the blood of Christ is sufficient for this task (9:14, 25–26).

Additional Notes

10:1 / For "shadow," see note to 8:5 (cf. Col. 2:17). There are two textual problems in this verse. The earliest manuscript of Hebrews (P⁴⁶) reads "and the image" for "not the very image," thus affirming that the Law is (only) the "image" (GNB **model**) of the good things to come. But both the structure of the sentence and the meaning of the word "image" (*eikōn*) argue against this reading. *Eikōn* is a manifestation of the reality (it is used of Christ in 2 Cor. 4:4 and Col. 1:15) and stands in contrast to the shadow (GNB **faint outline**) rather than being essentially synonymous with it. See Metzger *TCGNT*, p. 669. The second variant involves the verb "is impossible" for which some understood a plural subject (i.e., the sacrifices). The correct subject grammatically, however, is "the Law," and therefore the singular form is to be preferred. The Greek word translated **real things** (*pragma*) occurs elsewhere in Hebrews only in 6:18 and 11:1. See Maurer, *TDNT*, vol. 6, pp. 638 f. For **sacrifices** (*thysia*) and **offered** (*prospherō*), see note on 5:1. The Greek underlying **forever** is *eis to diēnekes*; for the translation "continually," see BAGD, p. 195. **Who come** (*proserchomai*) is again language of the cultus (cf. RSV "draw near"). See note on 4:16. On the important word **make perfect** (*teleioō*), see note on 2:10.

10:2-3 / The "conscience" of the worshiper is frequently in our author's mind. See note on 9:9. The Greek word for **worshiping** (*latreuō*) connotes service in the cultus. See note on 8:5. For the importance of "once and for all" (here, *hapax*), see note on 7:27. The verb **purified** is in the perfect tense, suggesting cleansing in the past with results lasting into the present. On the verb here, *katharizō*, which again has a cultic meaning, see note on 9:23. Behind GNB's **to remind** is the noun "remembrance" (*anamnēsis*), a word occurring in Hebrews only here. The somewhat ambiguous Greek, which does not spell out who is reminded, is correctly interpreted by GNB's **people** (in keeping with the consciousness of sin mentioned in v. 2).

10:4 / A tradition about the inefficacy of sacrifices had already emerged in the OT Scriptures. One of these passages, indeed, is about to be quoted (see v. 6). In addition to Ps. 40:6, see Ps. 51:16, 1 Sam. 15:22, and the following passages from the Prophets: Isa. 1:11; Hos. 6:6; Amos 5:21–22; Mic. 6:6–8 (cf., too, Jesus' use of this perspective in Matt. 9:13; Mark 12:33). Thus the readers would have been familiar with this polemic, although not with the way in which our author utilizes it. Judaism, after the fall of Jerusalem, was able on the basis of this polemic to assert the reality of forgiveness without animal sacrifices. For our author, however, it is the blood of Christ that obviates the need for the blood of animals and answers its final inadequacy. On the phrase **the blood of bulls and goats**, see 9:12, 13, 19.

22

Old and New in Psalm 40:6–8

For this reason, when Christ was about to come into the world, he said to God:
"You do not want sacrifices and offerings,
but you have prepared a body for me,
⁶You are not pleased with animals burned whole on the altar
or with sacrifices to take away sins.
⁷Then I said, 'Here I am, to do your will, O God,
just as it is written of me in the book of the Law.' "

⁸First he said, "You neither want nor are you pleased with sacrifices and offerings or with animals burned on the altar and the sacrifices to take away sins." He said this even though all these sacrifices are offered according to the Law. ⁹Then he said, "Here I am, O God, to do your will." So God does away with all the old sacrifices and puts the sacrifice of Christ in their place. ¹⁰Because Jesus Christ did what God wanted him to do, we are all purified from sin by the offering that he made of his own body once and for all.

In this section we encounter another brilliant example of the author's christological exegesis of the OT. As he likes so much to do (cf. 2:6-9; 3:7–4:10), he first cites the OT text and then presents a midrash, or running commentary, on the passage, by which he supports the argument he is pursuing. In this instance that argument involves the transitory character of the levitical sacrifices and the permanent character of what Christ has done. The author has found an ideal text for his purposes. With Christ as his hermeneutical key, he expounds the deeper meaning of the text, which can now be seen retrospectively in a new way through the fulfillment brought by Christ.

10:5-7 / Although not stipulated in the original text, GNB is correct in adding **Christ** and **to God**. It is clear from the quotation and what follows that our author understands Christ to be the speaker in the psalm. **About to come** (lit., "coming") **into the world** indicates that from the author's perspective it is the pre-existent Christ who speaks through the psalmist. The quotation is from Psalm 40:6–8 and follows the LXX closely. An important difference between the LXX and the Hebrew text of Psalm 40:6, however, is LXX's **you have prepared a body for me** for "you have given me ears to hear you" (lit., "ears you have dug for me"). The LXX translator apparently understood an allusion to the creation of Adam in the words "ears you have dug for me," for in the sculpting of a body from clay, ears must be dug out. Thus he translated the expression from Hebrew idiom into language that would more readily be understood in the Hellenistic world: **you have prepared a body for me**.

Animals burned whole on the altar is GNB's expansive translation of "whole burnt offerings." **Here I am, to do your will** may also be translated "I have come to do your will," which may be a more appropriate translation given the fact that the Messiah was regularly described as "the coming one" (cf. the opening words of v. 5; John 6:14; 11:27). **The book of the Law** is literally "the roll of the book" (cf. Ezek. 2:9, LXX).

The meaning of the psalm passage in its own historical context seems clear. A pious Israelite, perhaps David or a Davidic king, stresses that what is important to God is not sacrifices but obedience. God has given ears to hear and to obey. Thus the psalmist goes on to say, "How I love to do your will, my God! I keep your teaching in my heart" (cf. Jer. 31:33). From his Christocentric perspective the author understands Christ to be the speaker of these words. In addition to the actual content of the present passage, he may have thought of the psalm as messianic because of its Davidic associations and also because of certain of its phrases, for example, "sing a new song" (v. 3), "the good news that you save us" (v. 9), "news of salvation" (v. 10; cf. v. 16). In the exegesis of the passage provided by our author in the following verses, it becomes clear how appropriately it can be applied to Christ and his work. For our author, Christ is the goal of the OT Scriptures; the fulfillment brought by him is the justification for christological interpretation of the OT.

10:8 / The midrashic commentary on the psalm text begins with a requotation of the opening (**first**, lit., "earlier") sentences, telescoping them into one sentence and omitting the clause about the preparation of a body. The author adds the reminder that these sacrifices were divinely ordained: "which are offered according to the Law." GNB re-expresses this in an independent sentence: **He said this even though all these sacrifices are offered according to the Law**. The OT itself recognizes the inadequacy of the levitical sacrifices, though not in the sense that our author does, despite the fact that it contains the Mosaic legislation that requires those sacrifices.

10:9-10 / In contrast to animal sacrifices is the obedience of Christ. Again, the original citation is quoted: **Then he said, Here I am (O God is**

brought down from the citation and does not occur here in the text) **to do your will**. That the obedience of Christ to the will of God (cf. Matt. 26:39, 42; John 6:38) entails his own self-sacrifice has already been established by the author (most recently in 9:28). It is asserted again in verse 10 but only implied in verse 9. GNB takes what is implicit in the original, terse sentence, "he abolishes the first in order to establish the second," and makes it explicit: **So God does away with all the old sacrifices and puts the sacrifice of Christ in their place**. That GNB's constructed sentence is a correct paraphrase of our author's thought is evident from the statement in verse 10. The reference to abolishing the first to establish the second is very reminiscent of 7:12, 18–19 and 8:7, 13 where it is said that the former commandments and covenant must give way to the new. Here it is the sacrifices of animals that must give way to the sacrifice of Christ in obedience to God's will. The will of God referred to in the original quotation (and in its recurrence in v. 9) is identified at the beginning of verse 10 as that by which we are **purified** (GNB adds **all** and **from sin**).

GNB's **because Jesus Christ did what God wanted him to do** is a paraphrase of "by which will," the last word being the first of three deliberate allusions in midrashic fashion to the psalm quotation in verse 10. The second word drawn from the original quotation is **offering**. The **offering** that is acceptable to God because it fulfills his will is literally "of the body of Jesus Christ." It is in the word **body** that we have the third allusion to the original quotation. This reference to the **body** of Jesus calls to mind the emphasis in chapter 2 upon the "flesh and blood" he shared so that "he should die for everyone" and that "through his death he might destroy the Devil" (2:9, 14). According to our author the humanity of Jesus had as its purpose his atoning death, **the offering** of his **body**. It was this that occurred **once and for all**. This one sacrifice is the counterpart to, and fulfills altogether, the entire catalogue of animal sacrifices rejected in Psalm 40:6–7. For it is Jesus who has come to do the will of God, and in agreement with the teaching of the Scriptures: "just as it is written of me in the book of the Law." All of the OT in one way or another points to or prepares for the fulfillment of God's saving purposes accomplished through Christ.

Additional Notes

10:5–7 / The content of the psalm quotation as elucidated by the author shows how appropriately it can be said to refer to the one "coming into the world" in order to accomplish God's saving will. On "the coming one" as a messianic title, to which the present passage may well allude, see Schneider, *TDNT*, vol. 2, p. 670.

It has been suggested by some that the word **body** (*sōma*) in the LXX was caused by a scribe's misreading of the word "ears," which in Greek would only have involved mistaking the letters TI for M. Despite this interesting conjecture, however, it is more probable that **you have prepared a body for me** was a deliberate re-expression of the Hebrew original. The fact that a few later witnesses to the text of the LXX contain the word for "ears" rather than **body** (as the major witnesses have it) is to be explained as an attempt to bring about conformity with the Hebrew text. (The LXX otherwise follows the Hebrew text closely.) Our author's quotation of the LXX is also quite accurate. He does replace "you have not asked" (*aiteō*) with **you are not pleased** (*eudokeō*; cf. Ps. 51:16), thus sharpening the contrast with the good pleasure of his will. He also omits the LXX's verb "I delight" **to do your will**.

Four different words or phrases are used by the psalmist in referring to sacrifices. These are apparently meant to represent comprehensively the various kinds of levitical sacrifices. Thus the word for **sacrifices** (*thysia*), though it may describe sacrifices generally (as it does in 5:1; 7:27; 8:3; 9:9, etc.), here as in the OT probably indicates the peace offering. See C. Brown, *NIDNTT*, vol. 3, pp. 416-38. **Offerings** (*prosphora*), which also can have a general sense, in the levitical system means specifically "meal (or cereal) offering." This word is used in Hebrews only in the present chapter (vv. 8, 10, 14, 18). See K. Weiss, *TDNT*, vol. 9, pp. 65-68. The third word means explicitly "whole burnt offerings" (*holokautōma*). In Hebrews the word occurs again only in the requotation of the line from the psalm in v. 8 (and elsewhere in the NT only in Mark 12:33). The Greek underlying GNB's **sacrifices to take away sins** consists of two words "for sins" (*peri hamartias*), a phrase used regularly in the LXX for "sin offerings." This same phrase for sin offerings occurs in Hebrews in 5:3, vv. 8, 18, and 26 of the present chapter, and in 13:11 (see, too, Rom. 8:3). Thus as the psalmist attempted through his vocabulary to contrast the importance of obedience with the entire range of levitical sacrifices, so also our author must have been pleased to use this passage to contrast the entire catalogue of such sacrifices (note his repetition of it in v. 8) with the obedience of Christ and his final and definitive sacrifice. On the terminology of sacrifice, see C. Brown, *NIDNTT*, vol. 3, pp. 418-38.

10:8 / On the categories of sacrifices, see preceding note. The expression **according to the Law** occurs in Hebrews also in 7:5, 16; 8:4; 9:19, 22. In most of these instances, as here, there is the consciousness that what the Law stipulated was only of a temporary character. Now that Christ has brought fulfillment of the promises, the Law is no longer binding. This is stated forcefully and explicitly in v. 9.

10:9-10 / The verb translated **does away with** (*anaireō*) is a strong one, meaning to "abolish" or "destroy" (in Hebrews the word occurs only here). See BAGD, p. 54. Such strong language is in keeping with our author's perspective on the Mosaic Law, given the inauguration of the new covenant in Christ. The point of the present passage and others like it is that the OT had itself spoken of the fact that the sacrifice of animals was not a matter of ultimate significance. God required and had something in mind far greater than animal sacrifices, namely, the obedient sacrifice of Christ. And as he abolishes the one, so he "establishes" (*histēmi*) the other (used in this sense only here in Hebrews). See BAGD, p. 382. The word "will" (*thelēma*) drawn from the original quotation occurs only in the present passage in reference to Christ's obedience. It is found, however, in 10:36 and 13:21, where Christians are called to obey the will of God. **Purified from sin** translates the verb *hagiazō*, lit., "sanctify." See note on 2:11. Our being cleansed from sin is again shown to be directly dependent on Christ's sacrifice, i.e., **by the offering that he made of his own body**. The word **body** (*sōma*) is only used in the present passage in connection with Christ's sacrifice (but cf. 1 Pet. 2:24 and the implication in 13:11 f.). The offering of the body is simply another way of referring to sacrifice. Cf. Eph. 5:2: "as Christ loved us and gave his life for us as a sweet-smelling offering and sacrifice that pleases God." On "body" see S. Wibbing, *NIDNTT*, vol. 1, pp. 232–38. A final point to note in the present passage is the placement of the Greek word *ephapax*, **once and for all**, at the end of the sentence. This adds emphasis to the finality of Christ's sacrifice. For *ephapax*, see note on 7:27.

23

The Perfect Offering and the Fulfillment of Jeremiah 31:31–34

Every Jewish priest performs his services every day and offers the same sacrifices many times; but these sacrifices can never take away sins. [12]Christ, however, offered one sacrifice for sins, an offering that is effective forever, and then he sat down at the right side of God. [13]There he now waits until God puts his enemies as a footstool under his feet. [14]With one sacrifice, then, he has made perfect forever those who are purified from sin.

[15]And the Holy Spirit also gives us his witness. First he says,
[16]"This is the covenant that I will make with them
in the days to come, says the Lord:
I will put my laws in their hearts
and write them on their minds."
[17]And then he says, "I will not remember their sins and evil deeds any longer." [18]So when these have been forgiven, an offering to take away sins is no longer needed.

We now come to the final, climactic section of the central argument in the epistle. Yet again the author asserts the definitive character, and hence the finality, of Christ's sacrifice. In the early stages of this central argument Jeremiah 31:31–34 was quoted (in 8:8–12). Now as the argument is brought to a conclusion, the author returns to that passage, quoting again words from verses 33 and 34. He also makes use of a favorite text, Psalm 110:1, in this passage. In the last sentence it is pointed out that where the promise of Jeremiah has been fulfilled, the sacrificial system is necessarily at an end.

10:11 / Once again the repetitious character of the levitical priestly duties is stressed (cf. 7:27; 9:25; 10:1, 3). Every **priest** (GNB adds **Jewish**) **performs his services** (lit., "stands doing priestly service") **every day** (cf. Exod. 29:38). The very posture of standing suggests the ever-unfinished task performed by the priests, especially when in the next verse it is stressed that having accomplished his task of atonement, Christ "sat down" at God's right hand. The irony of the situation of the levitical priests is that these repeated **sacrifices**, by their very nature, **can never take away sins** (cf. v. 1 and 9:9). Such sacrifices are thus self-condemned.

10:12-13 / The expected contrast, involving the single, sufficient sacrifice of Christ is now set forth (cf. 7:27; 9:12, 26, 28; 10:10). The **one sacrifice for sins** offered by **Christ** (lit., "this one") is described with the word **forever** (GNB adds **an offering that is effective**). Psalm 110:1, one of the main OT texts employed in the book, is now again cited (cf. 1:3, 13; 8:1; 12:2). On this occasion, the author divides the quotation in order to indicate more effectively what has been accomplished and what yet remains to occur. What is now true is that Christ, having accomplished his priestly mission on earth, reigns as King at the right hand of the Father (cf. 1 Cor. 15:25). The second part of the quotation (v. 13) begins with "finally" or "beyond that" (GNB's **then**). What remains is the final vindication of Christ wherein his enemies are fully and finally subjected to him (cf. 9:28). This motif will become an important basis for exhortation in succeeding sections of the epistle (cf. vv. 25, 27, 35, 39; 12:28 f.). The point here, however, is that Christ's atoning work is complete, as the following verse now emphasizes.

10:14 / The efficacy of Christ's single sacrifice is such that **he has made perfect forever** those who are sanctified by his work. As throughout the epistle, the word **perfect** is not to be understood as moral perfection, but as the complete realization of God's saving purpose. To arrive at this **one sacrifice** (cf. v. 12) and to experience its benefits is to arrive at the goal anticipated from the beginning of God's gracious activity among his people. As this sacrifice has a teleological character, so those who are **purified** by it have (cf. the cleansing of the conscience in 9:14) arrived at the fullness of salvation, the *telos*, promised and foreshadowed by all that preceded in the old covenant. It is for this reason that the results of this sacrifice last **forever** (cf. 7:25; 9:12, "eternal salvation"), in contrast to the temporary effects of the levitical sacrifices.

10:15-17 / Returning now to one of his key texts (Jer. 31:33-34), the author asserts that what he has argued is in precise accord with Jeremiah's prophecy concerning the new covenant. The **Holy Spirit** is regarded as the ultimate inspiration of the prophet Jeremiah's words; thus the Spirit bears witness through what he wrote (cf. 3:7; 9:8; 8:8). The quotation is given in two parts: the first predicts the reality of the new covenant positively, whereas the second (v. 17) refers to the blotting out of sins (with the strongest negatives, lit., "I will in no wise remember"). The effect is, on the one hand, to underline the promise of the new covenant with its internal dimension, and on the other, to point out the close interconnection between this promise and the experience of a new level of forgiveness. This is what has come about through the sacrifice of Christ.

10:18 / "But" (the word underlying GNB's **so**) where such promised things as these have become a reality, only one conclusion about the old system of sacrifices is possible. And thus climactically the author asserts that there is **no longer** any need for further sacrifices for sins. Fulfillment of Jeremiah's promise has come. Christ's sacrifice is the definitive, final, and fully efficacious answer to the universal problem of human sin.

Additional Notes

10:11 / A few important witnesses have "high priest" for **priest**, probably by influence from the similar verse in 7:27. The phrase **every day** (*kath' hēmeran*) is found also in 7:27 (cf. 8:13). Underlying "doing priestly service" is the verb *leitourgeō*, which is found only here in Hebrews (but cognate nouns are found in 8:2, 6 and 9:21). See note on 8:6. The perfect tense of "stands" and the present participle "doing priestly service" may point again to the existence of the Temple and its sacrificial ritual at the time the epistle was written. For a contrasting use of **many times** (*pollakis*), see 9:25 f. On **offers** (*prospherō*) and **sacrifices** (*thysia*), see note to 5:1. The verb for **take away** (*periaireō*) occurs only here in Hebrews (elsewhere in the NT epistles it is found in 2 Cor. 3:16).

10:12-13 / GNB's **and then**, although not in the original text, effectively expresses the significance of the aorist participle ("having offered"), which indicates action accomplished prior to the action of the main verb, **he sat down**. The point is clear: Christ's sacrificial work, his **one sacrifice for sins**, was sufficient and complete. The fact that he is finished with that work is underlined by the reference to his sitting down at God's right hand. The reference to **one sacrifice** (*thysia*, see note on 5:1) is paralleled by the **one sacrifice** (lit., "offering") in v. 14. In the Greek text the phrase translated **forever** (*eis to diēnekes*) can be understood to refer to Christ's offering or to his sitting at God's right hand. GNB's interpretation is probably correct since it is more in keeping with what is argued by the author elsewhere (cf. the same phrase for **forever** in v. 14 in reference to the results of Christ's sacrifice). For the great importance of Ps. 110:1, which is quoted here, see note on 1:3. GNB expresses the Hebraic "divine passive"—a passive verb where God is understood to be the acting subject—by a direct active

until God puts. The reality of a final victory fully realized is assumed because God is the agent who will bring it to pass.

10:14 / For **sacrifice** ("offering," *prosphora*), see note on 10:5. On the important verb **made perfect** (*teleioō*), see note to 2:10. On **purified from sin** (*hagiazō*), see note to 2:11.

10:15-17 / For the **Holy Spirit** as the speaker in OT Scripture, see note on 3:7. The first part of the quotation is introduced with **first he says** (lit., "after saying"), but the second lacks any introduction unless the opening "and" of v. 17 is meant to be such (GNB adds **and then he says**). The author makes only slight changes from the original quotation of this material in 8:10-11. He substitutes **with them** for "with the house of Israel," transposes the clauses about minds and hearts, and moves from there directly to the promise of the forgiveness, using two words **sins** and **evil deeds** (the latter, *anomia*, is probably written by the author on the analogy of the word translated **sins**, *adikia*, in 8:12). As in 8:10, GNB translates the semitechnical expression "after those days" with **in the days to come**.

10:18 / **When** (*hopou*) is not a temporal adverb here, but is a logical connective indicating the circumstances that lead one logically to the statement in the main clause: thus, "where this is true, this follows." Forgiveness of sins in the sense that Jeremiah prophesied it means that an offering or sacrifice for sin is no longer necessary. For **offering** (*prospherō*), see note on 10:5. The word for "forgiveness" (*aphesis*) occurs in Hebrews only here and in 9:22. See Bultmann, *TDNT*, vol. 1, pp. 509-512.

24

The Grounds for Faithfulness

HEBREWS 10:19-25

We have, then, my brothers, complete freedom to go into the Most Holy Place by means of the death of Jesus. [20]He opened for us a new way, a living way, through the curtain—that is, through his own body. [21]We have a great priest in charge of the house of God. [22]So let us come near to God with a sincere heart and a sure faith, with hearts that have been purified from a guilty conscience and with bodies washed with clean water. [23]Let us hold on firmly to the hope we profess, because we can trust God to keep his promise. [24]Let us be concerned for one another, to help one another to show love and to do good. [25]Let us not give up the habit of meeting together, as some are doing. Instead, let us encourage one another all the more, since you see that the Day of the Lord is coming nearer.

With his central theological argument concluded, the author turns now to some practical applications of what he has so effectively argued. Thus, as is true throughout his epistle, he is never content simply to present theology without showing its practical relevance to his readers. Indeed, he has had his Jewish readers in mind through all the argumentation of the preceding section. But now he comes again to their immediate situation. In this section he draws together motifs from the preceding several chapters and makes them the basis of his moving exhortation of his readers to faithfulness. They, as we shall be reminded of again in verses 26–36, are in danger of falling away from the truth of Christianity. The firm conviction of the author is that if they can but see the true significance of Christ and his work, draw upon the resources he has made available, and so take advantage of what is offered them, they will persevere and receive the reward God has for all his faithful people. This exhortation bears a striking resemblance to that in 4:14–16.

10:19-21 / These three verses contain the basis for the first of the three major verbs of exhortation in this section: "let us come near" (v. 22; cf. vv. 23, 24). In the original these verses constitute subordinate clauses dependent on the main clause at the beginning of verse 22. GNB turns them into separate sentences. The author begins the exhortation by addressing his readers as **brothers** (GNB adds **my**), as he has done in 3:1, 12 and will do in 13:22. From the logical connective **then** (or "therefore"), it is evident that the basis of the following exhortation depends in turn on the entire preceding argument. That argument has demonstrated that the way **into the Most Holy Place** has been opened by a forerunner (6:20), that is, **by means of the death** (lit., "blood") **of Jesus** (cf. 9:12, 14). This fact affords us **complete freedom**, a noun that can equally well be translated "confidence" or even "boldness." The point is that what had hitherto been the special awe-inspiring privilege of the high priest one day in the year—entry into the very presence of God—is now said to be the privilege of every member of the community of faith (cf. Eph. 2:18; 3:12). The originally literal language is now spiritualized and understood as available to Christian experience universally (cf. 1 Pet. 2:5). The old situation of the levitical priesthood and sacrifices indicated by its very nature that "the way into the Most Holy Place had not yet been opened" (9:8). But now it is evident that Jesus **has opened for us a new** and **living way** (cf. John 14:6).

This way is obviously **new**, both in its means and its effects. By **living** the author probably means something like "truly effective" or "enduring," in contrast to the ineffective and now defunct rituals of the past. This new way goes **through the curtain** that divided the Holy of Holies from the rest of the Holy Place or sanctuary. And now the author finds a rich symbolism in this reference to **the curtain** by identifying it with Christ's **own body** (lit., "flesh"). Probably the author here alludes to the tradition about the tearing of the curtain in two at the time of the crucifixion of Jesus—a tradition that eventually found its way into all three Synoptic Gospels. (Mark 15:38 and Matt. 27:51 specify that it was torn from top to bottom, that is by an act of God rather than men; cf. Luke 23:45.) The tearing of the curtain symbolized the opening of direct access to God's presence accomplished by Christ's sacrificial death on the cross. Thus, for our author, although he does not explicitly say so, the tearing of the Christ's "flesh" (and this may be why the word for flesh is used rather than the word for body) in the crucifixion may be analogous to the tearing of the curtain in the Temple. Through his death Christ opened the way to God's presence. It may be said that **we have a great priest** (cf. 4:14), one who has accomplished what no other high priest (which is what **great priest** means) could do by preparing a way in which all may follow. And those who do follow—his people—are described as **the house of God** (see 3:6). God's saving purposes are brought to fulfillment in Christ and Christ now reigns as Priest and King over those whom he has redeemed (**in charge of** is literally "over").

10:22 / The author has thus summarized what has been accomplished through Christ's work and he now exhorts his readers to take advantage of it. The first exhortation is **let us come near** (GNB adds **to God**). This is the spiritualized language of the Temple cultus, meaning now to come into God's presence through such things as worship and prayer. This is to be done in all sincerity ("a true heart") and in the "full assurance" of **faith**. And we are reminded of our acceptability which, as we know from the preceding chapters, depends fully upon the priestly work of Christ. We have been cleansed internally (**hearts that have been purified**, lit., "sprinkled"; cf. Ezek. 36:25, in the context of reference to the new covenant), so that we no longer have the **guilty conscience** (cf. 9:9, 14) from which the old sacrificial ritual could not free us. Again the language of the cultus is deliberately used to show how it finds its true fulfillment in the internal cleansing made possible by Christ. **Bodies washed with clean water**, refers not to Jewish lustrations (ceremonial washings for purification [e.g., 6:2]), but almost certainly to Christian baptism, which is the outward sign of the true, internal cleansing to which reference has just been made (cf. 1 Pet. 3:21; Eph. 5:26). It is this new cleansed state enjoyed by Christians, as well as the open way to God's presence, that results from the sacrifice of Christ.

10:23 / The second exhortation calls the readers to faithfulness, and thus the author returns to one of this major concerns in the letter, the danger that the readers will fall away from the truth (cf. 2:1–3; 3:12–14; 4:1; 6:4–6; 10:26–31). He accordingly encourages them to **hold on firmly** (lit., "without wavering") **to the hope we profess** (lit., "the confession of our hope"). This last clause refers to what is believed by these Jewish Christians (cf. 4:14) and the confident expectation for the future included in that belief. This is the faith that would have been confessed by these Christians at their baptism. What justifies our efforts at faithfulness is God's faithfulness: **we can trust God to keep his promise** (lit., "faithful is the one who promised"; cf. 11:11). What Christians believe, and the hope that is a part of that belief, may be trusted fully and held firmly, because God's faithful character is beyond questioning.

10:24–25 / The third exhortation in this section directs the readers to be concerned with the welfare of others in the community of faith. There is to be a "stimulating" or an "urging on" (this is the more accurate meaning of GNB's **to help**) to the basic Christian conduct of **love** (cf. 13:1) and **good** (lit., "good works"). It is worth noting that we have now encountered the three great virtues of faith (v. 22), hope (v. 23), and love in three successive verses (cf. 1 Cor. 13:13). The mutual encouragement that our author has in mind can occur, of course, only in the context of Christian fellowship. But some, perhaps even in this community, had been neglecting to come together. The avoidance of public meetings on the part of Jewish Christians may have been caused by the understandable desire to escape persecution, whether from the Romans or from the non-Christian Jewish community. Perhaps in the light of past experiences (see vv. 32–34) as well as threats concerning the imminent future (12:4), it was deemed wise to avoid attracting attention. Despite the twofold **let us** (both are added by GNB) in verse 25, no new exhortations are found here; rather, the material in this verse supports the exhortation of verse 24. The way in which the readers can manifest their concern for one another is through active participation in fellowship, on the one hand, and through mutual encouragement, on the other. Christians need each other, and especially in trying circumstances. The whole matter, moreover, is to take on a special urgency with the increasing sense of the imminence of the eschaton, as it is seen **that the Day** (GNB adds **of the Lord**) **is coming nearer** (cf. the quotation of Hab. 2:3 in v. 37).

Additional Notes

10:19-21 / The Greek word translated **complete freedom** (*parrhēsia*) often implies boldness or courage to do something otherwise regarded as dangerous, as here and in 4:16. This courage is based always on the sufficiency of the work of Christ. The word is used elsewhere in the NT in connection with drawing near to God's presence (see Eph. 3:12; cf. 2 Cor. 3:12; 1 John 2:28). Note 12:29: "our God is indeed a destroying fire." See Schlier, *TDNT*, vol. 5, pp. 871–86. Underlying the words **to go into** is the Greek word *eisodos* ("entrance"), which occurs only here in Hebrews and is used in referring to entering God's presence only here in the NT. **Most Holy Place** is literally "holy place" as in 9:8 and 25, but here, as there, the context points to the Holy of Holies. For the "blood of Jesus," see 9:12, 14; 10:29; 13:12, 20. For the importance of "blood" see note on 9:7. The verb for **opened** (*enkainizō*) is translated "went into effect" in 9:18, where the new covenant is in view. Here, in describing the basis of the new covenant, the translation "inaugurated" is also possible. The Greek word used here for **new** is *prosphatos*, which occurs only here in the NT. The adjective **living** is elsewhere used by our author to describe God, as it is often in the NT (3:12; 9:14; 10:31; 12:22). The word **way** (*hodos*) is used in exactly the same sense in 9:8 (but nowhere else in the NT does it refer to the approach to God's presence).

The word for **curtain** (*katapetasma*) occurs earlier in Hebrews in 6:19 and 9:3 ("second curtain"), but nowhere else except in the Gospel passages cited above. It is exegetically possible, and preferred by some commentators (e.g., Westcott, Montefiore; cf. NEB), to understand the words **through his own body** ("flesh") as referring to the **living way** rather than to the **curtain**. In this view the death of Jesus, made possible through the "flesh," is the **way** through which we have access to God. Although unexceptionable in itself and in agreement with the teaching of the epistle, this view is more awkward so far as the word order of the passage is concerned and ignores the probable allusion to the synoptic tradition about the tearing of the curtain. There is no need to press the function of the curtain in hiding or blocking out the presence of God. The view that the **curtain** is the flesh does not deny that the **living way** depends upon the "flesh" of Jesus. The difference is not much in the end. Just as one had to go through the curtain to get to the Holy of Holies, thus Jesus in his "flesh" (Col. 1:22) and through his sacrificial offering on the cross has become the mediator of the new covenant (9:15), the means whereby all may draw near to the presence of God. See N. A. Dahl, "A New and Living Way: The Approach to God according to Heb. 10:19–25," *Interp* 5 (1951), pp. 401–12; N. H. Young *"Tout' estin tēs sarkos autou* (Heb. 10:20): Apposition, Dependent or Explicative?" *NTS* 20 (1973), pp. 100–104. **Great priest** is used often for "high priest" in the LXX (cf. Num. 35:25, 28; Zech. 3:1; 6:11).

10:22 / The expression **sincere** ("true") **heart** occurs only here in the NT (3:12 describes the opposite kind of heart). The word for "full assurance" (*plērophoria*) occurs elsewhere in Hebrews only in 6:11, where it modifies "hope." The verb for purified ("sprinkled"), *rhantizō*, is used three times earlier in the preceding chapter in a cultic or ritualistic sense (9:13, 19, 21). Here in its only other occurrence in Hebrews it has a symbolic connotation. For a similar spiritual application of the cognate noun "sprinkling," see 1 Pet. 1:2. This is the only reference in the NT to a **guilty** (or "evil") **conscience**. The inward cleansing described in the language of the cultus is paralleled by an outward cleansing that is symbolic of the former. This is the only place in the NT where the literal word for **washed** (*louō*) is given a sacramental meaning. This language, too, although it alludes to Christian baptism, is drawn from the ceremonial cleansing of the levitical rituals (cf. Lev. 16:4). If this language is reminiscent of the ceremony for the ordination of the levitical priests (cf. Lev. 8:30; Exod. 29:4), it may then point to the qualification of the Christian to perform the "priestly" duties of the New Covenant, such as, for example, described in the present passage. The Greek words underlying **purified** and **washed** are perfect participles, describing the resultant state from the past experience of these realities.

10:23 / "Confession" in Hebrews consistently has the objective meaning of what is believed. See note on 3:1. Here the added description "of hope" orients us to the future aspects of our faith, a subject that will come to the fore later in this chapter (vv. 35–39). The word for "without wavering" (*aklinēs*) occurs in the NT only here. The faithfulness of God is a common motif in the NT (see 1 Cor. 1:9; 10:13;

2 Cor. 1:18; 1 Thess. 5:24; 2 Tim. 2:13). Sarah will be shown in 11:11 to be a model believer in the faithfulness of God.

10:24–25 / The word underlying GNB's **to help** (*paroxysmos*) is a sharp word with the nuance of "stirring up" (cf. RSV) or "spurring" (cf. NIV). Its only other occurrence in the NT is with the negative meaning of a sharp disagreement (Acts 15:39). With "good works" contrast the "useless works" of 6:1; 9:14. The Greek word for **meeting together** (*episynagōgē*) occurs elsewhere in the NT only in 2 Thess. 2:1. Some have argued that the prefix to this unusual word is an indication of some sense in which the gathering in view was in addition to the synagogue meetings. This, however, as Hughes points out, is to read too much into the word. See his note on the word, pp. 417–18. The author is a strong advocate of exhortation or encouragement (the Greek verb for **encourage** is *parakaleō*). In 3:13 he tells his readers to encourage or exhort one another every day. He exhorts his readers throughout the book and at the end refers to what he has written as a "message of encouragement" (13:22). The urgency of his request is the result of the approach of **the Day**. For the absolute use of "day" to indicate the arrival of eschatology proper, see 1 Cor. 3:3 (cf. 1 Thess. 5:4). On "day," see G. Braumann and C. Brown, *NIDNTT*, vol. 2, pp. 887–95. The delay of the return of Jesus became an increasingly difficult problem as Christians continued to suffer persecution (cf. vv. 36–39). As F. F. Bruce suggests, the statement about seeing the Day **coming nearer** may possibly reflect knowledge of the increasing predicament of Judea and Jerusalem. With the prophecy of Jesus in mind, the fall of Jerusalem may have been seen to be simply a matter of time (cf. 8:13), and from the perspective of the author and indeed all Christians of that era, the destruction of Jerusalem would have been thought to signal the appearance of the eschaton (cf. Matt. 24:3).

The Sin of Apostasy and the Reality of Judgment

HEBREWS 10:26–31

For there is no longer any sacrifice that will take away sins if we purposely go on sinning after the truth has been made known to us. [27]Instead, all that is left is to wait in fear for the coming Judgment and the fierce fire which will destroy those who oppose God! [28]Anyone who disobeys the Law of Moses is put to death without any mercy when judged guilty from the evidence of two or more witnesses. [29]What, then, of the person who despises the Son of God? who treats as a cheap thing the blood of God's covenant which purified him from sin? who insults the Spirit of grace? Just think how much worse is the punishment he will deserve! [30]For we know who said, "I will take revenge, I will repay"; and who also said, "The Lord will judge his people." [31]It is a terrifying thing to fall into the hands of the living God!

The reference to eschatology at the end of the preceding section leads naturally to the subject of the future judgment, and this is now used as a further motive to faithfulness and the avoidance of apostasy. The concern of this passage is similar to that of 6:4–8 (cf. 3:12).

10:26–27 / GNB reverses the clauses in this sentence, putting the main clause first. The words **if we purposely go on sinning** do not refer to ordinary sins, but to the most grievous and final sin, apostasy. This is the sin which by its nature puts the offender out of reach of God's forgiveness and therefore the sin from which there is no return. Verse 29 underlines the nature and the seriousness of the sin in question. That the sin involves a falling away is further indicated by the words **after the truth has been made known to us** (lit., "after having received the knowledge of the truth"). The parallel in 6:4 is clear: "they were once in God's light . . . they knew from experience that God's word is good, and they had felt the powers of the coming age. And then they abandoned their faith!" But for those who have turned their backs on the sacrifice of Christ—the sacrifice to which all other sacrifices pointed and upon which they depended for their temporary efficacy—then **there is no longer any sacrifice that will take away** (lit., "for") **sins**. One who rejects the sacrifice of Christ (v. 29) will find no other answer to the problem of sin. With resources exhausted (this is the point of the passage, even though GNB's words **all that is left** are added to the original), this person must face the prospect of God's wrath against sin (cf. 2 Pet. 2:21). And, for such a person the only perspective toward the final judgment must be **fear** in anticipation of the **fierce fire** of destruction that will come to **those who oppose God** (lit., "the adversaries"). The last words about fire consuming the adversaries seem to be based on the words of Isaiah 26:11 as found in the LXX.

10:28–29 / To bring his point home with even more forcefulness, the author now turns to a form of argumentation he used in 2:1–3 (and will use again in 12:25) wherein something shown to be true in the era of Mosaic Law is shown to be all the more true in the era of fulfillment brought by Christ. Thus disobedience to **the Law of Moses** was so serious a matter that **without mercy** (GNB adds **any**), on the evidence of **two or more** (lit., "three") **witnesses** (GNB adds **when judged guilty**), an offender was **put to death** (cf. Num. 15:30). But to transgress the Law of Moses, grievous though that may be, is not so serious an offense as to reject the work of Christ, once a person has received it as the truth. The language of verse 29 is very strong, but it is just this that is entailed in apostasy by its nature. **Despises** is literally "treads underfoot." Apostasy means that **the Son of God**—Jesus, the mediator of the new covenant—is counted worthless and treated with contempt. **Cheap thing** is literally "common." Apostasy means that **the blood of** the (GNB adds **God's**) **covenant** is reckoned to be common or unholy—this despite the fact that this blood **purified him from sin** (lit., "by which he was sanctified"). The apostate is one who **insults the Spirit of grace**. Apostasy is the equivalent of the unforgivable sin, the blasphemy of the Holy Spirit (e.g., Matt. 12:31 f.). It is evident, then, that apostasy involves the rejection and hence the mockery of the Son of God, the blood of the covenant, and the Spirit of grace. Obviously this sin must involve a person in even worse **punishment** than that which was applied under the Mosaic Law.

10:30–31 / The reality of judgment upon those who spurn the salvation offered by God is now emphasized by the quotation of two statements from Deuteronomy 32:35–36. The first of these is introduced with the words, **we know who said**. (GNB adds **who also said** before the second quotation). The identity of the speaker is made explicit by our author in the final words, **the living God**. That God will avenge himself against his enemies is, of course, a common theme in the OT and in Judaism. Thus, the second quotation can be found verbatim not only in Deuteronomy 32:36, but also in Psalm 135:14. The first quotation, which does not agree exactly with the LXX text of Deuteronomy 32:35, is, however, quoted in exactly the same form by Paul in Romans 12:19. The thought of the judgment of **the living God** is something that can only fill the heart with fear (cf. v. 27; 12:29; Matt. 10:28). Yet such must be the lot of those who repudiate their original faith.

Additional Notes

10:26–27 / The word for **purposely** (*hekousiōs*) or "willingly" occurs only here and in 1 Pet. 5:2 in the NT. In view is the clearly volitional character of an abandonment of the Christian faith. The verb underlying **sinning** (*hamartanō*) occurs elsewhere in Hebrews only in 3:17, where it also refers to willful rebellion against God. It was argued by some in the early church that the **sinning** referred to here included lesser sins than apostasy, namely, any sin that was done knowingly and thus in defiance of God's will (this in contrast to the sins of "those who are ignorant and make mistakes," 5:2; cf. Num. 15:29–31). In order to avoid such so-called postbaptismal sins, baptism was delayed until the end of one's life. It is obvious from the context, however, that the sinning in the author's mind involves a rejection of the central truths of the Christian faith. Grace and mercy remain available to the Christian who sins (4:16; 7:25). The unavailability of any further sacrifice for sins points thus not to the unavailability of mercy for the Christian who has sinned, but to the fact that the apostate has cut himself off from any possibility of forgiveness. Christ's sacrifice alone is the means of forgiveness. On "sacrifice for sins," see note to 10:5. "Knowledge of the truth" (*epignōsis tēs alētheias*), where the word "knowledge" is found in an intensive form, is an expression found also in the Pastoral Epistles (1 Tim. 2:4; 2 Tim. 2:25; 3:7; Titus 1:1). The position of the word **fear** (*phoberos*) makes it slightly emphatic. The word occurs elsewhere only in v. 31 and in 12:21 (where Moses trembles with fear in God's presence). Hebrews refers to **Judgment** (*krisis*) only here and in 9:27 (the verb form occurs in v. 30 and 13:4). The present passage, including vv. 30–31, reflects the widespread Jewish view concerning the ineluctable reality of apocalyptic judgment. Now, however, the ones who will experience the fury of this judgment are not the enemies of God and Israel generally (as in the language drawn from Isa. 26:11), but those who reject God's Son and the salvation that rests upon his work.

10:28–29 / Underlying the word **disobeys** is not one of the usual words for "disobey," but a word with stronger implications, more parallel with the potential apostasy that is in view in this passage: *atheteō* (lit., "set aside" or "nullify"). This verb occurs in Hebrews only here (but the cognate noun is found in 7:18, where it refers to the setting aside of the Mosaic Law concerning priesthood, and 9:26, where it refers to the removing of sin by the sacrifice of Christ). The reference to "two or three witnesses" deliberately recalls the OT practice as recorded in Deut. 17:6; 19:15 (cf. Matt. 18:16; 2 Cor. 13:1; and 1 Tim. 5:19 for an application of the principle in the early church). The word **punishment** (*timōria*) in v. 29 occurs only here in the NT. The verb for "tread underfoot" is found in Matthew referring to salt that has lost its savor and is cast out as worthless so that "people trample it" (Matt. 5:13), and referring to pearls cast before swine which proceed to "trample them underfoot" (Matt. 7:6). "The blood of the covenant" initially referred to the sealing of the covenant with Israel as, for example, in Exod. 24:8, which is quoted by our author in 9:20. In the argument of Hebrews, however, it is clear that the blood of the covenant refers now to the blood of Christ and the inauguration of the new covenant. See 7:22; 9:15–18; 10:12–18, and the reference in 13:20 to "the blood of the eternal covenant" (RSV). The word for "common" (*koinos*), which occurs only here in Hebrews (but cf. the participial form in 9:13), is a cultic word meaning "unclean" or "unholy" (cf. Mark 7:2; Acts 10:14; 11:8; Rev. 21:27). See Hauck, *TDNT*, vol. 3, pp. 789–97. For the verb "sanctified" (*hagiazō*), see note on 2:11. By **Spirit of grace** is meant the gracious Spirit, the one who is the vehicle of God's grace whereby we become participants in the saving acts of God. Thus, to insult the Spirit is to cut at the very means of experiencing the favor of God. The strong word for **insults** (*enhybrizō*) occurs in the Greek Bible only here. See Bertram, *TDNT*, vol. 8, pp. 305–6.

10:30–31 / The first quoted sentence does not agree exactly with the LXX of Deut. 32:35, which reads: "In the day of vengeance I will repay." But in Rom. 12:19 the quotation is given in a form exactly agreeing with the form here. The quotation also appears in a similar form in certain of the Targums (paraphrastic translations of OT writings into Aramaic; in view here are those known as Onkelos, Pseudo-Jonathan, Palestinian). It was widely known in the form cited here and indeed had probably become a proverbial saying by the first century. Both of these quotations express a common expectation in the OT Scriptures and first century Judaism. Thus, the point need not be argued, but only mentioned (cf. **we know who said**). The "hand" or "hands" of God is a common anthropomorphism used in describing God's activity (cf. 1:10; 2:7). On **terrifying thing** (lit., "fearful"), see note to v. 27. God is referred to as **the living God** in 3:12; 9:14; 12:22. It is a common Hebraic way of referring to God in his dynamic power and is found frequently in the NT. See note on 9:14.

26

An Exhortation to Endurance and Faithfulness

HEBREWS 10:32–39

Remember how it was with you in the past. In those days, after God's light had shone on you, you suffered many things, yet were not defeated by the struggle. [33]You were at times publicly insulted and mistreated, and at other times you were ready to join those who were being treated in this way. [34]You shared the sufferings of prisoners, and when all your belongings were seized, you endured your loss gladly, because you knew that you still possessed something much better, which would last forever. [35]Do not lose your courage, then, because it brings with it a great reward. [36]You need to be patient, in order to receive what he promises. [37]For, as the scripture says,

"Just a little while longer,
and he who is coming will come;
he will not delay.
[38]My righteous people, however,
will believe and live;
but if any of them turns back,
I will not be pleased with him."

[39]We are not people who turn back and are lost. Instead, we have faith and are saved.

O ur author again turns to exhortation. But now he bases his encouragement on the past successes of the readers in the most trying of circumstances. In this description of their history we obtain the letter's most explicit information concerning the addressees. We learn that they endured persecution in the past and came through it victoriously. Now they apparently face difficult times again, to the extent that (as we have previously noted) they are severely tempted to abandon their Christian faith (cf. 2:1–3; 3:12–14; 4:1, 11; 6:4–6; 12:3–11; 13:13). In his exhortation the author reminds the readers of their faithfulness in the past. They should not throw away that former success by yielding to the present pressures. If they endured in the past, they can endure both in the present and in the future, whatever it may hold. Past experience should be motivation for faithfulness in the present. The same faithful God will supply the needed resources—now, as then.

10:32-33 / The readers are reminded of **how it was with you in the past** (lit., "the former days"). The memories of the sufferings now to be mentioned must have been vivid by their very nature, although we have no way of knowing precisely how much earlier these events had taken place. This persecution was more probably that under Claudius in A.D. 49 than that suffered by the Roman community under the mad Nero in A.D. 64. If we are right that Hebrews was written in the early sixties, the events remembered may have occurred more than ten years earlier. This was clearly sometime after the Jewish readers had become believers in Christ, that is, **after God's light had shone on you** (lit., "having been enlightened"; cf. the same expression in 6:4). GNB paraphrases the remainder of the verse so as to put stress upon the victory of the readers: **you suffered many things, yet were not defeated by the struggle** (lit., "you endured a great struggle with sufferings"). What is described generally as a "great struggle" is given some detail in the following verses. They were made a public spectacle of, suffering verbal abuse and physical punishment. Apparently, however, the persecution had not resulted in martyrdom for the faith and thus cannot be the persecution under Nero in A.D. 64 when many were martyred in the Roman church. (The statement of 12:4, although referring to the present situation of the readers, presumably holds true for the past also.) And when the readers did not suffer directly, they shared (GNB adds **you were ready to join**) in the similar sufferings of others. The way in which they were "sharers" (as the text literally reads) is not altogether clear, but it apparently involved the support of others who suffered, at considerable personal sacrifice, as we see from the following verse.

10:34 / **You shared the sufferings of prisoners** (lit., "you suffered with the prisoners") seems to indicate that the readers were not themselves prisoners but nevertheless suffered because of the imprisonment of others. The exhortation of 13:3 reminds the readers of this very responsibility: "Remember those who are in prison, as though you were in prison with them." One aspect of the persecution involved the plundering of their **belongings** (GNB adds the word **all**). This they **endured** . . . **gladly** (lit., "accepted with joy") because they kept in mind that they had **something much better, which would last forever** (lit., "a better and abiding possession"). This reference to the superiority of an unseen, eternal reality will become an important motif in chapter 11 (cf. 11:10, 16, 40). The readers, in the midst of difficult circumstances, were thus able to make an unseen reality their priority and in light of it to endure great personal hardship and loss. Possibly it is the sharing of the sufferings of others referred to in these verses that was in the author's mind when he wrote in 6:10 that God "will not forget the work you did or the love you showed for him in the help you gave and are still giving to your fellow Christians." In 13:3 the author exhorts the readers to continue this identification with those who suffer.

10:35-36 / It is precisely this that the readers are now to remember and to take to heart. The author exhorts them not to **lose** (lit., "throw away") their **courage** or "boldness." This boldness, if it is exercised in the present situation, will enable the readers to endure as they have done in the past. It therefore has a great reward (GNB's **because it brings with it** is lit. "which has"). Above all, what the readers need is "endurance" (translated by GNB **to be patient**). This noun is formed from the same root as the verb "endured" in verse 32. They endured in the past times of hardship; they must endure now. Endurance is **the will of God** and is necessary in order to receive "the promise." The promise is left unspecified here, but it is obviously that eschatological hope of the final realization of God's saving purpose. It is what has been described in verse 34 as "a better and abiding possession" and what will be described in chapters 11 and 12 under different metaphors.

10:37-38 / A quotation from Habakkuk 2:3-4 is now offered without introduction except for the word **for** (GNB adds **as the scripture says**). Its appropriateness is evident. The time of suffering is a limited one and the return of the Lord is imminent. The author may understand Habakkuk's words concerning imminence quite literally, especially if persecution were increasing. The end of the age, it had been promised, would see an increase in the persecution of the righteous (cf. Matt. 24:9-14). But with the Lord's return in view, faithfulness becomes a special consideration. Habakkuk 2:4 is quoted here, but not with the same meaning as when Paul cites it in Romans 1:7 and Galatians 3:11. In these passages the stress is upon how a person becomes righteous, namely, by faith. Thus GNB appropriately translates: "The person who is put right with God through faith shall live." Here, however, the stress is upon the faithfulness of the righteous person (GNB's **my righteous people** is lit. "my righteous one"). **Will believe and live** is literally "will live by faith." That is, righteous people will live faithfully, their lives will be lived in accordance with their faith. These two emphases are complementary rather than contradictory. The possibility of our faith (whereby we are accounted righteous) and our faithfulness (whereby we live according to God's will) are both based upon the faithfulness of God on our behalf. It is clear from the context and from the chapter to follow that our author's stress here is on the necessity of faithfulness. It is this to which he calls his readers, lest they fall away in the midst of tribulation. If the righteous one (GNB adds **if any of them**, to agree with the plural, **people**) should **turn back** (or "shrink back"; cf. RSV), even though under pressure, the Lord will be displeased. The simple point is that God requires faithfulness or endurance of his people. This is the message the readers need desperately to hear and to heed. The displeasure of the Lord is equivalent to his wrath, already alluded to in verses 27–31.

10:39 / A brief one-sentence commentary on the meaning of the passage is now given in midrashic form, utilizing two key words from the quotation. The author here, as in 6:9, encourages the readers by believing not the worst, but the best, concerning them. He furthermore speaks of himself together with them in the plural and emphatic **we**. GNB omits the strong adversative "but" at the beginning of the verse. We are not, says the author tersely, "of those who shrink back [alluding to the word in Habakkuk] unto destruction, but "of faith [using the same word as in Habakkuk] unto the preserving of life." This is his way of encouraging his readers to positive thinking. If they are but true to their identity and take advantage of the resources God has provided, being motivated by the reality and imminence of their hope, they will find strength to endure the present crisis without falling away from the truth. The connection between endurance and the gaining of one's life is referred to in the context of persecution in Luke 21:19, where Jesus says: "Stand firm [lit., "by your endurance"] and you will save yourselves."

Additional Notes

10:32-33 / For "enlightened" (*phōtizō*), see note on 6:4. The word for "struggle" (*athlēsis*) occurs only here in the NT and is used figuratively to refer to the adversity which people must battle. The verb "endured" (*hypomenō*) occurs again in 12:2, 3, and 7 (the cognate noun occurs in 10:36 and 12:1). This word is very important in the author's message to his readers. See Hauck, *TDNT*, vol. 4, pp. 581–88. The noun "suffering" (*pathēma*) is used elsewhere in Hebrews only in referring to Christ's death (2:9, 10). Underlying GNB's **insulted** is the noun "reproaches" (*oneidismos*), which the author uses again in 11:26 and 13:13, where it is explicitly the Christian's bearing of the reproach of Christ. **Mistreated** is lit. "tribulations" (*thlipsis*), which although a common word in the NT occurs in Hebrews only here. GNB's **publicly** derives from *theatrizō*, a verb occurring only here in the NT that means "to make a public show" (NEB). Cf. the cognate noun "spectacle" (*theatron*) in 1 Cor. 4:9, describing the experience of the apostles. **Ready to join** translates the noun "sharers" (*koinonos*), a word occurring in Hebrews only here. For a parallel concept, "sharers in sufferings," see 2 Cor. 1:7, where the idea depends on Paul's doctrine of participation in the body of Christ (1 Cor. 12:4–5, 26).

10:34 / This verse contains two textual uncertainties. In the first, some manuscripts read "bonds" (*desmos*) instead of **prisoners** (*desmios*), some containing "my bonds" or "their bonds." Metzger attributes the loss of the Greek letter iota, producing "bonds," to a transcriptional error. Thus **prisoners** is to be preferred (cf. 13:3). See Metzger, *TCGNT*, p. 670. The second question involves the case of the reflexive pronoun "yourselves." It is probably accusative (*heautous*), thus producing GNB's **you possessed**, rather than dative (*heautois*), which would produce "possessing for yourselves," or "in yourselves." See Metzger, *TCGNT*, p. 670. The verb underlying **shared the sufferings** (*sympatheō*, lit., "suffered with") occurs only here and in 4:15 in the entire NT. For the concept, see the preceding note. The idea of "joy" (*chara*) in the face of personal suffering is reminiscent of James 1:2 and 1 Pet. 4:13 f. (cf. Matt. 5:11). The same word occurs again in 12:2, 11, and 13:17. See Conzelmann, *TDNT*, vol. 9, pp. 359–72. For the importance of **better** (*kreissōn*) in Hebrews, see note on 1:4. Although the language of an "abiding possession" is unique, the concept is very close to the reference in Matt. 6:20 to treasures in heaven which "moths and rust cannot destroy, and robbers cannot break in and steal." The participle "abiding" is used with the same significance in 13:14: "For there is no permanent city for us here on earth" (cf. 12:27, "remain").

10:35–36 / For **courage** or "boldness," see note on 3:6. The word for **reward** (*misthapodosia*) occurs in the NT only in Hebrews: in 11:26 it has a positive sense, as it does here (cf. 11:26 for almost the same word); in 2:2 it occurs in the negative sense of "retribution." Concerning the importance of "endurance" (*hypomonē*), see note on the verbal form of the same word in v. 32. Reference to the readers doing **the will of God** is again made in the great benediction of 13:20–21. The expression "receive the promise" occurs in 11:13 and 39 where it is denied that the partriarchs had already received it. For "promise" (*epangelia*) in Hebrews, see note on 6:15.

10:37–38 / The opening line in the quotation, **just a little while longer**, is not from Habakkuk, but is probably drawn from Isa. 26:20, unless it is a common, stereotyped expression. (Isa. 26:11 may have been alluded to in v. 27. See above.) The author takes some liberties in his citation of Hab. 2:3–4, which follows the LXX rather than the Hebrew. He adds a definite article to turn a participle into a substantive, **he who is coming**. "The coming one" was a title of the Messiah, Jesus, in the early church (cf. Matt. 3:11; 11:3). The author also transposes the clauses of Hab. 2:4 (which in the LXX begins with the words "But if any of them turns back") so that it is the righteous one who must directly confront the possibility of turning back and experiencing the displeasure of the Lord. The author thus accepts the messianic understanding of the passage (as in the LXX) but applies Hab. 2:4 to the Christian believer (despite the singular, "my righteous one"). Hence GNB's translation, **my righteous people**, is justified. This passage was commonly used in Jewish literature to strengthen belief in the realization of the promises to Israel. The Greek word "faith" (*pistis*) can also be translated "faithfulness." Some manuscripts of Hebrews have the pronoun "my" in another place, producing the reading "the righteous one will live by my faithfulness," as it is found in an important manuscript of the LXX(B). Some manuscripts of Hebrews (e.g., P^{13}) omit the pronoun "my" altogether (as does Paul in his use of Hab. 2:4). The better manuscripts of Hebrews, however, favor placement of the "my" with "righteous one" (e.g., P^{46}, Sinaiticus, A). See Metzger, *TCGNT*, pp. 670 f. The verb underlying **turns back** (*hypostellō*; cf. v. 39) may connote doing so "in concealment" (cf. the emphasis in 4:12–13). See Rengstorf, *TDNT*, vol. 7, pp. 597–99; T. W. Lewis, " '. . . And if he shrinks back' (Heb. x. 38b)," *NTS* 22 (1975), pp. 88–94.

10:39 / **Are lost** is derived from *apōleia*, a common NT word for "destruction," which in Hebrews occurs only here. The idea recalls the argument in vv. 27–29. **And are saved** translates lit. "unto the preserving (*peripoiēsis*) of life." The word "life" here is *psychē* (lit., "soul"). This word is used in a similar way in 12:3 and 13:17 (contrast 4:12; 6:19). What is meant here is obviously the opposite of "destruction." Thus the phrase may well connote the realization of new life in the eschaton. See Schweizer, *TDNT*, vol. 9, pp. 637–56.

27

The Nature and Importance
of Faith

To have faith is to be sure of the things we hope for, to be certain of the things we cannot see. ²It was by their faith that people of ancient times won God's approval.

³It is by faith that we understand that the universe was created by God's word, so that what can be seen was made out of what cannot be seen.

The mention of the importance of faith in the last two verses of the preceding chapter leads naturally to this famous chapter on faith. It is impossible to know whether the author is making use of a source, which he now takes over in part or totally, or whether he is composing a fresh catalogue of heroes on the model of existing examples. Extensive reviews of the history of Israel had been composed to substantiate a warning or to provide encouragement, and some of these would have been known to our author. As examples, we may mention Psalm 78; Wisdom of Solomon 10; Sirach 44–50; 1 Maccabees 2:51–64; and Acts 7.

The author's purpose in this magnificent section of his letter is to encourage his readers to emulate these heroes of faith, who on the basis of what they knew about God and his promises had the courage to move out into the unknown, with their hearts set upon, and their lives controlled by, a great unseen reality. The application of the chapters comes to full expression in the following chapter. This list of heroes is meant to provide the readers with strength and encouragement in their own difficult circumstances. According to our author, if there is a key to unlock the gate to effective Christian existence, it is to be found in the reality and the motivating power of faith.

11:1 / In his important opening statement, the author makes it plain that **faith** (GNB adds **to have**) is oriented to things not yet present or visible. Faith has in mind **the things we hope for**, that is, **the things we cannot** see. What then is the nature of faith concerning these things? The answer hinges on the meaning of two key words in this verse. Both words are capable of being interpreted subjectively or objectively. GNB opts for the subjective meaning in both cases, thus focusing on the assurance or inner certainty of faith with respect to things hoped for and not yet seen. Throughout this chapter, however, the emphasis concerning faith is not on the subjective confidence of the persons mentioned, but on the way in which they acted out, or gave expression to, their faith.

The argument is that faith results in conduct that points unmistakably to the reality of what is not yet seen. The first of these two words, which GNB translates **to be sure of**, is a noun that can be understood (as GNB does) in a subjective sense. Many translations choose this interpretation (RSV and NASB: "assurance"; NIV: "being sure"). It is equally possible, however, as well as more natural, to understand the word in an objective sense, as expressing the basis or foundation of things hoped for. Some translations follow this interpretation (KJV: "substance"; NEB: "gives substance"; JB: "guarantee"; cf. Geneva Bible: "Faith is that which causeth those things to appear in deed which are hoped for").

The second key word, which GNB translates **to be certain of**, is a noun that means "a proving" or "a means of proof." Many commentators have interpreted this word as referring to the subjective certainty or "conviction" of faith (cf. 10:22). But here too the objective sense is to be preferred, parallel with the first statement. The action produced by faith is a manifestation or a proving of the reality of things not yet seen. The objective interpretation of these two words is in agreement with one of the major emphases of the entire chapter, that is, that faith is active in obedience. But when faith manifests itself in this way, the unseen and the hoped-for become real. Faith expressed in this way can be said to objectify what is believed. This in turn strengthens faith itself (which is why faith and obedience must accompany each other).

The objective understanding of this verse, of course, presupposes the reality of subjective assurance (itself dependent on the experience of God's goodness) as the wellspring of acts of faith. But it is the expression of faith rather than the conviction of faith that is the author's point in this chapter. The obedient response of faith substantiates what is promised. Effective faith, although directed to future realities, also in a sense makes the future present. Faith that is authentic recognizes the reality of the unseen and allows itself to be governed by that reality. In a similar vein, Paul can write, "for we fix our attention, not on things that are seen, but on things that are unseen. What can be seen lasts only for a time, but what cannot be seen lasts forever" (2 Cor. 4:18). And he adds a little farther on, "for our life is a matter of faith, not sight" (2 Cor. 5:7). What our author provides here is not so much a technical definition of faith as it is a description of what authentic faith does and how God provides evidence in the practice of faith that what he promises will eventually come to pass. The future and unseen realities can be made real by Christians through faith. We may paraphrase this verse in the following words: Faith through its active character gives substance to, that is, expresses the reality of, things hoped for; it provides a demonstration of the truth of things not yet seen.

11:2 / GNB's **it was by their faith** explicates the literal "for by this," as does **people of ancient times** (lit., "the elders"). This last word is a common Jewish term with a variety of uses that here must take its meaning from the following list of heroes. GNB's **won God's approval** is highly interpretive for the simple "were well attested" (cf. NIV: "were commended for"). The same verb occurs in a similar statement in verse 39 that rounds out the list of the heroes of faith. These "men of old" (and some women too) are to be brought forward as specific illustrations beginning in verse 4, so that this verse can serve almost as a title for the remainder of the chapter.

11:3 / But the author begins his great catalogue with a reference to the origin of the created order, for here he finds an illustration of the very principle in faith that involves unseen reality coming to concrete expression. **The universe** (lit., "the ages") was brought into existence **by God's word** (cf. Gen. 1; Ps. 33:6, 9), with the obvious result that what we know and see **was made out of what cannot be seen** (lit., "not from things which appear"). Thus the creation itself involves a model similar to faith. It is the unseen reality that is prior to, and of more lasting importance than, the world we can see. Our understanding of the creation of the universe through the word of God is itself **by faith**. That is, here too we reckon the truth of an unseen reality, despite the account of creation given in Scripture. From the creation we may indeed know of God's power (Rom. 1:20) but not the manner of its creation, that is, that it was created by his word.

Additional Notes

11:1 / The word **faith** (*pistis*) is used more often in Hebrews than in any other NT book, occurring twenty-four times in the present chapter alone. It is clear that

faith in Hebrews involves active obedience rather than a passive belief in the truth of God. (Cf. the close relationship between unbelief and disobedience in 3:18 f.) This obedience obviously also involves trust. Thus the word **faith** in Hebrews approximates "faithfulness" (cf. 10:36–39). See Bultmann, *TDNT*, vol. 6, pp. 205-8. The Greek word underlying **to be sure of** (*hypostasis*) occurs elsewhere in Hebrews in two places. In the first of these (1:3) the word has an objective sense and is translated "being" by GNB: "the exact likeness of God's own being." In its second occurrence (3:14) the word may have a subjective sense and is translated "confidence" by GNB: "the confidence we had at the beginning." Even in this passage, however, an objective sense is possible (as Köster argues). The objective sense is probably to be favored in the present passage because it is more in keeping with the normal meaning of the word and the main thrust of the chapter. A third option, similar to the objective meaning of the word, has been suggested on the basis of the use of the word in contemporaneous secular papyri, where it means "title-deed" or "guarantee" (thus Moulton and Milligan, *The Vocabulary of the Greek Testament* [London: Hodder and Stoughton, 1930]). See G. Harder, *NIDNTT*, vol. 1, pp. 710–14 and Köster, *TDNT*, vol. 8, pp. 585–88. The second key word (*elenchos*), which underlies GNB's **to be certain of**, occurs only here in the NT. Against understanding the word as subjective persuasion, see Büchsel, *TDNT*, vol. 2, p. 476. Behind GNB's **the things we hope for** is the strong Christian word for "hope" (*elpizomenon*), which involves not wishful thinking, but confident expectation (cf. 6:11; 10:23; Rom. 8:24 f.). The reason for the confidence of this hope—and indeed of our faith itself—is the faithfulness of God (cf. 10:22 f.). Faith is explicitly related to what is unseen also by Philo (*On Dreams*, 1.68). What the author here means by the unseen will become clear as the chapter unfolds.

11:2 / The verb for "well attested" (*martyreō*) is used three times to refer to Scripture (7:8, 17; 10:15). In the present chapter it also occurs in the sense of being attested in Scripture, and perhaps also tradition (vv. 4, 5, 39). The word "elders" occurs only here in Hebrews. It lacks the technical meaning it has elsewhere in the NT, here meaning something like "forefathers." The listing of examples from the past illustrating some virtue or ideal is found not only in Jewish literature (see introduction to the present section) but also in Hellenistic, and particularly Stoic, literature.

11:3 / In the Greek text, this is the first of eighteen sentences where the initial word is *pistei* ("by faith"). Thus, the word receives emphasis by its very position in each of these sentences, and the repetition itself has a cumulative impact on the reader. Out of the twenty-four occurrences of the word "faith" in this chapter, this is the only time the author applies it to himself and his readers directly. The word for **understand** (*noeō*) is found only here in Hebrews, but is the same word used by Paul in Rom. 1:20 in a similar context. "The ages" (*aiōn*) is the same expression used in 1:2, but the word for "create" here (*katartizō*) is different from that used in 1:2 (it occurs elsewhere in Hebrews only in 10:5 and 13:21).

Although from 1:2 we know that our author views the Son as God's agency in creation, we do not have this Christology reflected in the reference to creation by the word. Rather than *logos* for "word" (as in John's *logos* Christology, John 1:1–3), here the Greek word is *rhēma*. Our author gives no sign of a knowledge of a *logos* Christology. On the significance of this verse for the doctrine of creation *ex nihilo*, see the excursus in Hughes, pp. 443–52. The new creation brought to pass in the preaching of and response to the gospel is described in the similar language of bringing something into existence out of nothing (cf. 1 Cor. 1:28). The God of creation is the God of the new creation and in the gospel he works a new miracle.

28

The Faith of Abel, Enoch, and Noah

HEBREWS 11:4–7

It was faith that made Abel offer to God a better sacrifice than Cain's. Through his faith he won God's approval as a righteous man, because God himself approved of his gifts. By means of his faith Abel still speaks, even though he is dead. ⁵It was faith that kept Enoch from dying. Instead, he was taken up to God, and nobody could find him, because God had taken him up. The scripture says that before Enoch was taken up, he had pleased God. ⁶No one can please God without faith, for whoever comes to God must have faith that God exists and rewards those who seek him. ⁷It was faith that made Noah hear God's warnings about things in the future that he could not see. He obeyed God and built a boat in which he and his family were saved. As a result, the world was condemned, and Noah received from God the righteousness that comes by faith.

Our author's catalogue of heroes of faith begins with three examples drawn from the early chapters of Genesis, from the time before the flood. These examples, like those that follow, are meant to inspire the readers to exhibit the same kind of faith (cf. 6:12). Common to all of them, and therefore to the whole chapter, is the fact that these heroes are motivated by the unseen reality of God and his purposes. Their faith finds expression in their obedient faithfulness.

11:4 / Throughout the chapter, as here, GNB translates the simple "by faith" with the phrase **it was faith that made.** Although the details of the Genesis account (Gen. 4:2–16) are far from clear, Abel's offering was for some reason acceptable to God whereas Cain's was not. We do not need to know the details, however, to accept our author's argument that **faith**— that is, unreserved commitment to the reality of God and the absolute character of his claims upon us—was the decisive difference. Cain in some way held back from God, whether in the offering itself or in his heart; Abel held nothing back, but acted in a way consistent with his inner conviction. It was this that made Abel's sacrifice **better** (this word is a general term of comparison that can mean "more adequate," "more acceptable"). GNB spells out **his faith** (for the literal pronoun "which") in the next two sentences in this verse. **Won God's approval**, as in verse 2, is literally "was well attested," referring to the account in Genesis, as is clear in the deliberate allusion to the words of the LXX of Genesis 4:4, **God himself approved of his gifts**. By his faith, and the action springing from it, Abel was thus attested as **a righteous man** (cf. v. 7). The first murder produced the first martyr, and Abel's innocent blood was not forgotten (12:24; Matt. 23:35; cf. Gen. 4:10). Having died for his faithfulness, Abel continues to speak the message of faith.

11:5 / If in Abel faith speaks through a dead man, in Enoch it speaks through one who never died. GNB rearranges the sentence structure, adding the word **instead**. GNB's threefold **taken up** of this verse is literally "translated," that is, conveyed from one realm to another. Genesis has very little to say about Enoch. Twice in the Hebrew text it is recorded that he "walked with God" (Gen. 5:22 and 24), which in the LXX is translated as "he pleased God." This expression, **pleased God**, is used by the author here and in the following verse. The words **nobody could find him** (lit., "he could not be found") **because God had taken him up** are a quotation from the LXX of Genesis 5:24. This reference to the translation of Enoch directly from this world to the next, made him, like Elijah, a very special figure in Jewish eschatology, where he was expected to appear again as one of God's special envoys. GNB adds **the Scripture says** to indicate that the words **he had pleased God** are drawn from Genesis 5. The important thing for our author is not the miraculous translation of Enoch but rather this statement about Enoch having pleased God (contrast 10:38: "I will not be pleased with him"). For this indeed is what it means to walk in faith (as the next verse argues). Thus without providing any detailed information, our author seizes upon the idea of "pleasing God" as indicative of the reality of faith. If we may say nothing else about Enoch, we can assert that his life was controlled by the unseen reality of God. The general application is made in the following verse.

11:6 / The author is now addressing his readers as much as he is commenting on the significance of Enoch. GNB's **no one can** is literally "it is impossible to." Enoch could live a life that pleased God only by his acceptance of the reality of God (**that God exists**, lit., "that he is"; cf. Exod. 3:14) and the conviction that God would reward him (lit., "that God is a rewarder"). But this orientation involves faith, since it involves what is not directly apparent to the senses (cf. v. 27, "as though he saw the invisible God"). The appeal to the readers is left implicit but is nonetheless real. Faith in this sense is fundamental to all religious experience (cf. Rom 10:14).

11:7 / In this third example of faith, Noah (Gen. 6:9–22) acts upon divinely revealed warnings **about things in the future that he could not see** (lit., "things not yet seen"). The author thus returns explicitly to the orientation of faith toward the unseen and the future (cf. v. 1). This is a dominant motif in the chapter (see note). In this specific instance, and in contrast to all the others in this chapter, the unseen and future involve the threat of imminent judgment rather than eschatological blessing. GNB's **he obeyed God** is literally "having reverent regard for [the divinely revealed warnings or commandments]." Noah accordingly prepared an ark in obedience to God, and to the ridicule of those around him, for (lit.) "the salvation of his house." For GNB's **as a result** the original has "through which" (i.e., faith). The faith of Noah served to highlight the unbelief of the world and thus to demonstrate the propriety of its condemnation. Noah in turn **received from God** (lit., "became an heir of") **the righteousness that comes by** (lit., "according to") **faith**. The language is at first glance the language of Paul (cf. Rom. 3:22, 24; 4:13). But in context it cannot be read in a Pauline way. The point is that Noah's faith expressed itself in action (cf. Gen. 6:9, 22; 7:1). Our author is not arguing the doctrine of salvation against the legalism of Judaizers but describing how righteousness is fundamentally a matter of faith in the unseen, leading to appropriate action. The key is not in the "believing" alone, as it is in Paul, but in faith as the cause of proper conduct. This for our author is the tradition of righteousness in which Noah became enrolled (cf. 10:38).

Additional Notes

11:4 / Two textual variants in this verse should be noted. First, P[13] and Clement of Alexandria omit the words **to God** (GNB's opening sentence). Although stylistic reasons argue for their omission, the textual evidence in favor of the words is nearly overwhelming, and thus they are to be retained. The second variant amounts to a harmonizing with the dative case of the words just mentioned, and the text would accordingly read "being well attested by his gifts to God." This would leave the participle unaccounted for grammatically, however, and thus despite some weighty textual support, the reading is to be rejected. On both of these variants, see Metzger, *TCGNT*, pp. 671 f. The greater acceptability of Abel's offering was more probably due to his inner responsiveness than to the offering itself. It is probably wrong to stress the quantitative aspect (as does Westcott) of the Greek word underlying GNB's **better** (*polys*), as though it were the size of the offering alone that mattered. Similarly it is probably incorrect to emphasize that Abel's sacrifice was of animals, whereas Cain's offering was of the fruits of the earth, and to find great significance in Abel's sacrifice as indicating a conscious sin offering or an early theory of atonement by blood. There is no hint of this in the text. Even the LXX is probably not to be followed when, departing from the Hebrew text, it attributes the unacceptability of Cain's offering to a ritual mistake: "not rightly dividing it" (Gen. 4:7, LXX). For the verb "be well attested" (*martyreō*), see note on v. 2 above. The word for **a righteous man** (*dikaios*) is the same word used in 10:38. It occurs again in Hebrews only in 12:23.

11:5 / The verb "translated" (*metatithēmi*), which occurs twice in this verse, derives from the LXX quotation (Gen. 5:24). It occurs in only one other place in Hebrews, 7:12, where GNB translates "changed" (referring to the priesthood). The cognate noun "translation" (*metathesis*) that occurs in this verse (lit., "before the translation") occurs also in 7:12 ("a change") and 12:27. The verb **pleased** (*euaresteō*), here and in the next verse, is drawn from the same LXX quotation. It occurs only once again in Hebrews (13:16). For later intertestamental references to Enoch, after whom a corpus of literature was named, see Wisdom of Solomon 4:10; Sirach 44:16; 49:14; Jubilees 10:17; and 1 Enoch 71:14 (these are writings originating in the intertestamental period and later, known collectively as apocrypha and pseudepigrapha).

11:6 / The concept of "pleasing" God is taken up from the LXX and applied generally to righteous living in the Christian church. Our author can use this language in a similar way (see 12:28; 13:16, 21; cf. Rom. 12:1 f.; 14:18; Phil. 4:18; Col. 3:20). **Comes to God** (*proserchomai*) is not used here in the technical way that it is elsewhere in the book (see note on 4:16). As important as the noun **faith** (*pistis*) is in this chapter, the cognate verb "have faith" (*pisteuō*) occurs only here. Its only other occurrence in Hebrews is in 4:3. The noun "rewarder" (*misthapodotēs*) occurs only here in the NT, but the related noun "reward" (*misthapodosia*) is found in 2:2; 10:35; and 11:26 (but only in Hebrews).

11:7 / The word underlying **God's warnings** (*chrēmatizō*) is a technical term for the reception of divine oracles. It occurs in Hebrews also in 8:5 and 12:25. Behind **he obeyed** is the Greek verb *eulabeomai*, which occurs only here in the NT. One meaning of the word is "to be afraid" or "concerned," but here it may well mean "to have reverent regard for." See *BAGD*, p. 322. The expression "heir of righteousness" (which occurs nowhere else in the NT) is reminiscent of "heirs of the promise" (6:17). The word "heir" (*klēronomos*) is found again in 1:2. When Paul refers to **the righteousness that comes by faith**, he uses *ek pisteōs* (e.g., Rom. 9:30; 10:6), and never *kata pistin* as in our text.

The reality of the unseen is a controlling theme in the present chapter, as may be seen from the following list:

v. 1—things hoped for, but not yet seen
    3—creation from what cannot be seen
    6—that God exists and rewards
    7—events yet unseen
    8—an unknown country
  10—the city with permanent foundations (cf. 13:14)
  13—from a long way off they saw (the things God promised)
  14—looking for a country
  16—the heavenly country
  26—kept his eyes on the future reward
  27—as though he saw the invisible God

Even beyond these explicit references, it is assumed that the heroes of faith act as they do because of their full conviction concerning the reality of God and his promises. The result is that from the world's perspective their conduct looks rash and unjustifiable.

29

The Faith of Abraham and Sarah

HEBREWS 11:8-12

It was faith that made Abraham obey when God called him to go out to a country which God had promised to give him. He left his own country without knowing where he was going. ⁹By faith he lived as a foreigner in the country that God had promised him. He lived in tents, as did Isaac and Jacob, who received the same promise from God. ¹⁰For Abraham was waiting for the city which God has designed and built, the city with permanent foundations.

¹¹It was faith that made Abraham able to become a father, even though he was too old and Sarah herself could not have children. He⁸ trusted God to keep his promise. ¹²Though Abraham was practically dead, from this one man came as many descendants as there are stars in the sky, as many as the numberless grains of sand on the seashore.

It was faith . . . children. He; *some manuscripts have* It was faith that made Sarah herself able to conceive, even though she was too old to have children. She.

I n the OT Abraham is the man of faith par excellence. According to Genesis 15:6, "Abram put his trust in the Lord, and because of this the Lord was pleased with him and accepted him." Paul can describe Abraham as "the spiritual father of all who believe in God" (Rom. 4:11; cf. Gal. 3:9). Our author understandably gives more space to him than to any other of the examples he brings forward. Three major episodes from Abraham's life come into view: the departure to the holy land, the later fulfillment of the promise of descendants, and, in verses 17–19, the sacrifice of Isaac. In all of these, faith is wonderfully illustrated. It was faith that enabled Abraham to overcome obstacles that from a human perspective were insurmountable. Our author's "by faith" formula is applied to Abraham four times: verses 8, 9, 11 (possibly referring to Sarah), and 17.

11:8 / In this first example (drawn from Gen. 12:1, 4) the essence of faith is beautifully and simply expressed. Abraham is called by God to go to a **country** (lit., "a place") **which God had promised to give him** (lit., "which he was about to receive as an inheritance"). Abraham obeyed and departed (GNB adds **his own country**), although he did not know **where he was going**. Abraham leaves the known and the familiar to be led wherever God leads him. He acts on the basis of God's promise alone, heading toward the unseen and unknown (cf. the definition of faith in v. 1). Abraham is thus controlled by God and his promise. This is exactly what faith entails and what our author wants his readers to emulate (cf. 13:13).

11:9 / In this one place GNB translates **by faith** literally. Despite the fact that he came to **the country that God had promised him** (lit., "the promised land"), he did not settle there as though that were his final goal. Indeed, he continued to live as a pilgrim in this world, **a foreigner** (Gen. 23:4) even in the land of promise, a dweller in **tents** (e.g., Gen. 12:8; 13:3; 18:1), rather than more permanent structures. And in this he was followed by his son and grandson (to be mentioned again in vv. 20–21), Isaac and Jacob, who were literally "fellow-heirs of the same promise" (cf. 6:17).

11:10 / The reason for this attitude of Abraham, so strange by the world's standards, is now made clear. He knew that what God ultimately had in store for his people transcended security and prosperity in a parcel of real estate on the eastern shore of the Mediterranean. The author now uses the metaphor of a city—no doubt with the eschatological image of the heavenly Jerusalem in mind (cf. v. 16; 12:22; 13:14; Rev. 21:2). Alternatively, he can speak of a heavenly country as its equivalent (v. 16). The city looked for by Abraham is described as one with **foundations** (GNB adds **permanent**)—that is, one that is stable and lasting—a city whose designer and builder is God himself. Our final goal, our eschatological hope, is not the accomplishment of human technology but is God's creation. Such is its reality, though yet to come and hence unseen, that our conduct in the present should be motivated by it. This point will receive elaboration in verses 13–16.

11-12 / The second example of Abraham's faith (drawn from Gen. 17:15–21; 18:9–15; and 21:1–7) involves the fulfillment of God's promise of descendants. Abraham put his trust in God's faithfulness. **He trusted God to keep his promise** is literally "since he counted as faithful the one who promised." This trust enabled Abraham and Sarah to accomplish the humanly unthinkable (cf. Abraham's response, Gen. 17:19; and Sarah's in 18:12 and 21:7). Thus despite his (and Sarah's) age and Sarah's (and his) barrenness, Abraham was **able to become a father** (lit., "received power to beget"). The result of faith in this instance was that **from this one man**, who was "worn out," "impotent," or "as good as dead," as the participle can be construed, came forth an abundance of offspring. This abundance, now seen as fulfillment, is deliberately described in the language of the covenantal promises to Abraham recorded in Genesis (see Gen. 15:5; 22:17; 32:12). God was faithful to his promise, and it was by their faith that Abraham and Sarah experienced God's faithfulness. Our author's argument here is very similar to Paul's in Romans 4:16 ff. There Paul refers to God as the one "who brings the dead to life and whose command brings into being what did not exist" (Rom. 4:17). He describes Abraham's body as "already practically dead" (4:19), using the same word as the author of Hebrews, and he describes Abraham's attitude in these words: "He was absolutely sure that God would be able to do what he had promised" (4:21).

Additional Notes

11:8 / Abraham is frequently celebrated as a hero of faith in Jewish literature. Thus, material generally parallel to the emphasis of the present passage may be found, e.g., in Sirach 44:19-21; Wisdom of Solomon 10:5; and Philo, *On Abraham* and *The Migration of Abraham*. Our author puts together faith and obedience in a way similar to James 2:14-26. Abraham not only has faith, but he acts congruently with that faith: he obeys God. The word used for **go out** (*exerchomai*) is the same verb used in the LXX of Gen. 12:1. The word "inheritance" occurs only here and in 9:15 in Hebrews. As it is used here, "inheritance" (*klēronomia*) refers to the land promised to Abraham (of which Isaac and Jacob are said to be "fellow-heirs" in v. 9). This is indeed the common use of the word, but our author can use it in a fuller sense, as in 9:15. See Foerster, *TDNT*, vol. 3, pp. 776-85.

11:9 / In the speech of Stephen in Acts 7 the same point is made. When Abraham went out to the land, "God did not then give Abraham any part of it as his own, not even a square foot of ground" (Acts 7:5). The verb underlying **lived as a foreigner** (*paroikeō*, "sojourn") is used frequently in reference to Abraham in the LXX, e.g., Gen. 12:10; 17:8; 19:9; 20:1; 26:3 (cf. the cognate noun "sojourner," *paroikos*, in Gen. 23:4). Abraham, however, is nowhere described in the LXX with the word "foreigner" (*allotrios*) as our author describes him. Two similar words are used in v. 13, "foreigners and refugees on earth." The Genesis narrative indicates several times that Abraham dwelt in a tent (e.g., Gen. 12:8; 13:3; 18:1 ff.).

11:10 / The metaphor of "a city" (*polis*) to come has Jewish antecedents and derives from the importance of Jerusalem. Philo uses the metaphor in describing the promise to Abraham (*Allegorical Interpretation* 3.83). Paul draws on this tradition when he refers to "the heavenly Jerusalem" in Gal. 4:26, and it is found in the Apocalypse in the reference to "Jerusalem, the Holy City, coming down out of heaven from God" (Rev. 21:10). The early Christian writer Hermas utilizes the image of the city in a way similar to, and perhaps dependent upon, Hebrews (*Sheperd*, Similitude I.1). The metaphor is used again by our author in v. 16 and 12:22 (cf. 13:14). It is the eschatological reality that awaits the people of God. This reality controlled Abraham (although of course he would not have been familiar with this later metaphor employed by our author). See Strathmann, *TDNT*, vol. 6, pp. 529–33. The reference to the **foundations** of the city may well be derived from Ps. 87:1 (cf. RSV). See too Rev. 21:14, 19 f. GNB's **designed and built** translates two rare nouns in the NT. The first of these, *technitēs* ("craftsman," "designer"), is found elsewhere in the NT only in Acts 17:29; 18:3; and Rev. 18:22; the second, *demiourgos* ("maker," "creator"), occurs only here in the NT. Philo uses both words (or their cognates) in describing God (e.g., *Who Is the Heir*, 133). In the *Epistle to Diognetus* the same two words are used to describe Jesus as the agent of creation (7:2), but this is perhaps by influence from Hebrews. The argument that God's people find their true home elsewhere than in the present world (cf. vv. 13–16) is found in several other places in the NT (e.g., Phil. 3:20: "We, however, are citizens of heaven, and we eagerly wait for our Savior, the Lord Jesus Christ, to come from heaven"; cf. 1 Pet. 1:1, 17; 2:11). An argument similar to that of the present passage is found in Hebrews 3:7–4:11, where entrance into the land of Canaan was found not to provide the rest that God had promised.

11:11-12 / A serious textual problem exists at the beginning of v. 11, which revolves around the subject of the verse: Is it Abraham or Sarah? GNB (with NIV; against RSV, NEB, and NASB) concludes, probably rightly, that Abraham is the subject. The strongest reason in favor of this conclusion is the fact that the language of v. 11, "received power to beget" is regularly used for the male and never for the female. The question then becomes how to construe the words "Sarah herself barren," or, as some MSS read, "Sarah herself." It is not necessary to take the words as an early gloss inserted into the text. The words can be explained as datives (which in the earliest MSS would have been indistinguishable from nominatives) and understood as referring to accompaniment, i.e., "with (barren) Sarah herself" (thus, among others, Michel and Bruce). They may also, however, be understood as nominatives and taken as a Hebraic circumstantial clause, "even though Sarah was barren" (thus Metzger [*TCGNT*] and the UBS committee). These natural possibilities, together with the normal meaning of the verb, make is unnecessary to argue in favor of Sarah as the subject. Further benefits from these solutions (keeping Abraham as the subject) are that they make it unnecessary to accept an unannounced shift in the subject (back to Abraham) in v. 12 and obviate the problem in the Genesis account that Sarah lacks faith (see especially Gen. 18:12–15).

Hughes's interesting suggestion that Sarah be understood as the subject and that the verb be taken as "establishing a posterity" seems strained and less satisfactory than the solutions suggested above. See Metzger, *TCGNT*, pp. 672 f. On the technical term "beget" ("to lay down seed"), see BAGD, p. 409. What was reckoned as true by Abraham—that the one who promised was faithful—is expressed by our author in exactly the same words in his exhortation to the readers in 10:23. (See note on that passage.) The participle lying behing GNB's **practically dead** (*nekroō*) occurs in exactly the same sense in Rom. 4:19 (the only other NT occurrence of the verb is in Col. 3:5, where, however, it has a different sense). The OT phrases about the abundance of **stars in the sky** and **grains of sand on the seashore** had, because of their occurrence in the Genesis passages, become very familiar metaphors for God's faithful blessing of Abraham.

30

The Transcendent Nature
of Hope

HEBREWS 11:13–16

It was in faith that all these persons died. They did not receive the things God had promised, but from a long way off they saw them and welcomed them, and admitted openly that they were foreigners and refugees on earth. ¹⁴Those who say such things make it clear that they are looking for a country of their own. ¹⁵They did not keep thinking about the country they had left; if they had, they would have had the chance to return. ¹⁶Instead, it was a better country they longed for, the heavenly country. And so God is not ashamed for them to call him their God, because he has prepared a city for them.

Our author interrupts his seriatim listing of heroes and their specific triumphs of faith in order to elaborate the material of verses 8–10. The perspective set forth here, wherein one lives in this world as an alien, is of the essence of faith as it is first described in verse 1. The things hoped for, although not yet seen, control the life of the person of faith. The OT saints looked for the reality God had promised. It was an eschatological reality, "a heavenly country," "a city" prepared by God. The implications for the author's Jewish readers and their present situation are clear. Indeed, it is just this kind of faith that views life as a pilgrimage that the author desires for his readers.

11:13–14 / The heroes of faith mentioned thus far, like those about to be mentioned (cf. v. 39), died without receiving **the things God had promised** (lit., "the promises"). They died **in faith**, that is, having lived their lives under the controlling influence of a reality yet distant and unexperienced, they faced death in that same spirit. Their believing response to what lay in the future is described by the author in the picturesque language of their having seen it **from a long way off** and having **welcomed** it (John 8:56). It was their orientation toward the promises that enabled them to regard their present status as only temporary and to describe themselves as **foreigners and refugees on earth** (Gen. 23:4; 47:9; 1 Chron. 29:15; Ps. 39:12). Their true home accordingly lay elsewhere, and thus they sought for themselves **a country of their own** (lit., "fatherland," "homeland"). Although the author does not use the language of shadow and reality here (as in 8:5 and 9:23 f.), he could easily have done so. The promises and the experience of temporal, earthly blessings were for these persons only the shadow or copy of the transcendent eschatological reality to come.

11:15-16 / Abraham and his family could, of course, have returned to Mesopotamia if they had continued to regard that land as their true home. But this was not what was in their thoughts or what motivated their lifestyle. Nor should it be in the minds of the readers (see 10:39). It was not their absence from Mesopotamia that caused Abraham and his family to refer to themselves as strangers and exiles. What they looked for was a **better**, a **heavenly** place (the word **country** does not actually occur in these verses; GNB carries it forward from v. 14). The author again refers to a **city** that God **has prepared** for them (cf. v. 10). This is an eschatological expectation, not a temporal one. The point of the words **God is not ashamed for them to call him their God** (cf. Exod. 3:6) is simply that God is faithful to his promises. Their expectation may thus be referred to as an already existing reality. Indeed, it is already being experienced by the church (12:22), as well as something yet to come in all its fullness (Rev. 21:2).

Additional Notes

11:13-14 / Here the opening word in the Greek is not *pistei*, "by faith," as it is regularly in this chapter, but *kata pistin*, lit., "in accordance with faith." No important difference is meant by this change, which is probably due to the following verb, "they died." It is not "by faith" because faith does not explain their dying. It is rather **in faith** or "in accordance with faith" that they died, i.e., with their hearts set upon the goal that God promised them. It is clear according to this verse (13) that Abraham did not experience God's promises in their deepest sense. Earlier (6:15) our author indicated that Abraham did receive a kind of initial fulfillment of the promises. But that initial fulfillment was far short of the true intent of the promises. By identifying the expectation of Abraham with that of the church (cf. vv. 39–40), our author again underlines the unity of salvation history. The verb underlying **receive** (*komizō*) occurs elsewhere in Hebrews in 10:36 and 39 together with the noun "promise" (cf. also 11:19). The Greek for **from a long way off** (*porrōthen*) occurs only here and in Luke 17:12 in the NT. **Welcomed** (*aspazomai*), which may also be translated "greeted," occurs again in its normal sense twice in 13:24. **Admitted openly** is from *homologeō*, a verb that occurs again in 13:15 ("confess"). The word **refugees** (*parepidēmos*) is used in a similar way in 1 Peter (1:1, 2:11) to describe the life of the Christian in this world. 1 Peter 2:11 links this word with *paroikoi*, "aliens," instead of *xenoi*, **foreigners**. (Our author uses the cognate verb *paroikeō*, "lived as a foreigner," in v. 9.) **Looking for** reflects the strong verb *epizēteō*, "seek," which occurs in exactly the same sense in the exhortation of 13:14. The word "fatherland" occurs only here in Hebrews (cf. Luke 4:24).

11:15-16 / The patriarchs were faithful in their expectancy. Therefore they did not desire to return to Mesopotamia. This stands in sharp contrast to the generation that wandered in the wilderness and failed to enter God's rest (4:6), but who instead desired to return to Egypt. **Long for** translates *oregomai*, a rare word in the NT (occurring elsewhere in the NT only in 1 Tim. 3:1; 6:10). **Better**, a key word in Hebrews, is most often used to contrast the old covenant with the superior new covenant (see note on 1:4). For **heavenly** (*epouranios*), see note on 3:1. What is in view is that transcendent and perfect reality that awaits the saints of God (cf. 1 Cor. 2:9; Rom. 8:18). When Jesus quotes Exod. 3:6, "I am the God of Abraham, and the God of Isaac, and the God of Jacob" (Matt. 22:32), he adds that "He is not God of the dead, but of the living." This suggests, in a way similar to the present passage, that the patriarchs will through the resurrection inherit the transcendent promises that God had spoken to them. God's purpose "was that only in company with us would they be made perfect" (v. 40). The **city** that God has prepared has already been referred to in v. 10. See note on that verse.

31

Abraham's Offering of Isaac and the Faith of Isaac, Jacob, and Joseph

It was faith that made Abraham offer his son Isaac as a sacrifice when God put Abraham to the test. Abraham was the one to whom God had made the promise, yet he was ready to offer his only son as a sacrifice. [18]God had said to him, "It is through Isaac that you will have the descendants I promised." [19]Abraham reckoned that God was able to raise Isaac from death—and, so to speak, Abraham did receive Isaac back from death.

[20]It was faith that made Isaac promise blessings for the future to Jacob and Esau.

[21]It was faith that made Jacob bless each of the sons of Joseph just before he died. He leaned on the top of his walking stick and worshiped God.

[22]It was faith that made Joseph, when he was about to die, speak of the departure of the Israelites from Egypt, and leave instructions about what should be done with his body.

The third and perhaps the most remarkable example of Abraham's faith is now set forth: the offering of Isaac. To this are added brief references to Isaac, Jacob, and Joseph. The faith of all these men is seen in their confident orientation to the future and the unseen (cf. v. 1).

11:17-18 / The story of the testing of Abraham's faith related here is drawn from Genesis 22:1–14 and became very important in Jewish tradition under the title "The Binding of Isaac." Although Abraham had bound Isaac and, in obedience to God, was about to slay him as a sacrifice, God intervened at the last instant. Thus it is legitimate to translate, as GNB does, **he was ready to offer** (lit., "he offered"). **When God put Abraham to the test** is an expansive translation for the simple "being tested." As our author points out, the testing took on an unusual significance since Abraham **was the one to whom God had made the promise** (lit., "who had received the promises"). This is emphasized by the quotation in verse 18 that explicitly names Isaac as the one through whom the promise of descendants would be realized. This quotation is drawn from Genesis 21:12 and may be literally translated as "In Isaac shall your seed be named." Abraham endured a most severe form of testing but through it demonstrated his faith, that is, his absolute, unshakable confidence in the reliability of God's promises.

11:19 / From Abraham's point of view, God's power was such that if necessary the sacrificed Isaac could be raised by God **from death** (lit., "from the dead"). The next clause is difficult to interpret exactly. It reads literally "from whence he received him in a parable." This may mean no more than that since Isaac was as good as dead at the point of being sacrificed, it is "as though" (**so to speak**) he had been raised from the dead. There may, however, be a deliberate allusion here to Isaac as an anticipation of the resurrection of Christ. For, like Abraham, God sacrificed his only son, whom he has now received again from the dead through the resurrection. Thus the binding of Isaac may foreshadow not only the sacrifice of Christ but also his resurrection.

11:20 / By faith Isaac was able to **promise blessings for the future to Jacob and Esau** (lit., "concerning things to come blessed Jacob and Esau"). Isaac, who received the same covenant as Abraham, spoke confidently of the future (Gen. 27:28 f., 39 f.) because he trusted God's promises. He therefore stands with his father in the lineage of faith.

11:21 / In a similar way, the dying Jacob blessed the sons of Joseph. The reference to the blessing of the two sons of Joseph, rather than to the blessing of his own twelve sons (Gen. 49), is probably by the prompting of the preceding reference to Isaac's blessing of Jacob and Esau. Jacob, however, unlike Isaac, deliberately sought to bless the younger of the two, Ephraim (Gen. 48:15 ff.). The last sentence in this verse is taken practically verbatim from the LXX of Genesis 47:31 (**walking stick** is lit. "staff"). It is difficult to know why the author includes this sentence. Perhaps he regards Jacob's attitude of worship as particularly appropriate to his faith.

11:22 / As in the two preceding examples we again are presented with a glimpse of a hero of faith who is close to his death (lit., "dying"). Thus these examples illustrate vividly the statement in verse 13 about dying "in faith." Because of his faith in the faithfulness of God, Joseph had knowledge of the future and was able to speak of (lit.) "the exodus of the sons of Israel" and give directions (lit.) "concerning his bones" (see Gen. 50:24 f.), which like Jacob's, were to be brought to the promised land.

Additional Notes

11:17–18 / The author's language in v. 17 is close to the language of Gen. 22. "The binding of Isaac" is referred to in some Jewish liturgies for the New Year. For allusions to this story, see too, Sir. 44:20; Wisd. of Sol. 10:5; 4 Macc. 16:20 (cf. 13:12). The reference to **only son**, language that does not occur in the Genesis narrative, may reflect indirect influence of the Christology of the early church, in which of course the title was very important. Paul may build upon Gen. 22 in Rom. 8:32, and some have thought that John 8:56 may have this story in mind (cf. John 3:16). The word for **only son** (*monogenēs*) does not occur in the Genesis narrative according to the LXX. There (Gen. 22:2) Isaac is referred to as "beloved (*agapētos*) son," a closely related word and an apparently alternative translation of the same Hebrew word. The use of the expression "only son" in reference to Christ occurs only in the Johannine literature of the NT. (For "beloved son," see Mark 1:11; 9:7; 12:6, and parallels.) Isaac, of course, was not Abraham's only son—but he was the only son of Sarah and the only son of the so-called line of promise as the next verse unequivocally points out. James (2:21 f.) also refers to Abraham's offering of Isaac as an example of one whose "faith was made perfect through his actions." For Isaac as a type of Christ in early Christian literature (e.g., Barnabas 7:3), see references in Hughes, pp. 485 f. The Greek verb **ready to offer** (*prospherō*) can also be described as an inceptive imperfect tense, "he began to offer," without completing the deed. "The promises" again connotes not simply those of a temporal quality, but more particularly the transcendent expectations they foreshadowed. See note on 4:1. On the importance of the present passage for the author's perspective, see J. Swetnam, *Jesus and Isaac: A Study of the Epistle to the Hebrews in the Light of the Aqedah* (Rome: Biblical Institute Press, 1981).

11:19 / **Reckoned** (*logizomai*) means to "count as true." It occurs here in Hebrews, but is used frequently in connection with Abraham in Rom. 4. Resurrection is not an important idea in Hebrews (the resurrection of Christ is explicitly referred to only in 13:20). The ascension of Christ, which of course presupposes his resurrection, plays the most important part (see note on 1:13 and the importance of Ps. 110:1 in the book). The word "parable" (*parabolē*) was used earlier by the author in 9:9 (where GNB translates: "this is a symbol"). It is possible that when the author writes "from whence [the dead] he received him," he is thinking of the generation of Isaac from one who was "practically dead" (v. 12; so Westcott). Abraham's faith may then be interpreted to mean that God has the power to raise up another son like Isaac from Sarah. Yet in the Genesis narrative Abraham seems to believe that it is Isaac who will somehow be spared (Gen. 22:5, 8). Thus, it is more likely that Abraham believed in the power of God to raise Isaac from the dead if need be. And so, symbolically (**so to speak**), he did receive Isaac back from the dead, whereby Isaac foreshadows the resurrection of Christ. Paul's words about the power of the God in whom Abraham believed are pertinent: "the God who brings the dead to life and whose command brings into being what does not exist" (Rom. 4:17).

11:20 / The verb underlying "things to come" (*mellō*) is used frequently in Hebrews to indicate the eschatological hope of the faithful (see 1:14; 2:5; 6:5; 10:1; 13:14). "Blessed" (*eulogeō*) in this context refers to the important Hebrew custom of passing the promise, and the privileged position that goes with it (cf. 6:14), from one generation to another. Thus a father who is nearing death blesses his son or grandson (as Abraham blessed Isaac, Gen. 25:11; Isaac blessed Jacob, Gen. 27:27 ff.; and Jacob blessed Joseph, Gen. 48:15, and Ephraim and Manasseh, Gen. 48:20). See Beyer, *TDNT*, vol. 2, pp. 754–65.

11:21 / On the word "blessed," see preceding note. Although the LXX has Jacob leaning upon his staff, the Hebrew of Gen. 47:31 says he "bowed himself upon the head of the bed" (RSV). The words for "bed" and "staff" consist of the same three consonants (*mth*) vocalized differently. The Masoretes of the early Middle Ages chose the vowels for "bed," and so it has come to us in our Hebrew Bibles. The physical object leaned upon is of little significance; what matters is the attitude and pose of worship that points to Jacob's faith.

11:22 / Joseph's faith can be abundantly illustrated from a variety of episodes in his life. Understandably he became much celebrated for the character of his life (e.g., Philo, *On Joseph*; *Testament of Joseph*; Josephus, *Ant.* 2.9 ff.; Ps. 105:17 ff.; Wisd. of Sol. 10:13 f.; 1 Macc. 2:53; Acts 7:9 f.). Joseph's faith not only made him confident of the eventual deliverance of the sons of Israel, but also gave occasion for him to give instructions about his own remains. These instructions were duly accomplished, according to Exod. 13:19 and Josh. 24:32. On the unusual use of the Greek word *mnēmoneuō* (**speak of** or "mention"), see BAGD, p. 525.

32

The Faith of Moses
and the Israelites

HEBREWS 11:23–29

It was faith that made the parents of Moses hide him for three months after he was born. They saw that he was a beautiful child, and they were not afraid to disobey the king's order. ²⁴It was faith that made Moses, when he had grown up, refuse to be called the son of the king's daughter. ²⁵He preferred to suffer with God's people rather than to enjoy sin for a little while. ²⁶He reckoned that to suffer scorn for the Messiah was worth far more than all the treasures of Egypt, for he kept his eyes on the future reward.

²⁷It was faith that made Moses leave Egypt without being afraid of the king's anger. As though he saw the invisible God, he refused to turn back. ²⁸It was faith that made him establish the Passover and order the blood to be sprinkled on the doors, so that the Angel of Death would not kill the first-born sons of the Israelites. ²⁹It was faith that made the Israelites able to cross the Red Sea as if on dry land; when the Egyptians tried to do it, the water swallowed them up.

Moses is a hero of faith who is of central significance in Judaism, and he thus naturally assumes an important place in our author's catalogue. The author selects a few of the more important events, beginning with his survival as an infant because of his parents' faith and concluding with a general reference to the exodus and the peoples' participation in the same faith Moses had. Again the emphasis is on the unseen and God's faithfulness to what he promised.

11:23 / The very life of Moses was dependent upon faith from the beginning. As a newborn baby, he was saved by the faith of his parents. It was at great personal risk that they disobeyed Pharaoh's commandment that sons born to Hebrew parents were to be put to death (Exod. 1:22), yet **they were not afraid**. They trusted God and his faithfulness, and **for three months** they kept their son hidden (Exod. 2:1 ff.). The reference to the child as **beautiful** is drawn directly from the LXX (cf. Acts 7:20). Our author could have gone on to stress the parents' faith in setting the infant afloat in a basket and the remarkable reward of that faith when his own mother was called to be his nurse.

11:24-26 / The fruit of faith has been shown in several ways thus far: for example, confidence concerning the unknown and the future; obedience to the difficult and unexpected command of God; courage in the face of fear. Now the author illustrates how faith enables personal self-denial in the choice of suffering rather than pleasure. Moses refused what would have been the dream of most: **to be called the son of the king's** (lit., "Pharaoh's") **daughter**. Instead he **preferred** (lit., "choosing") to identify with the suffering of his people (Exod. 2:11 f.; cf. Acts 7:23 ff.). To stay in Pharaoh's court would have meant the enjoyment of pleasures, that is, immediate gratification, albeit only **for a little while**. Any such choice by Moses would have involved turning his back on the needs of his people and hence had to be described as **sin**. The key to Moses' behavior, so strange by the world's standards, is stated in verse 26. He was motivated by **the reward** (GNB adds **future**). This is the same word used in 10:35, also in a context referring to suffering. With that ultimate or transcendent reward in view, Moses counted it true that to suffer reproach **for the Messiah** led to greater wealth **than** (GNB adds **all**) **the treasures of Egypt**. The words **for the Messiah** are of course anachronistic, reflecting categories of thought much later than the time of Moses. Given the continuity of God's saving purposes, however, when Moses suffered reproach for his loyalty to the people of God, in principle he may be said to have suffered reproach for loyalty to Christ (cf. 13:13).

11:27-28 / Like his parents (v. 23), Moses was unafraid of the mighty Pharaoh. This passage refers not to Moses' flight from Egypt after killing the Egyptian but, as the context suggests, to his leading the people of Israel out of Egypt in the exodus (Exod. 12:51). Again alluding back to the opening verse of this chapter, the author describes Moses' accomplishment through faith in these words: **As though he saw the invisible** (GNB adds **God**), **he refused to turn back** (lit., "he persevered"). The mention of perseverance may be taken to refer to the entire sequence of events that culminated in the exodus itself. Moses was motivated by his conviction of the reality of what is unseen. In keeping with the thrust of the entire chapter, it is probably the transcendent hope that is in view, which, to be sure, in the final analysis depends upon the existence of God (v. 6) and his faithfulness. Verse 28 moves from the general to the specific, the means by which the deliverance of the Israelites was effected. Faith made **the Pass-**

over (Exod. 12:12 f., 21–30) a possibility. **Order the blood to be sprinkled on the doors** is GNB's expansion of "the sprinkling of the blood." **The Angel of Death** is literally "the destroyer," who because of the sprinkled blood **would not kill** (lit., "touch") **the first-born sons of the Israelites** (lit., "their [first-born]"). Thus it was Moses' faith that caused him to obey God. He acted in confidence with respect to God's faithfulness. The result was the deliverance of the Israelites and the punishment of the Egyptians.

11:29 / **The Israelites** exhibited the same kind of faith as Moses did. They were confident that God would deliver them and thus prove himself faithful to his promises. It was this faith that enabled them under Moses' leadership **to cross the Red Sea** in the miracle of the dividing of the waters (Exod. 14:21–29). But the Egyptian pursuers had no such faith and thus came to their end when they tried to follow the Israelites. Thus the events of the exodus—that central deliverance of God's people in the OT—were possible only by faith.

Additional Notes

11:23 / The Hebrew text of Exod. 2 refers only to the mother of Moses, not his **parents** (lit., "fathers") as in the LXX. Some of the language of this verse reflects the language of the LXX narrative. The word **beautiful** (*asteios*) occurs in the NT only here and in Acts 7:20, where in dependence upon the LXX it also describes the infant Moses. In the latter passage, Moses is said to be "beautiful before God" suggesting that *asteios* in our verse means something more than mere physical beauty. Thus in our passage **beautiful** should perhaps be understood as "acceptable" or "well-pleasing" to God, in which case the parents may have somehow understood that God had a special purpose for their son. See BAGD, p. 117. The word for **order** (*diatagma*, "edict") occurs only here in the NT. Cf. the present verse with Acts 7:17–22.

11:24–26 / **When he had grown up** also reflects the language of Exod. 2:11 (Acts 7:23 mentions the age of "forty"). Moses, of course, is a much celebrated figure in Jewish literature (see, e.g., Philo, *Life of Moses*; Josephus, *Ant.* 2.230 ff.; Sir. 45:1 ff.). The particular Greek verb underlying **suffer with** (*synkakoucheomai*) occurs only here in the entire NT. The word for "enjoyment" (*apolausis*) is found elsewhere in the NT only in 1 Tim. 6:17. A point similar to that made by our author in **for a little while** (*proskairos*) is made by Paul using the same Greek word in 2 Cor. 4:18: "What can be seen lasts only for a time, but what cannot be seen lasts forever." *Proskairos* is used similarly in 4 Macc. 15:2, 8. The deceptive character of sin is mentioned in 3:13 (cf. 12:1). For Moses it would have been **sin** (*hamartia*) to remain in his privileged position in Egypt, since God had a work for him to do. (This is in contrast to Joseph, whose calling was to remain in his high position in Egypt in order to help his brothers; cf. Gen. 43–50.) **The treasures of Egypt** were famous for their immeasurable wealth. But in Moses' perspective they paled into insignificance. He therefore willingly suffered **scorn** (*oneidismos*) **for the Messiah** (*christos*). The scorn or reproach God's people receive from their enemies is a familiar idea, both in the OT and NT. The same word is used in passages such as Ps. 69:9 and 89:50 f. (the latter even connects the reproach with "your anointed one," *christos*). The suggestion of some commentators that Moses himself is "the anointed one" toward whom the reproaches were directed is not convincing. Rather, when Moses suffers the reproach of Pharaoh's court, he suffers the reproach of God's people and thus of the Messiah who is one with his people. Clearly the use of the word **Messiah** here is a deliberate device employed by the author with his readers in mind. For they indeed are called to suffer reproach for *the* Christ (13:13), whose coming is already an event of the past. Any abuse they may suffer is not significant when compared to what God has prepared for them. The argument is the same as that of 2 Cor. 4:17: "And this small and temporary trouble we suffer will bring us a tremendous and eternal glory, much greater than the trouble" (cf. Matt. 5:11 f.). The word for **reward** (*misthapodosia*) occurs only in Hebrews. The same root is found in v. 6 where God is described as a "rewarder." See note on 10:35.

11:27-28 / The major reason this passage is probably not a reference to Moses' initial flight from Egypt is that according to Exod. 2:14, and contrary to our passage, Moses *was* afraid of Pharaoh when he fled. It was not yet the time for God's deliverance of his people (cf. Acts 7:25). The words **as though he saw the invisible God** are possibly, but not necessarily, an allusion to the vision of the burning bush (Exod. 3:2–6). They can equally well be understood as simply a repetition of the importance of faith's orientation to the unseen (which of course includes the reality of God; cf. 1 Tim. 6:16). For the importance of the unseen, see vv. 1, 3, 7. The verb "persevered" (*kartereō*) occurs only here in the NT. On the disputed meaning of the word, see BAGD, p. 405. See also Grundmann, *TDNT*, vol. 3, p. 617. The endurance or perseverance in view here is that displayed in Moses' struggle with Pharaoh for the deliverance of his people. **Establish** is GNB's effective rendering of the perfect tense of *poieō* ("make" or "do"). Our author has in mind not only the original event, but the institution of the Passover. (He does not pick up the christological implications of the Passover, as Paul does for example, in 2 Cor. 5:7.) On the **Passover** (*pascha*), see Jeremias, *TDNT*, vol. 5, pp. 896–904. The "sprinkling (*proschysis*, which occurs only here in the NT) of the blood" is often referred to in Hebrews, but in connection with the Day of Atonement rather than the Passover, and using a different word (*rhantizō*). "Destroyer" (*olethreuō*) is drawn from the LXX and occurs only here in the NT (but cf. the cognate in 1 Cor. 10:10). In the Exodus story, the "messenger of destruction," as the Hebrew may be rendered, destroyed the first-born of both men and beasts. See J. Schneider, *TDNT*, vol. 5, pp. 167–71.

11:29 / **The Red Sea** is "the sea of reeds" according to the Hebrew text of Exodus (cf. 13:18). The deliverance is celebrated in the "Song of Moses" (Exod. 15).

33

The Faith of Rahab and Countless Others

HEBREWS 11:30–40

It was faith that made the walls of Jericho fall down after the Israelites had marched around them for seven days. [31]It was faith that kept the prostitute Rahab from being killed with those who disobeyed God, for she gave the Israelite spies a friendly welcome.

[32]Should I go on? There isn't enough time for me to speak of Gideon, Barak, Samson, Jephthah, David, Samuel, and the prophets. [33]Through faith they fought whole countries and won. They did what was right and received what God had promised. They shut the mouths of lions, [34]put out fierce fires, escaped being killed by the sword. They were weak, but became strong; they were mighty in battle and defeated the armies of foreigners. [35]Through faith women received their dead relatives raised back to life.

Others, refusing to accept freedom, died under torture in order to be raised to a better life. [36]Some were mocked and whipped, and others were put in chains and taken off to prison. [37]They were stoned, they were sawn in two, they were killed by the sword. They went around clothed in skins of sheep or goats—poor, persecuted, and mistreated. [38]The world was not good enough for them! They wandered like refugees in the deserts and hills, living in caves and holes in the ground.

[39]What a record all of these have won by their faith! Yet they did not receive what God had promised, [40]because God had decided on an even better plan for us. His purpose was that only in company with us would they be made perfect.

Our author continues his catalogue of heroes of faith with a reference to the fall of Jericho and the faith of Rahab. At this point, however, he realizes that he will be unable to continue the same degree of thoroughness, and he thus proceeds to mention a few more specific names and then to speak generally about the ways in which true faith manifests itself. Many persons of faith experienced great victories through deliverance from their enemies; others experienced victories through their ability to endure suffering and martyrdom. But through faith all are victorious in one way or another. The author rounds out this long essay on faith by pointing to the fact that all these prior heroes of faith were unable to arrive at the final goal of blessing and fulfillment apart from those who, like his readers, believe in Christ in the present. The family of faith, as can now be seen, is one. The application to the readers follows in chapter 12.

11:30 / The second example of the faith of the Israelites as a people (cf. v. 29) is the conquest of Jericho. By faith they (GNB adds **the Israelites**) **marched around** (lit., "circled") the walls of the city (Josh. 6:12–21). They trusted what God said he would do through this otherwise apparently foolish behavior. By their faith and obedience God thus accomplished his purpose through them.

11:31 / It is perhaps something of a surprise to find Rahab **the prostitute**, a non-Israelite, mentioned alongside the great names of righteous Israelites (cf. James 2:25). But she too, most remarkably, had come to have faith in the God of Israel, perhaps by hearing of the victories of Israel and the power of Israel's God (Josh. 2:11). She acted in faith when she received the **spies** (GNB adds **Israelite**) with **a friendly welcome** (lit., "with peace"). In doing so she put her own life in danger, but the outcome was that she and her family escaped the destruction that came upon the city and its disobedient inhabitants (Josh. 2; 6:17, 23). Despite her unrighteous profession to that point, Rahab manifested the faith that counts upon the reality of the unseen.

11:32-35a / Realizing that he has only begun to mention examples from the OT, the author laments that he cannot continue. He then simply lists six names and refers to **the prophets** as others whom he could discuss if time permitted. We do not know why these specific names are mentioned. The list appears to be arbitrary, and the names are not listed in exact chronological order. The first four names are from the book of Judges: **Gideon** (6:11–8:32); **Barak** (4:6–5:31); **Samson** (13:2–16:31); and **Jephthah** (11:1–12:7). Although not of equal importance, all these men demonstrated their faith in God, and it is recorded (except for Barak) that the Spirit of the Lord came upon each of them. **David** and **Samuel** are of course much better known (from the books of Samuel), as are **the prophets**, among whom must be included not only those whose names are associated with canonical books, but also Elijah and Elisha.

The exploits that follow are not in any particular order and do not parallel the names just mentioned in any structured way. Rather, the author now describes in general language the various kinds of victory won through faith. These and other unmentioned heroes **fought whole coun-**

tries and won (lit., "conquered kingdoms"); this is probably an allusion to the victories recorded in Joshua and Judges, but may include David's. Did what was right (lit., "wrought righteousness") may simply refer to the obedience of these faithful persons. Received what God had promised (lit., "received the promises") may refer either to a degree of fulfillment they experienced in their lifetimes or to the reception of further promises concerning the future. The reference to stopping the mouths of lions could refer to Samson (Judg. 14:6), David (1 Sam. 17:34 f.), or most conspicuously, Daniel (Dan. 6:22). Put out fierce fires suggests Shadrach, Meshach, and Abednego (Dan. 3:1–30). Escaped being killed by the sword (lit., "the mouth of the sword") can refer to several of the prophets, for example, Elijah (1 Kings 19:2–8) or Jeremiah (Jer. 36:19, 26). The references to the weak becoming strong and the defeat of foreign armies (cf. v. 33) are general enough to apply to many OT personalities. The women who received their dead (GNB adds relatives and to life) are clearly the non-Israelite widow of Zarephath (1 Kings 17:17–24) and the Shunammite woman (2 Kings 4:25–37) both of whom had their sons raised from the dead (by Elijah and Elisha respectively). At the beginning of verse 35 GNB adds through faith, picking up the phrase again from verse 33. In the case of the widow of Zarephath, it was Elijah's faith that made the raising possible.

11:35b–38 / The others here do not stand in contrast to the names (and "the prophets") of verse 32, but in contrast to all those who experienced victories of the kind described in the immediately preceding verses. For some through faith experienced victories of another kind. They suffered all kinds of evil and even martyrdom. But these were only apparent defeats. In actuality they were triumphs of faith expressed in the faithfulness of total commitment. It is of great importance for the readers, and for all Christians, to understand that the life of faith does not always involve success by the world's standards. The faithful person does not always experience deliverance; faith and suffering are not incompatible. Faith, however, sanctifies suffering, and there is in the midst of apparent defeat the appropriation of the promise of the future. The author offers his readers no guarantee of an easy Christianity. If in their "struggle against sin" they have "not yet had to resist to the point of being killed," as the author will say in 12:4, there can be no assurance that they may not yet have to do so. The immediate, temporal outcome (which after all can only be temporary) is not the important thing. Faith is what finally matters.

Again in this passage the author speaks generally, leaving the reader opportunity to think of whatever appropriate names may come to mind. Those who refusing **freedom** accepted **torture** (GNB adds **died under**) with a future resurrection in mind seems most naturally to point to the Maccabean martyrs, although it is impossible to restrict the reference to them. The apocryphal book of 2 Maccabees in particular refers to many examples of this kind of faith, which made people accept death rather than the laws of the anti-Jewish Antiochus Epiphanes during his attempt to destroy Judaism, 167–164 B.C. (e.g., Eleazar; see 2 Macc. 6:18–7:42). **Be raised to a better life** is literally "obtain a better resurrection." This stands in deliberate contrast to the "resurrection" referred to in the first half of the verse. The difference is between resuscitation and eschatological resurrection, which entails a new order of life altogether.

Mocking and scourging have frequently been the lot of the righteous, as has been imprisonment. The readers were well aware of this from their firsthand experience (cf. 10:33). Among the prophets, Jeremiah comes to mind immediately as an example of this kind of suffering (Jer. 20:2, 7 ff.; 37:15; cf. 1 Kings 22:26 f.). Some were **stoned** (e.g., Zechariah, 2 Chron. 24:21; cf. Matt. 23:37); some died **by the sword** (cf. 1 Kings 19:10, and contrast those who by faith "escaped being killed by the sword," v. 34). The unusual reference to being **sawn in two** may derive from the tradition concerning the martyrdom of Isaiah by this method (see the intertestamental writing known as *The Ascension of Isaiah*, 5:11–14). Those who wandered **clothed in skins** and were forced to live in the wilderness **in caves and holes in the ground** are probably not the prophets, such as Elijah (2 Kings 1:8), but again the Israelites persecuted by Antiochus during the Maccabean era. This fits well with the description of them as **poor, persecuted, and mistreated**. They fled to the wilderness, according to 1 Maccabees 2:29–38, because of the evils Antiochus brought upon them. GNB's added words, **like refugees**, are thus appropriate. **The world was not good enough for them** is GNB's unusual translation for "of whom the world was not worthy." The underlying irony is found in the incongruity of God's faithful servants being forced to live like animals.

11:39–40 / The opening words echo verse 2. "These all," named and unnamed, "having been well attested" (a more literal translation than GNB's **what a record . . . these have won**) through their faith **did not receive what God had promised** (lit., "the promise"). Herein lies a paradox. God's faithful people of the past, remote and recent, have lived their lives in accordance with the promise of a great unseen, future reality. Although some experienced a degree of fulfillment in history, none has arrived at the ultimate goal, "*the* promise." That final, eschatological fulfillment has been delayed up until the present. The reason for this is now given by our author. God's people of every age constitute a unity and must arrive at the perfection of the *telos* together. **Only in company with us would they be made perfect** is literally "lest without us they should be made perfect" (GNB adds the words **his purpose was**).

Of course a basic aspect of the delay is the newness of what God has accomplished through the work of Christ. Since for our author all that preceded Christ is related to him as promise is related to fulfillment, no attainment of the *telos* has been conceivable until the present. **God had decided on an even better plan for us** (lit., "God foresaw [or provided] something better for us"). That "something better" is the new covenant with all of its blessings, which is "for us" in distinction from those of the past only because we are the privileged who have received it through the historical process. But in a more fundamental sense it belongs to all the faithful from every age. We have begun to taste of its fruit already in the present—these "last days" (cf. 1:2) of realized eschatology—but we together with those faithful heroes of the past will yet experience the consummation of God's purposes, which may now, all being prepared, occur at any time. The realization of "perfection," the arrival at the *telos* of his purposes, will be the portion of all who through faith count upon the reality of what is hoped for and unseen, and who through faith give expression to that conviction by their everyday living. Faith is the dynamic of the life that pleases God.

Additional Notes

11:30 / The author could equally well have mentioned Joshua as a man of faith at this point. His name is presupposed, just as Moses' name is in the preceding verse. This is the only reference in the NT to the capture of Jericho.

11:31 / The story of Rahab became popular in Jewish tradition. She became a beloved figure as the first proselyte to the Jewish faith. She is even found in the genealogy of Christ as the mother of Boaz (who married another famous non-Israelite, Ruth) in Matt. 1:5. Rahab's house was an ideal hiding place for the two spies, since in addition to being readily open during the evening, it was built into the city wall.

11:32–35a / The words about the lack of time to speak fully of the great heroes of faith could strengthen the hypothesis that Hebrews, in large part if not totally, is a homily (as is suggested by 13:22 and the repeated exhortations of the book). But this kind of expression is not uncommon in purely literary works of the time (e.g., Philo, *On the Special Laws*, 4.238; *On Dreams* 2.63; *The Life of Moses* 1.213).

The Greek participle underlying GNB's **to speak** (*diēgoumenon*) is masculine and makes the hypothesis concerning Priscilla as the author of the book correspondingly more difficult. On the other hand, the masculine participle may simply be formal, or if Priscilla left the book anonymous she may also have been wise enough to change the gender of the participle so as not to reveal its feminine origin. Samuel's name may be put after David's because of his natural association with the prophets (cf. Acts 3:24). This is the only occurrence in the NT of the names **Gideon**, **Barak**, **Samson**, and **Jephthah**. The phrase "wrought righteousness" (*eirgasanto dikaiosynēn*) occurs elsewhere in the NT only in Acts 10:35 and James 1:20. **Received** here is from *epitynchanō*, as in 6:15. See note to 6:15, and cf. similar words for "receive" in vv. 13 and 17 above. The motif of "from weakness to strength" is found frequently in the NT (e.g., Rom. 4:19 f.; 8:26; 1 Cor. 1:27–29; 2 Cor. 12:9-10; Eph. 6:10; Phil 4:13). The "resurrection" whereby these women received back their sons is in contrast to a "better resurrection" in v. 35b. The two references to "resurrection" (*anastasis*) in this verse are the only occurrences of the word in Hebrews, except for 6:2.

11:35b–38 / The perspective of this passage is similar to the main burden of the book of Revelation, namely confidence in the reality of God and his faithfulness to his promises despite deep suffering that seems to contradict all that is believed. As in the past, so in the present, it is faith that sustains God's people in their tribulation. The Greek verb for **torture** (*tympanizō*) refers to being beaten to death on the rack. It occurs only here in the NT. **Freedom** (*apolytrōsis*) is the same word as the key term "set free" or "redeem" in 9:15 (see note); here it is used nontechnically. For the significance of the word **better** (*kreittōn*) in Hebrews, see the note on 1:4. The expectation of resurrection for those who suffer martyrdom comes to expression most powerfully in the Jewish tradition in connection with the persecution under Antiochus in the document known as 4 Maccabees (from probably the first century). The mocking and scourging here is reminiscent of the language describing the treatment of Jesus according to the passion narratives (cognate verbs occur: e.g., *empaizō*, "mock"—Matt. 27:29 ff.; Mark 15:20 ff.; Luke 23:11, 36; *mastigoō*, "scourge"—John 19:1; cf. Matt. 20:19; Mark 10:34; Luke 18:33). This may be in the author's mind when he writes 12:3. In v. 37 a large number of manuscripts include after (although some have it before) **sawn in two** the additional verb "were tempted" (*epeirasthēsan*). This verb, however, does not make much sense in the immediate context of explicit martyrdom. Following the important P[46] and a few other witnesses, we are probably safe if we accept the shorter reading. See Metzger *TCGNT*, pp. 674 f. The tradition about Isaiah being sawn in two (according to some, with a wooden saw) is also attested in the Babylonian Talmud (Yebamoth 49b; Sanhedrin 103b) and in certain Christian writers (e.g., Justin, *Dialogue* 120; Tertullian, *On Patience*, 14). For the imagery of v. 38, although in a different context, see Rev. 6:15. The terrain of Palestine provides abundant **caves and holes** in which to hide.

11:39-40 / For "being well-attested" (*martyreō*), see note on v. 2. The word for **receive** here is *komizō*, which occurs also in 10:36 with the singular "the promise." In v. 13 we have a statement quite parallel to the present one: "They did not receive (*komizō*) the things God had promised" (lit., "the promises," plural). The singular and plural of the word promise (*epangelia*) are thus readily interchangeable, referring to the same thing. On "promise" see note to 6:15. GNB's **had decided on** translates the Greek verb *problepō* (which occurs only here in the NT), where the root idea of "foresee," because of the sovereignty of God, has practically become "select" or "provide." This was God's purpose from the beginning. See BAGD, p. 703. For the great importance of **better** (*kreittōn*) as it is used in Hebrews, see note on 1:4. **Be made perfect** (*teleioō*) in Hebrews has a strong teleological orientation. It refers to arriving at the goal of God's saving purposes. See note on 2:10.

34

Looking to Jesus
as the Perfect Pattern

HEBREWS 12:1–3

As for us, we have this large crowd of witnesses around us. So then, let us rid ourselves of everything that gets in the way, and of the sin which holds on to us so tightly, and let us run with determination the race that lies before us. ²Let us keep our eyes fixed upon Jesus, on whom our faith depends from beginning to end. He did not give up because of the cross!

On the contrary, because of the joy that was waiting for him, he thought nothing of the disgrace of dying on the cross, and he is now seated at the right side of God's throne. ³Think of what he went through; how he put up with so much hatred from sinners! So do not let yourselves become discouraged and give up.

With the glorious history of the faithful in mind, our author turns now to his readers. The standard of faith has been set by the record of God's faithful people in the past, who moved out into the unknown with confidence and who endured hardship without giving up their expectation of a future fulfillment of the promise. But the author now comes to the supreme example of this kind of faith in Jesus—the name that must be the climax of any list of heroes of faith. Jesus himself endured great suffering without losing sight of the glory that was to come. The readers, together with Christians of every era, are called to walk in the steps of faith that characterized the saints of the past and the one who has now been made Lord. Only such an attitude of faith can sustain them in the adversities they may be called to face.

12:1 / The first, and therefore emphatic, word of the original text is a strong inferential particle "therefore" (reflected in GNB's delayed **so then**). The exhortation now to be given is based on the reality expounded in chapter 11. The community of faith is such that it figuratively surrounds us as a **crowd** (lit., "cloud"; GNB adds **large**) **of witnesses**. **Witnesses** here does not mean observers of the present conduct of Christians but rather those who testify or give evidence of the victorious life of faith.

They show that it is possible to live by faith. Motivated by the preceding catalogue of examples, the readers are themselves to live the life of faith. The exhortation is given in figurative language: **Let us run with determination** (lit., "perseverance") **the race that lies before us**. But if the race is to be run (cf. the same imagery in 2 Tim. 4:7), we must put away **everything that gets in the way** (lit., "every weight" or "impediment"). The author does not specify any impediments; it is understood that anything that hinders the life of faith as it has been portrayed in the preceding chapter is to be laid aside. One clear obstacle to the life of faith, however, is **sin**, here described as that **which holds on to us so tightly** (lit., "easily ensnaring"). The relation between sin and unbelief has already been the subject of our author's attention (cf. 3:12, 18 f.). Our susceptibility to sin (cf. Rom. 7:21) must not be allowed to thwart us in our pursuit of the goal (cf. 11:25). Taking courage from past examples, the readers are exhorted to complete the course upon which they have embarked.

12:2 / An even more significant example of the life of faith is to be found in Jesus, now described as the one **on whom our faith depends from beginning to end** (lit., "the pioneer and perfecter of the faith"). The word for "pioneer" is the same word used in 2:10 ("originator," or "author," of salvation; cf. Acts 3:15). Is there a sense in which Jesus can be described as the "originator" of faith? Like Paul (Gal. 3:23–26; cf. John 1:17), our author believes that the people of God could indeed live by faith in past generations, but that in a fundamental sense the possibility—or at least the validity—of faith in any era depended and depends upon the work of Christ. That is, because Christ is so central both to the promise and to the fulfillment, because he brings into existence the hoped-for *telos* (and is therefore "the perfecter" of faith), he is also the "originator" or "founder" of faith. As "perfecter" of faith, he brings it to its intended goal. Thus, whether one talks about faith as a possibility or as the experience of fulfillment, all depends upon Jesus. For this reason, Christians must keep looking away from this world to him. He is not only the basis, means, and fulfillment of faith, but in his life he also exemplifies the same principle of faith that we saw in the heroes of chapter 11. Thus, by faith he counted upon the reality of future **joy** and "endured the cross" (GNB has apparently paraphrased these words in **he did not give up because of the cross** and adds **on the contrary**). He assessed the present circumstances in light of the glorious future, and so **thought nothing of the disgrace of dying on the cross** (lit., "despised the shame"). He died as a despised criminal (cf. Phil. 2:8). And that future joy is already his in a preliminary way for **he is now seated** at God's right hand. This description of Christ in the language of Psalm 110:1 alludes throughout the book to the completeness of his work (cf. 10:11 f.).

12:3 / The readers are encouraged to consider Jesus as the one who suffered (GNB adds **what he went through**), who endured so much **hatred** (lit., "hostility") **from sinners**. In this sense Jesus is a model of all the suffering of the righteous at the hands of the enemies of God. Consideration of what Jesus endured will prevent the readers from growing weary and losing heart. Following Jesus as their model, they can endure the most trying of circumstances.

Additional Notes

12:1 / The initial word *toigaroun* may be translated "for that very reason" (see BAGD, p. 821) and may refer particularly to the immediately preceding statement (11:40) that "only in company with us would they be made perfect." The saints of God, both past and present, must arrive at the goal together and therefore it is up to the readers to emulate the faith of their forebears. Only in this way can the people of God as a unity experience the eschatological consummation of God's purposes. The word "cloud" (*nephos*) is used commonly in Greek literature to indicate a "host" or "company." This is the only occurrence of the noun "witness" (*martyr*) in Hebrews, except for the quotation of Deut. 17:6 in 10:28. The Greek word had not yet acquired the meaning of "martyr" as one who gives his life for what he believes, which it came to have by the second or third century. See Strathmann, *TDNT*, vol. 4, pp. 504–12. The word for "impediment" (*onkos*) occurs only here in the Greek Bible. See Seesemann, *TDNT*, vol. 5, p. 41. A textual variant to the Greek word underlying GNB's "which holds onto us so tightly" (*euperistatos*) is found in the early and important P⁴⁶, which has *euperispastos*, "easily distracting." The latter reading may have occurred, however, because of some uncertainty about the meaning of the former word (which is not found elsewhere in the NT, the LXX, or Greek writers prior to the NT). F. F. Bruce (p. 350) quotes E. K. Simpson who defines the word as meaning "*so prone to hamper or trammel.*" This has an appropriate significance in the present context. See Metzger, *TCGNT*, p. 675. Athletic imagery is used frequently in the NT to describe the kind of discipline and dedication needed to live the Christian life (see especially 1 Cor. 9:24–27). This same imagery of the athletic contest is used in describing the sufferings and martyrdoms of the Maccabean age in 4 Macc. 17:9 ff. On the metaphorical language of "running a race," see too Gal. 2:2; 5:7; Phil. 2:16. "Perseverance" or "endurance" (*hypomonē*) is an important need of the readers (cf. 10:36). If there is a demanding course **that lies before** (*prokeimai*) **us**, there is also a great hope that is also said to lie before us (6:18, using the same verb; cf. the same verb in describing the joy **waiting for** Jesus in v. 2).

12:2 / The exhortation **let us keep our eyes fixed on Jesus** continues the metaphor of a race, where the runner must avoid distraction of every kind (cf. "looking unto God," 4 Macc. 17:10; cf. Acts 7:55). In this case, however, Jesus is appealed to as not merely another example, but as one whose whole existence revolves around faith. GNB's **our faith** is better taken literally as "the faith" or "faith" in a more general sense. He is the pioneer and perfecter of not simply the faith of Christians, but faith of every era. For "pioneer" (*archēgos*), see note on 2:10. The word for "perfecter" (*teleiotēs*) is found only here in the Greek Bible and does not occur in Greek literature prior to the NT. Our author, however, uses several cognate words (see notes on 2:10; 6:1; 7:11). See Delling, *TDNT*, vol. 8, pp. 86–87. Jesus is referred to in Rev. 1:5 (cf. 3:14) as "the faithful witness" (*ho martys ho pistos*). On "faith," see note to 11:1.

Some have thought that to say that Jesus endured the cross for **the joy that was waiting for him** is to base Jesus' obedient death upon an unworthy motive. They accordingly prefer to interpret the preposition *anti* to mean, as it can, "instead of" rather than "for" (cf. NEB margin: "in place of the joy that was open to him"). This objection, however, fails to understand that the stress on the future hope of the Christian is exactly the point that the author has made to his readers throughout the preceding chapter, and that he wishes to underline here. Furthermore, to say that Jesus was motivated by the joy that was to be his afterwards in no way need exclude the motives of obedience to the Father and the procurement of salvation for the world. Indeed, the **joy** that Jesus was to experience is inseparable from the accomplishment of God's saving purposes, and thus in a fundamental sense it is a shared joy (cf. John 17:13). Our author has already pointed out that the purpose of the incarnation was the death of God's Son and hence the deliverance of the world from sin and death (cf. 2:10, 14 f., 17).

Crucifixion was one of the most despicable forms of death in the Roman world. Roman citizens were automatically protected against this form of capital punishment, which was thought suitable only for barbarians. Jesus disregarded totally the shame attached to it. See E. Brandenburger, *NIDNTT*, vol. 1, pp. 391–403. Among the several allusions to Ps. 110:1, this is the only time the verb for **seated** occurs in the perfect tense (the other occurrences are aorists). The emphasis is on the present reign of Christ as the corresponding fulfillment of **the joy that was waiting for him**. On the importance of Ps. 110 for our epistle, see note on 1:3.

12:3 / The particular word used here for **think of** (*analogizomai*, "consider") occurs only here in the NT. The object of the verb, as in v. 2, is the one who suffered rather than the sufferings. The perfect tense of the Greek participle underlying **went through** ("endured," *hypomenō*) suggests the completed results from Jesus' endurance of the cross. The word "hostility" (*antilogia*) in connection with the cross may allude to the derision of Jesus' enemies (e.g., Matt. 27:39; cf. Ps. 22:7 f.). A textual variant supplies a plural instead of a singular reflexive pronoun, resulting in the hostility of sinners being directed "against themselves." This, however, makes little sense and thus is probably to be rejected despite its superior textual attestation. See Metzger, *TCGNT*, p. 675. The language of this verse bears some resemblance to the LXX of Num. 17:2 f. (16:38 in English translations of the OT). The Greek vocabulary of the last sentence in this verse indicates "weariness" (GNB's **discouraged**, *kampō*) and "losing heart" (GNB's **give up**; lit., "fainting in your souls," ASV). The thought of what Jesus endured should deliver the readers from falling into this plight. And we know from earlier passages in the epistle that our author is apprehensive for our readers in this regard (cf. 3:12; 4:1; 6:4 ff.; 10:26 ff., 35).

35

The Purpose of Chastening

HEBREWS 12:4–11

For in your struggle against sin you have not yet had to resist to the point of being killed. ⁵Have you forgotten the encouraging words which God speaks to you as his sons?

"My son, pay attention when
    the Lord corrects you,
    and do not be discouraged when
    he rebukes you.
⁶Because the Lord corrects
    everyone he loves,
    and punishes everyone he accepts
    as a son."

⁷Endure what you suffer as being a father's punishment; your suffering shows that God is treating you as his sons. Was there ever a son who was not punished by his father? ⁸If you are not punished, as all his sons are, it means you are not real sons, but bastards. ⁹In the case of our human fathers, they punished us and we respected them. How much more, then, should we submit to our spiritual Father and live! ¹⁰Our human fathers punished us for a short time, as it seemed right to them; but God does it for our own good, so that we may share his holiness. ¹¹When we are punished, it seems to us at the time something to make us sad, not glad. Later, however, those who have been disciplined by such punishment reap the peaceful reward of a righteous life.

As we have seen, a main purpose of our author throughout the book is to call his readers to faithfulness in the midst of adverse circumstances. Near the end of his epistle he exhorts them to "go forth to him [Jesus] outside the camp and bear the abuse he endured" (RSV). Although no members of the community have yet suffered martyrdom, the future may involve just that. Any perspective like this, which affirms suffering as the duty of the faithful, must develop a theology of suffering wherein suffering can be understood in a positive light. That is the purpose of the present section. Suffering, far from being a contradiction of the Christian's status, as the world is inclined to think, is actually a mark of his or her true status. Suffering is necessarily involved in sonship and is not a contradiction of God's love.

12:4 / **Struggle against sin** here signifies, as the context indicates, not the battle of the Christian to keep from sinning (cf. v. 1), but the struggle to avoid apostatizing. It may refer as much to the sin of the enemies of God who persecute his people as to the potential sin of apostasy with the readers themselves. It is this that they are to resist. There have indeed been difficult times in the past (cf. 10:32–34), and perhaps also in the present, but resistance for the readers has not yet come to **the point of being killed** (lit., "blood"). In that regard they have not equalled the suffering of the supreme paradigm of faith who, as the preceding verses emphasize, went to the cross and paid the ultimate price.

12:5-6 / It is possible to understand the opening sentence as either a question or a statement (that is, "you have forgotten"). That the readers are somewhat discouraged is clear. The difficulties they face are such that the author wants to remind them of the place of suffering in the life of faith. They need to remember again **the encouraging words** (lit., "encouragement") in Scripture which speak of **sons** (GNB adds **God** and **his**). The quotation is from Proverbs 3:11 f. GNB's **pay attention** is literally "do not think lightly of." The word used by GNB, **punishes** (and "punishment" in the following verses), seems to lack the positive connotation required in the present context. What is really in view is a kind of "discipline" that trains a person in obedience. This is the way they are to perceive the adversity they are experiencing: it is a mark of the Lord's love (cf. Rev. 3:19), on the one hand, and of their sonship, on the other. They are therefore not to become **discouraged** (cf. v. 3).

12:7-8 / Having presented the OT quotation, the author now provides another midrashic commentary in which he utilizes the actual words of the quotation to present his argument (for earlier examples of this procedure, see 2:6–9; 3:7–4:10; 10:5–11). This can be seen in the threefold use of the words "punish" (or "punishment") and "sons" (or "son") in these verses. The root of the word "discipline" (or "punish") also occurs once in each of the next three verses. The readers are first exhorted to **endure** their suffering as **punishment** (GNB adds **a father's**) and the sign that God is dealing with them as **sons** (GNB adds **his** and **your suffering shows that**). The author continues with a rhetorical question that points to the universality of the disciplining of sons by their fathers. Indeed, he adds, without the experience of this kind of discipline (**as all his sons are**, lit., "of which all have become partakers"), one must count oneself as an illegitimate rather than an authentic son. In short, it is a part of authentic sonship (and not the contradiction of it) to experience the discipline of God as Father. We may recall what is said of Christ in 5:8: "But even though he was God's Son, he learned through his sufferings to be obedient."

12:9-10 / In these verses our author draws his analogy further, using an *a fortiori* form of argument (from the lesser to the greater). So far as our **human fathers** (lit., "fathers of our flesh") are concerned (GNB adds **in the case of**), they disciplined us and yet **we respected them**. What seems to be meant by this is that we accepted the discipline without questioning either the authority of our literal father or our status as legitimate children. All the more then should we be submissive **to our spiritual Father** (lit., "the Father of spirits") and thus **live** (lit., "will live"). "The Father of spirits" is our Creator, to whom we owe our existence in an ultimate sense. As we are submissive to his discipline so will we live in the sense of experiencing the life of the eschaton (cf. 1 Cor. 11:32). The contrast contained in v. 10 makes a similar point. We should be more receptive to God's disciplining than we were even of our human fathers. They disciplined us **for a short time** (lit., "a few days"), that is, during our childhood, and used as their standard only what subjectively **seemed right to them**. The implication is that God disciplines us throughout our life and in accordance with his own knowledge of **our good** (GNB adds **own**), with the final goal of our **sharing his holiness**. In actuality our character is being formed by the experience of suffering. We are being purified and made to share the holiness of God, especially as revealed in his Son (cf. Rom. 8:29). By connecting suffering with holiness, our author sanctifies suffering as something that has a very special purpose in the life of the Christian.

12:11 / The author readily admits that, while it is being experienced, the discipline of suffering seems to produce sorrow rather than joy. Yet with the perspective of time the true purpose of such suffering will make itself plain, for those who have suffered will receive **the peaceful reward** (lit., "fruit") **of a righteous life** (lit., "righteousness"). Righteousness, then, is the portion of those who accept the discipline of suffering from their Father's hand. The point of this verse is the same as that of 2 Corinthians 4:17, where Paul writes: "And this small and temporary trouble we suffer will bring us a tremendous and eternal glory, much greater than the trouble" (cf. the closely related emphasis of 1 Pet. 1:6 f.; 4:12–14).

Additional Notes

12:4 / "Resistance to the point of death" is a common motif in Jewish literature, describing absolute commitment and endurance in a struggle against opponents. Our author is exceptional in using the word "blood" rather than "death," but it is fairly certain that he means martyrdom rather than merely the sustaining of wounds. The particular word for **struggle** used here (*antikathistēmi*) occurs only here in the NT. The same is true of the word translated **resist** by GNB (*antagonizomai*). On the use of **sin** (*hamartia*) as referring to apostasy, see especially 10:26 f. See W. Günther, *NIDNTT*, vol. 3, pp. 577–83.

12:5–6 / In the quotation our author again follows the LXX nearly verbatim (he adds **my** after the initial **son**). The LXX follows the Hebrew quite closely except for some slight deviation in the last line. There the LXX has added a verb (GNB's **punishes**) and translates the Hebrew verb "delights" with the Greek word "receives" (GNB's **accepts**). The added verb strengthens the obvious parallelism with the first line of Prov. 3:12 (Heb. 12:6). It is interesting to note that Philo quotes this same passage in an argument very similar to our author's, in which suffering is shown to benefit the recipient and is to be regarded as a blessing (*On the Preliminary Studies*, 175).

12:7–8 / The words for "discipline" (GNB's **punishment**) are drawn from the same root (verb: *paideuō*; noun: *paideia* and *paideutēs*). Words derived from this root occur twice in the original quotation, and no less than six times in the author's midrashic exposition of the passage (three times in vv. 7–8). On the positive significance of *paideia* here, as "education for eternity," see Bertram, *TDNT*, vol. 5, pp. 621–24. The imperative **endure** (*hypomenō*) is the same verb used in vv. 2 and 3 in describing Jesus' endurance of the cross. The readers are thus called to endure as he endured (cf. 10:36). In v. 8 the word **all** (*pantes*) was probably also suggested to the author by its occurrence in the original quotation (v. 6). The point of the author is not merely that all God's sons are disciplined, but that all sons universally are disciplined by their fathers. True sons were disciplined by their fathers in order to become worthy heirs; illegitimate sons (**bastards**; *nothos*, which occurs only here in the NT) were not able to inherit and thus were not worth the trouble of such training. Thus those who suffer discipline have not only their true sonship established, but also their status as heirs.

12:9–10 / The *a fortiori* form of argument is used often by our author (cf. 2:2 ff.; 9:14; 10:29; 12:25). The analogy between our human fathers and our "heavenly father" is found several times in the teaching of Jesus (e.g., Matt. 7:9–11; 21:28–31; Luke 15:11–32). The expression "fathers of our flesh" stands in contrast to "the Father of spirits." The former refers clearly to our literal, human fathers; the latter to our Creator in an absolute sense, and for the Christian in the more specific sense as the Father to whom they have become sons through the new covenant. The phrase "the Father of spirits" (*patēr tōn pneumatōn*) is similar to "the God of the spirits of all flesh" in Num. 16: 22 and 27:16 (cf. "the Lord of spirits" in the *Similitudes of Enoch*, 1 Enoch 37 ff.; cf. 2 Macc. 3:24). No anthropological dualism (wherein God is the Creator only of our spirits) is intended by our author. See Schweizer, *TDNT*, vol. 7, pp. 141 f. In v. 9 our fathers are described as "correctors" (*paideutēs*), a word that occurs elsewhere in the NT only in Rom. 2:20. The future tense of the verb **live** orients the reader to an eschatological expectation as does the full realization of the sharing of **his holiness** (v. 10) and the reaping of **the peaceful reward** of righteousness (v. 11). This is akin to the statement in Acts 14:22 that "We must pass through many troubles to enter the Kingdom of God." The mention of the fact that our fathers disciplined us only **for a short time** in itself suggests the lesser importance of the discipline of our fathers compared to that of God our Father. The advantage of the Father's disciplining is our participation in his **holiness** (*hagiotēs*), an unusual Greek word that is found elsewhere in the NT only in 2 Cor. 1:11.

12:11 / The ultimately beneficial character of suffering, despite its present pains, is a familiar motif in the Bible (cf. Ps. 119:67, 71, for benefits in the present life; 2 Thess. 1:5–8 and Matt. 5:10–12, for benefits in the life of the future). Underlying GNB's **disciplined** is the Greek word *gymnazō*, which means lit. "trained." Thus the author returns to the athletic games for his imagery at the end of this passage. The fruit of righteousness is called peaceful (*eirēnikos*) because it is the resolution of the "struggle" (v. 4) brought about by the sufferings of the present time. The latter must always find their truest answer in eschatology proper, but this cannot be allowed to weaken the author's emphasis on the experience of realized eschatology, to which he will turn in 12:18 ff.

36

A Challenge to Holiness and Faithfulness

HEBREWS 12:12–17

Lift up your tired hands, then, and strengthen your trembling knees! ¹³Keep walking on straight paths, so that the lame foot may not be disabled, but instead be healed.

¹⁴Try to be at peace with everyone, and try to live a holy life, because no one will see the Lord without it. ¹⁵Guard against turning back from the grace of God. Let no one become like a bitter plant that grows up and causes many troubles with its poison. ¹⁶Let no one become immoral or unspiritual like Esau, who for a single meal sold his rights as the older son. ¹⁷Afterward, you know, he wanted to receive his father's blessing: but he was turned back, because he could not find any way to change what he had done, even though in tears he looked for it.ʰ

h. he looked for it; *or* he tried to get the blessing.

In the light of the positive view of suffering set forth in the preceding section, the author now again gives a pastoral exhortation to his readers. They are to get on with the business of living the Christian life and to resist the temptation to return to their former ways, though such a retreat may appear to be less troublesome. A negative example, Esau, is provided as a further warning to the readers. This exhortation has much in common with preceding ones (e.g., 2:1–3; 4:1–2; 6:1–6; 10:32–36), but if anything, it carries even more persuasive power because of the material surveyed in chapter 11 and the argument of 12:1–11.

12:12-13 / The unusual imagery of the language of verse 12 is drawn from the LXX of Isaiah 35:3 where the context speaks of eschatological fulfillment, and the following sentence reads: "Tell everyone who is discouraged, 'Be strong and don't be afraid.' " The exhortation of this verse, as the context in Isaiah indicates, is thus very pertinent to the condition of the readers. There is only one verb in the Greek of verse 12, **strengthen** (GNB adds **lift up**; cf. NIV: "strengthen your feeble arms and weak knees"). GNB's **tired** may also be translated "drooping" (so RSV, NEB); **trembling** is literally "weak." The thrust of the exhortation is that the readers should take heart and thereby receive strength to face their difficult circumstances. The opening words of verse 13 are drawn from the LXX of Proverbs 4:26 (GNB's **keep walking on** is literally "make . . . for your feet") where the parallel line is "order your ways aright." The reference to **the lame foot** (lit., "what is lame") probably came to the author by the prompting of the words of Isaiah 35:3 in verse 12. Where there is weakness and drooping limbs there may also be lameness (see too Isa. 35:6). And if we associate avoidance of lameness with **straight paths**, **foot** (as in GNB) may, in keeping with Proverbs 4:26, be thought of to go along with **hands** and **knees**. **Disabled** is literally "turned aside," probably in the sense of "dislocated" (cf. RSV: "put out of joint"). Thus, if the readers make their paths straight, living in a way that is pleasing to God, what is lame and painful will be healed, rather than aggravated. The metaphorical language of these verses, from what we know elsewhere in Hebrews, may be assumed to constitute a graphic portrayal of the condition of the readers.

12:14 / The exhortation of this verse appears to be more general, much like that found in other NT epistles. The readers are told to "pursue" (which GNB translates **try to be at**) **peace with everyone** and holiness (GNB translates **a holy life**). The language "pursue peace" stems from Psalm 34:14 and is found also in Romans 14:19 and 1 Peter 3:11 (cf. Heb. 12:18; 2 Cor. 13:11; 2 Tim. 2:22; 1 Thess. 5:13). The exhortation to holiness, of course, is common in the NT. Holiness has already been set forth as the goal of the Christian in verse 10. If we remember that suffering and holiness are connected, the one producing the other, we may see the present exhortation as specifically pertinent to our readers. To **see the Lord** refers to eschatology: "But we know that when Christ appears, we shall be like him, because we shall see him as he really is" (1 John 3:2). It is worth noting that in two successive beatitudes Jesus refers to "the pure in heart" who will "see God" and the peacemakers who will be called "sons of God" (Matt. 5:8-9).

12:15 / The exhortation in this verse is directed to what is apparently the main concern of the author. Again and again we have seen this concern emerge (e.g., 2:1 ff.; 3:12 ff.; 4:1 ff.; 6:4 ff.; 10:23, 26 ff., 35). Here he appeals to the responsibility of the community for each of its members. Thus they are to **guard against** anyone (this last word is omitted by GNB) **turning back from the grace of God** The members of the community are to be accountable for one another (which may also be the point made in 10:25). The exhortation is restated in the language of Deuteronomy 29:18 about a **bitter plant** (lit., "root") that can grow and **poison** (lit., "defile") others around it. The appropriateness of the allusion is plain from the following verse in Deuteronomy (29:19): "Make sure that there is no one here today who hears these solemn demands and yet convinces himself that all will be well with him, even if he stubbornly goes his own way. That would destroy all of you, good and evil alike." The lapse of one member (or more) of the community will have its inevitable effect on others and is therefore to be prevented insofar as it is possible.

12:16-17 / The reference made in the preceding exhortation to the danger of "turning back from the grace of God" is now reinforced by the example of the unfortunate Esau. The community is to attempt to prevent anyone from becoming like him. Esau is described as **unspiritual** (lit., "irreligious") because he traded **his rights as the older son** (lit., "birthright") for a meal of bread and pottage (Gen. 25:33 f.). In this regard Esau is the antithesis of the heroes of faith in chapter 11. He trades off what is unseen and what lies in the future for immediate gratification in the present (cf. 11:25 f.). He thus forfeited the inheritance that was his right as the first born. Later Esau bitterly regretted his decision because when **he wanted to receive** (lit., "inherit") **his father's** (lit., "the") **blessing**, he was rejected. But there was no going back on his decision, no way **to change what he had done** (lit., "no way of repentance"). Repentance was not a possibility although he sought it with **tears** (Gen. 27:30–40). This warning concerning Esau's sad plight is reminiscent of the author's warning to the readers in 6:4 ff. (cf. 10:26 f.) about the impossibility of repentance for those who abandon the faith. Esau found no way back from his decision; the readers must learn from this how serious apostasy is, and not count upon an easy return to Christianity in more convenient times.

Additional Notes

12:12-13 / The imagery of Isa. 35:3 appears to have exercised influence on other writers besides the author of Hebrews. Thus Sirach also refers to "drooping hands and weak knees" (25:23; cf. 2:12; Zeph. 3:16; Josephus *Ant.* 6, 35). The word that describes **knees** as "tired" (*paralyō*) is used to describe the paralyzed man healed by Jesus in Luke 5:18–26. The word translated **strengthen** (*anorthoō*) occurs elsewhere in the NT only in Luke 13:13 and Acts 15:16. The rare word for **paths** (*trochia*), drawn from Prov. 4:26, occurs only here in the NT. **Lame** (*chōlos*) is the commonly used word in the NT, occurring only here in Hebrews. "Turned aside" (*ektrepō*) occurs elsewhere in the NT only in the Pastorals where it regularly means "to go astray." Perhaps in light of v. 15 an echo of this meaning may be seen here (note, too, **straight paths**). The common verb **healed** (*iaomai*) occurs only here in Hebrews.

12:14 / In the great benediction of 13:20 f. God is referred to as "the God of peace." The word for "holiness" in this verse (*hagiasmos*) is usually translated "sanctification" in the NT (e.g., the RSV of Rom. 6:19, 22; 1 Cor. 1:30; 1 Thess. 4:3). This word occurs only here in Hebrews. Its meaning, however, is not different from the related word used in v. 10. Sanctification is a state of holiness, and it is this that the readers are to pursue. Holiness is set forth as an essential requirement of the Christian particularly in 1 Pet. 1:15: "Be holy in all that you do, just as God who called you is holy," words that are followed by a quotation from Leviticus (11:44 f.; 19:2). See too Matt. 5:48. On the eschatological vision of God, see Rev. 22:4.

12:15 / Underlying GNB's **guard** is the Greek word *episkopeō*, which has the sense of "overseeing" or "caring for." This word (and its cognate noun), which here apparently refers to the responsibility of the entire community, soon becomes applied specifically to the official church leadership. The only other occurrence of the verb in the NT is in 1 Pet. 5:2. Underlying GNB's **turning back** is the Greek word *hystereō* (lit., "fall short"), the same verb used in the same connection in 4:1. The expression **the grace of God** occurs earlier in 2:9 where it refers to the atoning death of Jesus. Our author's words **causes many troubles** (from the verb *enochleō*) probably represent a minor corruption of the LXX text (which reads *en cholē* "in gall"). GNB reflects the influence of this better LXX text (and the Hebrew text of Deut. 29:18) in the words **with its poison**, which have no exact counterpart in the Greek text of our author. Because "trouble" and "gall" are fairly similar in meaning, the slight alteration of the LXX text is not serious. The result of such a "bitter root" in the community is lit. "that the many become defiled." The word "defiled" (*miainō*) here is used for both ceremonial (John 18:28; 1 Macc. 1:63) and moral (Titus 1:15) uncleanness. In the present context the defilement has to do with tendencies toward apostasy.

12:16–17 / As with his examples in chap. 11, the suitability of the example of Esau for the author's point is so striking that it is easy to imagine the diligence with which he searched his OT for appropriate illustrative material. It is debatable whether both **immoral** and **unspiritual** are to be understood as referring to Esau. That our author has a concern about sexual immorality among the readers seems clear from 13:4. It is also clear that Esau is portrayed in Jewish tradition as guilty of sexual immorality (see Strack-Billerbeck for examples). In the present context the second word is obviously appropriate. Esau was "irreligious" (*bebēlos*) because he had no regard for his lineage or for the covenant promises associated with that lineage. This is in obvious contrast to the portrayal of Jacob in 11:21. When Esau is said to have **wanted to receive his father's blessing**, what is meant of course is the restoration of his birthright as the first-born son.

He was turned back (*apodokimazō*) may perhaps be better translated "declared disqualified" (cf. BAGD, p. 90). The word for "repentance" (*metanoia*) occurs in a similar connection in 6:6. It is difficult to know whether the antecedent of **it** (*autēn*) at the end of v. 17 is "repentance" or the **blessing**, both of which are feminine nouns. The difference, however, is only slight, since the "repentance" was after all designed to repossess the **blessing**. Futility in one meant futility in the other, and thus either could have been the source of Esau's anguish.

37

The Glory of
the Christian's Present Status

HEBREWS 12:18–24

You have not come, as the people of Israel came, to what you can feel, to Mount Sinai with its blazing fire, the darkness and the gloom, the storm, [19]the blast of a trumpet, and the sound of a voice. When the people heard the voice, they begged not to hear another word, [20]because they could not bear the order which said, "If even an animal touches the mountain, it must be stoned to death." [21]The sight was so terrifying that Moses said, "I am trembling and afraid!" [22]Instead, you have come to Mount Zion and to the city of the living God, the heavenly Jerusalem, with its thousands of angels. [23]You have come to the joyful gathering of God's first-born sons, whose names are written in heaven. You have come to God, who is the judge of all mankind, and to the spirits of good people made perfect. [24]You have come to Jesus, who arranged the new covenant, and to the sprinkled blood that promises much better things than does the blood of Abel.

In one of the most remarkable passages in the whole book, the author presents a vivid contrast between Mount Sinai and Mount Zion, between the essential character of the old and new covenants. In so doing he provides a startling portrait of the readers' possession in and through Christ. It would be difficult to find a more impressive and moving expression of realized eschatology in the entire NT. The author's purpose is to enlarge the horizons of the readers to enable them to comprehend the true glory of what they participate in as Christian believers. What they are presently tempted to return to, their former Judaism, pales significantly in the comparison (cf. 2 Cor. 3:4–18). Those who have been to Mount Zion can never contemplate a return to Mount Sinai.

12:18 / In order to make the reference quite clear, GNB adds to the text the two phrases **as the people of Israel came** and **to Mount Sinai**, words that would hardly have been needed by the original readers, who would have recognized the allusion immediately. The vocabulary of this and the following verse is drawn to a large extent from the LXX accounts of Moses on Sinai (esp. Deut. 4:11; 5:22–25; Exod. 19:12–19). The manifestations of God's presence on Sinai were tangible, that is, they could be experienced by the senses. The **fire**, **darkness**, **gloom**, and **storm** made a vivid impression on the Israelites.

12:19–20 / They also heard **the blast of a trumpet** and **the sound of a voice** (lit., "a voice speaking words"). According to the Exodus narrative (20:19) the people indicated to Moses their fear of God's voice: "If you speak to us, we will listen; but we are afraid that if God speaks to us, we will die." This same fear is also recorded in Deuteronomy (5:25): "We are sure to die if we hear the Lord our God speak again." It was not only the actual hearing of God's voice that frightened the Israelites, but also the stern commands he uttered. Our author provides an example in the prohibition against touching the holy mountain. The awesome and absolute holiness of God's presence was unapproachable. Even an animal was to be **stoned** (GNB adds **to death**) if it touched the mountain (the quotation is from Exod. 19:13). The result of the Israelites' fear was that they wanted **not to hear another word**.

12:21 / According to our author even Moses was filled with fear at the spectacle of the theophany at Sinai. The words attributed to him are not found in the OT. The closest resemblance to them is found in Deuteronomy 9:19 where, after the rebellion of the Israelites in the wilderness, Moses says, "I was afraid of the Lord's fierce anger." The author's picture of the giving of the Law at Sinai, then, is one in which fear and the sternness of God's commands predominate. This picture stands in very great contrast to the picture of the new covenant situation the author now presents.

12:22 / The opening of this verse picks up the opening verb of verse 18. The perfect tense of this verb, **you have come**, indicates arrival some time in the past with continued enjoyment of the results of that arrival in the present. By the use of this tense the author clearly means to stress that what he is about to describe is in some way already enjoyed by the readers. They have come to **Mount Zion**, a mountain of even greater significance than the mountain alluded to in the preceding verses. **Mount Zion** is synonymous with Jerusalem in the OT (e.g., 2 Sam. 5:6 f.; 2 Kings 19:21; Ps. 2:6; 9:11). Here it is further described as **the heavenly Jerusalem**, that eschatological expectation referred to in Revelation 21:2 (cf. Gal. 4:26; 2 Bar. 4:2 ff.), and **the city of the living God**, a city already mentioned by our author as Abraham's true goal (11:10; cf. 11:16). In 13:14 he will write: "we are looking for the city which is to come." Thus the readers already enjoy in the present the eschatological city of the future (cf. Eph. 2:6). Here again we encounter the tension seen earlier in the epistle between realized and future eschatology (e.g., 1:2; 4:3; 6:5; 9:11; 10:1). Christians have experienced fulfillment, but fulfillment short of consummation. The readers are also said to have come to **thousands** (lit., "myriads" or "tens of thousands") of **angels** (GNB adds **with its**). In Deuteronomy 33:2, "ten thousands of holy ones" are associated with the appearance of the Lord at Sinai; in Daniel 7:10, "ten thousand times ten thousand" serve before the throne of God. These hosts are also present in the city, the heavenly Jerusalem (cf. the marriage supper of the Lamb, Rev. 19:6).

12:23 / GNB's **you have come** resumes the verb at the beginning of verse 22. The readers have come to the **gathering** of those who have been "called out" to form the people of God, as his **first-born**, whose names are inscribed in heaven (cf. Luke 10:21). This most probably refers to the believers of the new covenant era. Together this community of believers in Christ constitutes the **first-born** in that they have become the heirs of the promise (cf. Rom. 8:17). The Jerusalem Bible captures the sense of the passage well: "with the whole Church in which everyone is a 'first-born son' and a citizen of heaven." The readers, in short, **have come** (GNB resumes the original verb) into the very presence of God, the one **who is the judge of all**. Despite the awesome reality of God as judge (cf. v. 29), they have no need to be afraid, like the Israelites who were afraid at Sinai even of God's voice, because through Christ they now are free to approach God even in his role as **judge**. With this freedom we may compare the boldness of the Christian's free access into God's presence through the sacrificial work of Christ (e.g., 4:16; 6:19; 7:25; 10:19 ff.). **The spirits of good** (lit., "just") **people made perfect** is probably a reference to the OT people of God. They are referred to as **spirits** because they await the resurrection. More particularly they are described as having been **made perfect** in that, together with the readers and all Christians, they have arrived at the goal, the city of God, the final purpose of God that was first expressed to them, albeit in shadowy figures. This is in accord with what the author wrote of the OT saints in 11:40.

12:24 / The readers, finally, **have come** (GNB again resumes the verb of v. 22) **to Jesus who arranged** (lit., "the mediator of") **the new covenant**.

This climactic fact is the very basis of all that has been described beginning in verse 22. And the reference to **the new covenant** here recalls the reader to one of the author's central arguments (7:22; 8:6–13; 9:15). The **sprinkled blood** of Jesus refers to his sacrificial work of atonement. This imagery has also been utilized by our author earlier in his writing in describing the levitical practice (9:13 f., 19, 21), but also once in describing the work of Christ (10:22; cf. 1 Pet. 1:2). The blood of Jesus **promises much better things** (lit., "speaks better") than **the blood of Abel**. In 11:4 our author took note of Abel, writing that "by means of his faith Abel still speaks, even though he is dead." Here, however, the reference appears to be to Genesis 4:10 where the blood of Abel is said to be "crying out to me from the ground, like a voice calling for revenge." This is the message of the blood of Abel. But the blood of Christ speaks of better things—most conspicuously of the forgiveness of sins associated with the inauguration of the new covenant (8:12; 10:17 f.). Christ's atoning blood speaks of the end of the old covenant and the establishment of the new. It is this blood that has brought the readers to the benefits of the new covenant and to their present glorious status wherein they have begun to experience the fulfillment, the goal of God's saving purposes, the city of the living God, the heavenly Jerusalem.

Additional Notes

12:18 / A number of manuscripts include together with **what you can feel** the word "mountain" (*oros*), thus "a mountain that can be touched." The best manuscripts, however, omit the word, and its presence in some is probably due to the influence of v. 22. The perfect tense of the verb **have come** implies "to come to and remain at." This same tense is even more significant in the positive statement beginning in v. 22, where the verb is repeated. Only the words for **feel** (*psēlaphaō*) and **gloom** (*zophos*) are not drawn from LXX descriptions of the Sinai theophany.

12:19-20 / The reference to **the blast of a trumpet** and **the sound of a voice** are again drawn from the LXX of Exod. 19:16. According to the LXX of Exod. 19:13 the man or beast who touched the mountain was to be stoned or shot through with a dart. In both forms of execution the one killed is thus kept at a distance. This is in keeping with the dangerous potential for "contamination" by God's holiness (cf. 2 Sam. 6:7), even at second hand. See E. Pax, *EBT*, pp. 372–75. Some irony may be seen in the fact that although Sinai and the attendant phenomena are described as "tangible," yet neither man nor animal was in fact allowed to touch the mountain.

12:21 / The word for **sight** (*phantazō*) occurs only here in the NT. In Hellenistic literature the word is used to describe the "spectacle" of a theophany. See BAGD, p. 853. Possibly the reference to Moses' fear and trembling is drawn from Jewish traditional materials concerning the giving of the Law at Sinai (cf. Acts 7:32, but there the trembling is in connection with the burning bush).

12:22 / The literal Mount Zion and Jerusalem because of their great importance eventually came to be understood as archetypes of the greater eschatological reality to come. On **Zion** and the new **Jerusalem**, see Lohse, *TDNT*, vol. 7, pp. 319–38. For **city of the living God**, see note on 11:10. F. F. Bruce points out that the main verb **you have come to** implies conversion (the root occurring here, *proselēlythate*, produces the English word "proselyte"). A difficult question of interpretation hinges on whether the Greek word *panegyris* ("festal gathering") is to be taken with what precedes, "the myriad of angels" (RSV, NIV, JB) or with what follows, "the community of the first-born" (KJV, ASV, NEB, and GNB's **joyful**) or whether it is to be understood independently. It is almost certainly not to be taken independently since all other discrete entities referred to in the list are connected with **and** (*kai*), whereas there is no connective preceding *panegyris* here. The fact that there is a connective *kai* following it, however, makes it most natural to associate the word with the angels (e.g., NIV: "thousands upon thousands of angels in joyful assembly"). See Hughes's detailed note, pp. 552–55. On *panegyris*, see Seesemann, *TDNT*, vol. 5, p. 722. On the presence of angels in the heavenly realm and in an eschatological setting, cf. Revelation, which has the highest occurrence of references to angels of any NT book. See H. Bietenhard, *NIDNTT*, vol. 1, pp. 101–3, and note on 1:4 above.

12:23 / Much debate has taken place concerning the meaning of **gathering of God's first-born sons**. Such different possibilities as the following have been suggested: angels, OT saints, the first Christians, Christians who have died, and Christian martyrs. The accompanying reference to the **names written in heaven** makes it improbable that angels are meant, since this expression always refers to believers (e.g., Phil. 4:3; Rev. 3:5; 13:8; 20:15). The **first-born** could be interpreted to be the OT saints—first-born in the sense of preceding Christians. But given our author's convictions about the new covenant, it is improbable that he would restrict this title to the people of the earlier covenant (cf. James 1:18, which refers to Christians as "a kind of first fruits"). On **first-born** (*prōtotokos*), which refers to Christians only here in the NT, see Michaelis, *TDNT*, vol. 6, p. 881; Hughes, pp. 552–55; and note to 1:6 above. Moreover, the author's deliberate use of the word *ekklēsia* ("community") for **gathering** may be intended to point to the church (ASV, NIV, and JB translate "church"). The word *ekklēsia* in itself, of course, does not necessarily signify "church"; it can, as in the only other occurrence of the word in Hebrews (2:12), simply mean "congregation" or "assembly." See K. L. Schmidt, *TDNT*, vol. 3, pp. 501–36.

Earlier our author described the community of believers, of which the readers are a part, as "the house of God" (3:6). Here it is they who are said to comprise the city of God. This is the only place in Hebrews where God is called **judge** (*kritēs*), although the idea occurs several times (e.g., 2:3; 4:1; 6:8; 9:27; 10:27, 30 f.; 12:29). The word **spirits** is not to be taken as a technical term of biblical anthropology (to be distinguished from soul), but simply as referring to the spiritual or immaterial part of man's being. See Schweizer, *TDNT*, vol. 6, pp. 445 f. The word underlying GNB's **good** (*dikaios*) was used earlier by the author in 10:38 (in the quotation of Hab. 2:4) and in 11:4 where Abel is described as "a righteous man." The word is thus ideal to describe the heroes of faith mentioned in chap. 11. It is possible, however, as some have argued (e.g., Delitzsch, West-cott, Hughes), that this clause refers universally to people of faith in all eras, old and new. See W. J. Dumbrell, " 'The Spirits of Just Men Made Perfect,' " *EQ* 48 (1976), pp. 154–59. On the verb **made perfect** (*teleioō*), so important to our author, see note to 2:10.

12:24 / The word for "mediator" (*mesitēs*) is also used in referring to Jesus in 8:6 and 9:15. See note on 8:6. The word for "new" in **new covenant** here is *neos* rather than *kainē*, as it is in the other references to the new covenant in the epistle (8:8, quoting Jer. 31:31; 9:15), but no difference is intended by this synonym. For "covenant," see note on 7:22. For the sprinkling of blood (the noun *rhantismos* occurs only here in Hebrews), see notes on 9:7 and 9:13. This is the last occurrence of the word **better** (*kerittōn*) in the epistle. On this very important word for our author, see note to 1:4.

38

A Final Warning Concerning Rejection

HEBREWS 12:25-29

Be careful, then, and do not refuse to hear him who speaks. Those who refused to hear the one who gave the divine message on earth did not escape. How much less shall we escape, then, if we turn away from the one who speaks from heaven! [26]His voice shook the earth at that time, but now he has promised, "I will once more shake not only the earth but heaven as well." [27]The words "once more" plainly show that the created things will be shaken and removed, so that the things that cannot be shaken will remain.

[28]Let us be thankful, then, because we receive a kingdom that cannot be shaken. Let us be grateful and worship God in a way that will please him, with reverence and fear; [29]because our God is indeed a destroying fire.

Our author turns once again to warning his readers not to lapse from their Christian faith and commitment. This warning, however, is wonderfully counterbalanced by stress on the ultimate security of those who remain faithful. The options are thus finally put before the readers with the utmost clarity. If they reject the truth of the gospel they shall not escape judgment. But if they persevere in their faith, they are to know that they are the recipients of a kingdom that has no end. This passage, which rounds out so powerfully the argument that began in 2:1 with a passage so strikingly similar to the present one, is essentially the conclusion of the author's main argument and appeal. Chapter 13, as we shall see, functions more as an appendix to what precedes than an extension of the argument any further.

12:25 / This verse and the next build upon the contrast drawn between Sinai and Zion in the preceding passage. The author has presented virtually the same argument several times already (2:1 ff.; 4:21 f.; 10:28 f.). Arguing from the lesser to the greater (*a fortiori*), he points to the obvious and painful reality of the judgment experienced by the Israelites in their disobedience to the covenant at Sinai and then to the proportionately greater judgment deserved by those who turn away from the greater revelation of the new covenant. In the present instance, the Israelites refused to hear God's voice (cf. v. 19 f.), not only literally, but in the sense that they did not obey his commands (cf. 3:17 f.). It was God's voice they refused to hear when he spoke to them on earth through his servant Moses (see Deut. 5:4 f.). And to refuse God's word is to reject God himself. Thus the opening warning is that the readers not "reject him who speaks" (GNB adds **to hear**). GNB's **the one who gave the divine message** (lit., "revelation," or "warning") **on earth** in the events of Sinai just described (vv. 18–21) should probably not be understood as Moses, but as God speaking through Moses. If, therefore, the readers abandon their faith, they **turn away from** (lit., "reject") **the one** (GNB adds, probably correctly, **who speaks**) **from heaven**. That is, they refuse God's word from heaven, the gospel and all that is entailed in the fulfillment it brings. Our author wrote at the beginning of his epistle that "in these last days he has spoken to us through his Son" (1:2). This is the word from heaven that the readers are tempted to reject. But the greater the light, the more serious is its rejection. The readers are therefore to **be careful** not to reject the truth they have received.

12:26 / **At that time** refers to the giving of the Law at Sinai. It was the voice of God that then **shook the earth** (cf. v. 19; Exod. 19:18; Ps. 68:8). The **now** refers not to the past giving of the promise, but to the present expectation of its imminent fulfillment. God **has promised** a future shaking of the earth, and now that we are in the last days, that event can be expected in the near future. The quotation is from Haggai 2:6 (cf. 2:21). What is in view in these words from Haggai is the judgment that will take place in connection with the coming of the eschaton. The future shaking of the heavens has already been mentioned by our author in his quotation of Psalm 102:25–27 in 1:10–12 (cf. Matt. 24:29).

12:27 / Our author again provides a brief midrashic commentary for his readers. The words **once more** from the quotation are explained as referring to the eschatological judgment (unlike the earlier "shaking"), and this shaking involves the purging of **the created things** (lit., "as things made") so that (or "in order that") only what **cannot be shaken will remain**. But what can be shaken will be and this is what makes the prospect of eschatological judgment such a fearful thing (cf. v. 29).

12:28–29 / The readers, however, have good reason to be **thankful**, for they are the recipients of an unshakable **kingdom**. **Kingdom** here refers to what may be described as the fruit of the new covenant. Thus, like the reality of the kingdom of God mentioned frequently in the NT, it is the experience of the reign of God made possible by the reconciling grace of God in Christ. It thus is the new quality of life, the new existence, made possible through the fulfillment of the promises of a new covenant. Since this is the result of God's work it remains secure through any future shaking of the world. By this thankful frame of mind (GNB repeats the original exhortation, **let us be grateful**) and the faithful response that will accompany it, we will **worship** (or "serve") **God** in such a way as to **please** him, namely, in a way that produces **reverence and fear** (or "awe"). Reverence and awe remain appropriate words even for the worship and service of the Christian, for God is "the judge of all" (cf. v. 23), and in the eschatological judgment, he is **a destroying fire** (cf. 10:30 f.). This description of God is a quotation from Deuteronomy 4:24 (cf. Deut. 9:9), where Moses is exhorting the people to faithfulness to the covenant. God remains the same despite the new circumstances of the new covenant. In light of all this, the readers are to be thankful for what is theirs in Christ, and to put out of mind all thoughts of lapsing from their Christianity to their former way of life.

Additional Notes

12:25 / GNB removes "if" from before **those who**, turning the subordinate clause of the original into a declarative statement. The *a fortiori* form of the argument is more obvious from the original, which reads "how much more shall we not escape." The same verb for **be careful** (*blepō*) is used earlier in 3:12 in a similar connection. The fact that the verb for **refused** (*paraiteomai*) is the same as that used in v. 19 (GNB's **begged**) lends some support to the conclusion that it is God's voice and not Moses' that is refused. GNB, however, appears to accept the arguable conclusion (held, for example, by Moffatt and Montefiore) that it is Moses' voice **on earth** that is not heard. More probably it is God's voice through Moses that is in view here. The word **speaks**, since it is the same verb as in the preceding verse, may readily be associated with the "better things" there mentioned. In the Greek text the words **those** and **we** are emphatic. The verb **escape** (*ekpheugō*) is the same as that used in the parallel passage in 2:3. GNB's **gave the divine message** translates the same verb (*chrēmatizō*) used in 8:5 and 11:7, both of which refer to God speaking (to Moses and Noah respectively). **Heaven** is clearly regarded as the abode of God (e.g., 8:1; 9:24; 12:23). **Turn away** translates *apostrephō*, which is practically synonymous with "apostatize" (cf. Titus 1:14).

12:26 / The perfect tense of the Greek underlying **has promised** indicates the continuing validity of the promise. The quotation follows the LXX of Hag. 2:6

very closely. Our author adds the words **not only** and **but** and transposes the order of **heaven** and **earth** with a resultant emphasis on the shaking of **heaven**. On the general expectation of an eschatological shaking of heaven and earth, see passages such as Isa. 2:19, 21; 13:13 (cf. 2 Pet. 3:10; Rev. 16:18 ff.; 21:1). See Bornkamm, *TDNT*, vol. 7, pp. 196–200, and Bertram *TNDT*, vol. 7, pp. 65–70. The present experience of realized eschatology (see note on 1:2) leads naturally to an expectation of the imminence of eschatology proper.

12:27 / More extensive midrashic treatments of OT quotations can be seen in 2:8 f.; 3:12–4:10; 8:13; 10:8–10; and 12:7–11. The argument is that the words **once more** indicate something yet to come. From our author's perspective this must refer to eschatological judgment of the created order. This judgment has as its goal the revealing of what **cannot be shaken**, what is a permanent part of the new creation already (cf. 13:20 "the eternal covenant"). GNB's **removed** (lit., "removal") translates *metathesis*, a word that occurs twice earlier in Hebrews (7:12, where it refers to "a change in the law," and 11:5, where it refers to the taking up of Enoch).

12:28–29 / The only other place in Hebrews where **kingdom** is used positively, in the sense of "God's kingdom," is in the quotation of Ps. 45:6 in 1:8. Our author, if he is not dependent upon the gospel tradition, may have drawn the term from such a passage as Dan. 7:27. The present participle "receiving," which underlies GNB's **receive**, suggests a careful balance between present and future eschatology. We are in the process of receiving the kingdom now; we will receive it finally in the future. The verb for **worship** is *latreuō*, used earlier in describing the service of the levitical priests (e.g., 8:5; 9:9; 10:2; 13:10; cf. the cognate noun in 9:1 and 6), but here, as in 9:14, it is used spiritually to describe the life of the Christian. See Strathmann, *TDNT*, vol. 4, pp 58–65. The adverb underlying **in a way that will please him** (*euarestōs*) occurs only here in the NT (the cognate adjective occurs in 13:21, however). **Reverence** (*eulabeia*) occurs only here and in 5:7 in the NT. See note on 5:7. The word for "awe" (*deos*) occurs only here in the Greek Bible. God in his role as judge is described several times in the OT in the imagery of a consuming fire (e.g., Isa. 26:11; 33:14; Zeph. 1:18; 3:8). Our author has earlier used this imagery in 10:27.

39

A Call to Ethical Living

Keep on loving one another as Christian brothers. ²Remember to welcome strangers in your homes. There were some who did that and welcomed angels without knowing it. ³Remember those who are in prison, as though you were in prison with them. Remember those who are suffering, as though you were suffering as they are.

⁴Marriage is to be honored by all, and husbands and wives must be faithful to each other. God will judge those who are immoral and those who commit adultery.

The author has concluded the main part of his epistle, having argued his points with convincing forcefulness, and now turns to various matters he desires to mention before concluding. Chapter 13, therefore, is like an appendix to what precedes. This is not to say, however, that the material in this chapter is unrelated to the main part of the epistle. Indeed, some of the author's main concerns are again touched upon here, but in a somewhat different way, fleetingly, and so as to bring out the practical significance of what has already been argued. At the same time, much material is similar to the general ethical exhortation found in the final sections of other epistles of the NT. Despite the unusual way Hebrews begins, these specific and concluding exhortations give the work the character of a letter. The opening verses of this chapter are particularly of that character, although some items may well have a special bearing on the readers.

13:1 / This short verse reads literally "Let brotherly love continue." Love, of course, is the basis of all Christian ethics. Jesus sums up the Law in the twofold command to love God and one's neighbor as oneself (Matt. 22:37–40; Mark 12:29–31; cf. Rom. 13:9 f.). Love is all-important to the Christian, greater even than faith or hope (1 Cor. 13). Its importance is a constant theme of the NT. The particular stress here upon love between **Christian brothers** is also found, for example, in John 13:34; Romans 12:10; 1 Thess. 4:9; and 1 Peter 1:22. The exhortation to love one another has already been given by the author: "Let us be concerned for one another, to help one another to show love and to do good" (10:24). Love is always shown in concrete acts—acts such as the author now mentions.

13:2 / Hospitality to **strangers** was important in the early church, especially in a time when facilities for travelers were few and often not reputable. Thus, exhortations such as the present one are found in several places in the NT (e.g., Rom. 12:13; 1 Pet. 4:9; cf. 1 Tim. 3:2; 5:10; Titus 1:8). Probably it is traveling Christian workers who are primarily in view (see especially 3 John 5–8). **Welcome . . . in your homes** is literally "show hospitality." The reference to **some** in the past who had unknowingly shown hospitality to angels alludes to the famous story of Abraham's hospitality in Genesis 18:1–8 (cf. 19:1 ff.), but possibly also to Gideon (Judg. 6:11–22), Manoah, and the mother of Samson (Judg. 13:3–21), and Tobit (Tob. 5:4–9). The motif is therefore a familiar one in Jewish tradition.

13:3 / The remembering of prisoners and empathy with those who suffer (the second **remember** is added by GNB) had already been admirably displayed by the readers in the past (10:33 f.; cf. 6:10). They are called to exhibit these Christian virtues (cf. Matt. 25:36) again as present or imminent circumstances may warrant. GNB's **as though you were suffering as they are** is literally "as you yourselves being in a body." Barclay's paraphrase brings the point out clearly, "for you have not yet left this life, and the same fate can happen to you." This identification with those who suffer is again a common NT motif (e.g., 1 Cor. 12:26; Rom. 12:15).

13:4 / From our author's statement that **marriage** is to be held in honor, we may infer that he is countering the influence of an asceticism that forbade marriage in the name of a supposedly higher way of holiness. But as in Judaism, so also in Christianity the material world created by God is good and such extreme asceticism is unnecessary. Human sexuality is itself good. Sexual promiscuity, of course, is out of the question: **husbands and wives must be faithful to each other** (lit., "[let] their marriage bed [be] undefiled"). In common with Paul's strictures (cf. 1 Cor. 6:9; Eph. 5:5; Col. 3:5), our author emphasizes that the immoral and the adulterous will receive the judgment of God.

Additional Notes

13:1 / The extent to which the key themes of chap. 13 reflect the concerns of the body of the epistle is effectively demonstrated by F. V. Filson, *"Yesterday": A*

Study of Hebrews in the Light of Chapter 13, SBT(2) 4 (London: SCM, 1967). On the diverse character of the material, however, Filson notes that chap. 13 contains twenty imperatives on fifteen separate topics. In addition to the present passage, the word for "brotherly love" (*philadelphia*) occurs in the NT only in Rom. 12:10; 1 Thess. 4:9; 1 Pet. 1:22; and 2 Pet. 1:7 (twice). In Hellenistic literature the word generally refers to love for blood brothers and sisters; in Christian literature it refers particularly to love for those who share Christian faith. See BAGD, p. 858.

13:2 / The word for "hospitality to strangers" (*philoxenia*) occurs elsewhere in the NT only in Rom. 12:13; the cognate adjective "hospitable" (*philoxenos*), however, occurs among the qualifications for bishops listed in 1 Tim. 3:2 and Titus 1:8, and also 1 Pet. 4:9. Hospitality to strangers was highly esteemed in the Hellenistic world as well as in Jewish tradition. Zeus was regarded as the protector of the oppressed foreigner, and he and other gods are said to have visited the world in the guise of a stranger. Hospitality to strangers is also advocated by Jesus, who puts it alongside such things as feeding the hungry, clothing the naked, and visiting the imprisoned (Matt. 25:35, 38, 44). Clement of Rome, reflecting his knowledge of Hebrews, praises Rahab not only for her faith but also for her hospitality (*philoxenia*). See 1 Cl. 12:1 (cf. 10:7 and 11:1 for Abraham and Lot respectively). The *Didache* (chaps. 11 and 12) supports hospitality to Christian evangelists (who are to be received "as the Lord"), but also recommends measures against the abuse of such hospitality. On the whole subject, see Stählin, *TDNT*, vol. 5, pp. 1–36.

13:3 / Visiting the imprisoned was also a virtue in certain Hellenistic circles (esp. among the Stoics). In the ancient world Christians had established an excellent reputation for themselves as exercising charity to those in prison, as well as for helping the suffering. Christian motivation in this regard stemmed directly from the teaching of Jesus (cf. Matt. 25:31–46). Cf. F. F. Bruce, pp. 391.

13:4 / It is possible that the asceticism countered in this passage stems from a Gnostic orientation that has as its starting point the claim that matter, and hence the body, is evil. Marriage is thus to be avoided by those who would cultivate the life of the spirit. This form of asceticism is argued against elsewhere in the NT (e.g., 1 Tim. 4:3). This provides some support for T. W. Manson's thesis that Hebrews was written to the same Gnostic-influenced community in the Lycus Valley to which Colossians is addressed. R. Jewett has adopted this viewpoint in his commentary. On the other hand, a similar asceticism, but with very different presuppositions, was held by the Essenes such as those who formed the community at Qumran. Hughes uses this to support his theory that the readers were influenced by the Essene perspective. "Undefiled" (*amiantos*) is the same word used in 7:26 to describe the holiness of Christ our High Priest (cf. 1 Pet. 1:4 where it describes the Christian's inheritance.) The word **immoral** (*pornos*) refers specifically to sexual immorality (cf. the same word in 12:16). In 1 Cor. 6:9 this word is joined, as here, with "adulterer" (*moichos*).

40

The Security of the Believer

Keep your lives free from the love of money, and be satisfied with what you have. For God has said, "I will never leave you; I will never abandon you."	⁶Let us be bold, then, and say, "The Lord is my helper, - I will not be afraid. What can anyone do to me?"

A further exhortation pertaining to the love of money leads the author to a general statement about the security of the believer, a statement that must have carried special significance for the readers given what they were facing or were about to face.

13:5 / The **love of money** is a danger to be avoided by those who would live by faith. It brings further evil with it (1 Tim 6:9 f.) and reflects an improper attachment to this transitory world. In the past the readers had exhibited the proper attitude when they endured the loss of their property gladly "because you knew that you still possessed something much better, which would last forever" (10:34). The readers are therefore to be **satisfied** with what they have. This is again a common theme in the NT (cf. 1 Tim. 6:6 ff., where Christians are exhorted to remain content with the bare necessities of life). As is true of so much of the ethical teaching of the early church, this emphasis also derives from the teaching of Jesus (cf. Matt. 6:24–34; Luke 12:15). The readers, however, are to go beyond simple contentment with what they have. They are to find their security totally in God. The quotation introduced with the words **God** (lit., "he himself") **has said** is from Deuteronomy 31:6 (and again in v. 8). Our author, however, has altered the third person of the original ("he will") to the more vivid first person ("I will"). The same promise, but with slightly different wording, is made in the first person in Joshua 1:5 (cf. also Gen. 28:5; 1 Chron. 28:20). Whereas material possessions are by their nature subject to loss and thus unworthy of ultimate commitment, God and his saving purpose are unchanging.

13:6 / GNB's **let us** is in keeping with the tone of exhortation in the passage. The text, however, may also be interpreted as an indicative statement (e.g., "we say," NIV; "we can say," RSV). The quotation is drawn verbatim from the LXX of Psalm 118:6. Our author affirms the faithfulness of the Lord in every circumstance and thus argues that there is no place for fear of what **anyone** (lit., "man") can do against the Christian. The appropriateness of this reminder for the readers is clear. If they are called to suffer not only personal loss, as in the past, but even the loss of life (cf. 12:4), they are to remember that God is with them and that they participate in a kingdom that cannot be shaken (12:28). With **the Lord** as their **helper** the readers can thus face every eventuality that may threaten them.

Additional Notes

13:5 / The single Greek word underlying **free from the love of money** (*aphilargyros*) occurs elsewhere in the NT only in 1 Tim. 3:3 in the list of qualifications for a bishop. The verb for **be satisfied** (*arkeō*) occurs in 1 Tim. 6:8 where the same point is made by Paul. The emphasis on contentment with one's present belongings finds a parallel in the Stoic teaching of self-sufficiency. Paul also exemplified this attitude in his life (see Phil. 4:11 f.). The same verb for **abandon** (*enkataleipō*) occurs in 2 Cor. 4:9, where Paul refers to being "persecuted, but not forsaken" (RSV). The OT quotation in this verse agrees exactly with the quotation as found in Philo, *On the Confusion of Tongues* 166. Rather than indicating direct dependence of our author on Philo, probably this reflects a common form of the quotation in the preaching of Hellenistic Judaism.

13:6 / GNB's **be bold** translates a Greek verb (*tharreō*; cf. *tharseō*) that indicates "courage" or "confidence." It occurs elsewhere in the NT only in 2 Cor. (5:6, 8; 7:16; 10:1, 2). See Grundmann, *TDNT*, vol. 3, pp. 25–27. In the quotation from Ps. 118:6 our author follows the LXX verbatim; the latter closely follows the Hebrew original. (Paul's statement in Rom. 8:31 may be an allusion to the same passage.)

41

A Call to Faithfulness
and a Warning Against
False Teaching

HEBREWS 13:7–9

Remember your former leaders, who spoke God's message to you. Think back on how they lived and died, and imitate their faith. ⁸Jesus Christ is the same yesterday, today, and forever. ⁹Do not let all kinds of strange teachings lead you from the right way. It is good to receive inner strength from God's grace, and not by obeying rules about foods; those who obey these rules have not been helped by them.

Yet again our author calls his readers to faith. This leads him in turn to refer to the one whom he has earlier described as "the author of faith" (12:2). The constancy of Jesus Christ is a motive for the readers to have faith as well as to avoid false teaching.

13:7 / The **leaders** referred to in this verse are those of the past (hence GNB's addition of the word **former** is justified), who proclaimed **God's message** (lit., "the word of God") to the readers. Our author refers to the present leaders of the community in verses 17 and 24. GNB's **think back on how they lived and died** is a paraphrase of what is literally "consider the outcome of their way of life." Like the heroes of chapter 11, they were people of **faith**. That is, they remained true to their convictions through all difficult circumstances (perhaps including the events described in 10:32–34). The "outcome of their way of life" is not to be understood as martyrdom (cf. 12:4), but simply as a manifestation of faithfulness. Holding these examples before them, the readers are called to **imitate their faith** (cf. 6:12).

13:8 / This remarkable verse does not intend to represent Jesus in the abstract and timeless categories of Platonic thought. It is not meant as a description of the transcendent and eternal nature of Jesus Christ. The main point of the verse is that because of his past and present work Jesus Christ is sufficient to meet all needs that Christians face. This is apparent not only from the context but also from the actual structure of the verse, which reads, literally, "Jesus Christ yesterday and today is the same, and until the ages." His work of **yesterday**, the sacrificial and atoning work as High Priest, has been expounded at length by our author. That is the very basis of Christianity. **Today** his work continues in the intercession he makes for us at the right hand of God (7:25; cf. 4:14–16). It is also true, as a kind of surplus, that the future of the readers remains secure. The faithfulness of Christ in the past and present will find its counterpart in the future when he returns to consummate the saving purposes of God (9:28). The faithfulness of Jesus Christ is unchanging (cf. 7:24) and is thus something upon which the readers may depend in living the life of faith.

13:9 / The constancy of Jesus Christ should in itself put the readers on guard against innovative and **strange teachings** that can lead them away **from the right way** (lit., "carry away"). The author now specifies what he has in mind. He desires his readers to reject teachings about **foods** insofar as it is alleged that they have to do with the spiritual well-being of Christians. GNB's **to receive inner strength** is literally "for the heart to be strengthened." Strength for the Christian comes not by the partaking or nonpartaking of certain foods, but by **grace** (GNB adds **God's**). GNB adds the words **obeying rules about** (and their counterpart in the next clause) in order to make the meaning clearer. Our author has already argued the transitory character of the dietary laws of Judaism (9:10). The argument is applicable here. But because the doctrines are described in this verse as **strange**, it seems unlikely that the dietary restrictions of Judaism are in view in the present context. More probably, here as in verse 4 our author may be countering teachings derived from the influence of an early Jewish Gnosticism or the general religious syncretism of the time (perhaps involving the partaking of a sacrifice; cf. v. 10). Compare Colossians 2:16; 1 Timothy 4:3 ff. **Those who obey these rules** (lit., "who are walking in them") do not profit thereby. Paul takes a similar attitude toward these dietary teachings (cf. 1 Cor. 8:8; Rom. 14:17). Thus the readers are not to let themselves be carried away by such teachings. **God's grace** is all they need for strength to do his will and to live as they ought.

Additional Notes

13:7 / The participial noun for **leaders**, here and in vv. 17 and 24 (*hēgoumenoi*, from *hēgeomai*), occurs also in such passages as Luke 22:26 and Acts 15:22. See Büchsel, *TDNT*, vol. 2, pp. 907–9. Possibly **leaders** here refers to the founders of this community of believers, described in 2:3: "those who heard him proved to us that it is true." The aorist tense of the verb underlying **spoke** (*laleō*) points clearly to completed action in the past. The expression "the word of God" (*ho logos tou theou*) occurs also in 4:12, but in a different sense. Here it is equivalent to the gospel. GNB's **think back on** translates the verb *anatheoreō*, which can mean "observe" in a literal sense (as in Acts. 17:23, the only other occurrence in the NT), but is here used figuratively in the sense of "consider." The Greek word for "outcome" (*ekbasis*) can mean "the end of" in the sense of death, but here means "successful outcome." The only other NT occurrence is in 1 Cor. 10:13, where it means "escape." See BAGD, pp. 237 f. "Way of life" is from *anastrophē*, a common NT word meaning "conduct" or "behavior." The reference to **faith** (*pistis*) calls the readers' minds back to chap. 11. The former leaders of their community exhibited the same commitment to the reality of the unseen. See above on 11:1.

13:8 / It is arguable that **yesterday** refers not to the work of the incarnate Christ, but simply to the experience of Christ's provision by the "former leaders" mentioned in the preceding verse. It is certainly to be understood by the readers that because of the constancy of Jesus Christ he will provide for them just as he did for their former leaders. But the form of this verse, which sounds much like a weighty creedal statement, makes it probable that more than this is meant. The word **yesterday** (*echthes*) can be used to mean "the past as a whole." BAGD, p. 331. The Greek phrase underlying **forever** (*eis tous aiōnas*, lit., "unto the ages") occurs frequently in Hebrews (cf. 5:6; 6:20; 7:17, 21, 24, 28). The present verse presupposes the eternal character of Jesus as God's Son, which has already come to expression in the quotation from Ps. 102 in 1:12: "But you are always the same and your life never ends" (cf. Rev. 1:17 f.).

13:9 / The concern about the dangers of false teaching is most prominent in the Pastoral Epistles in the NT (cf. 1 Tim. 4:16; 6:3 f.; Titus 1:8). On **grace** (*charis*), see note to 4:16. For a parallel use of the Greek verb for "strengthen" (*bebaioō*), see 1 Cor. 1:8; 2 Cor. 1:21. (In Hebrews 2:3 the same verb is used in a different sense.) For the heart as the center of man's religious life, see Behm, *TDNT*, vol. 3, p. 608–14. On **foods** (*brōma*), see Behm, *TDNT*, vol. 1, pp. 642–45. The notion of "walking" (*peripateō*) is used commonly in Hebraic idiom for conduct, particularly the following of the stipulations of the Law.

226

42

Christ's Sacrifice and the Spiritual Sacrifices of Christians

HEBREWS 13:10-16

The priests who serve in the Jewish place of worship have no right to eat any of the sacrifice on our altar. [11]The Jewish High Priest brings the blood of the animals into the Most Holy Place to offer it as a sacrifice for our sins; but the bodies of the animals are burned outside the camp. [12]For this reason Jesus also died outside the city, in order to purify the people from sin with his own blood. [13]Let us, then, go to him outside the camp and share his shame. [14]For there is no permanent city for us here on earth; we are looking for the city which is to come. [15]Let us, then, always offer praise to God as our sacrifice through Jesus, which is the offering presented by lips that confess him as Lord. [16]Do not forget to do good and to help one another, because these are the sacrifices that please God.

The sacrificial work of Christ has put the Christian in a new and privileged position, free from the Mosaic or any other dietary legislation, and dependent only upon grace. This definitive sacrifice should produce an appropriate response: in the first instance, willingness to suffer abuse such as Christ suffered, but secondly, willingness to serve others. In this remarkable passage the author recapitulates earlier argumentation and focuses on the practical working out of these truths in the lives of his readers.

13:10-11 / Our author returns here to a familiar theme: the typological relationship between the sacrificial ritual of the levitical priesthood and the definitive sacrifice of Christ. His first point here is that those who continue in that outmoded sacrificial system cannot partake of the true and final sacrifice. This point is confirmed typologically in the fact that **the bodies** (GNB adds **of the animals**) of those animals whose blood was offered **for sins** (GNB adds **to offer it as a sacrifice**) were **burned outside the camp** (see Lev. 4:21; 16:27). Just as the priests could not eat of those sacrificial animals, so they cannot partake of the sacrifice which they foreshadowed. **The priests** (lit., "those") who render service in the **Jew-**

ish place of worship (lit., "the tent") thus may not **eat** from this altar (GNB adds **of the sacrifice on**). The word **eat** here is almost certainly to be taken in a figurative sense to mean to partake of the benefits of the sacrifice of Christ. That is, within the framework of the old system, they cannot partake of the fulfillment brought by the sacrifice of Christ. This is true of the priests and **the High Priest** (GNB adds **Jewish**), but by implication true of all those who participate in their work. Thus for the readers to return to Judaism would mean the forfeit of the benefits of Christ's work. They, like the priests, would be excluded from partaking of the **altar**, that is, the work of Christ. This argument will lead in verse 13 to the appeal to leave Judaism behind.

13:12-13 / Reference to the burning of the bodies of the sacrificial animals "outside the camp" leads our author to a further interesting typological parallel. Jesus **died** (lit., "suffered") **outside the city** (lit., "gate"). The crucifixion—that fulfillment of the OT sacrifices wherein he sanctified **the people . . . with his own blood**—took place outside the city walls (John 19:20; cf. Matt. 21:39). This analogy is now given an application to the readers in the author's exhortation to join Jesus **outside the camp**. That is, they are called to leave behind the security and comfort of Judaism and in so doing to **share his shame** (lit., "bearing his reproach"; RSV: "bear the abuse he endured," cf. 12:2). The readers are called to endure the persecution that will come their way when they remain true to their Christian faith. This exhortation is thus a restatement of the author's concern for the readers expressed throughout the book (e.g., 2:1; 3:12; 4:11; 6:4 ff.; 10:35; 12:3).

13:14 / Another way the author expresses the kind of commitment he is asking of his readers is by emphasizing the transitory character of all earthly cities. We have no abiding city **here** (GNB adds **on earth**). Like Abraham, and with all Christians, the readers seek an abiding city, "the city with permanent foundations" (11:10; cf. 11:16). To be sure, through the fulfillment brought by the finished work of Christ, they have in a sense already come to that city, the heavenly Jerusalem (12:22). Yet although "realized eschatology" (see commentary on 9:11) is a present reality, eschatology in the strictest sense of the word remains an expectation of the future. Thus, like the heroes of faith the readers are to be controlled by an unseen, future reality (cf. 11:1). By implication, the importance of the literal Jerusalem, symbolic of the Temple and the levitical sacrifices, must give way to that of the heavenly Jerusalem. But it is exactly the latter that the readers will not participate in if they remain in the Judaism of the literal Jerusalem (cf. v. 10).

13:15–16 / There are forms of sacrifice—spiritual, and not literal—that are still pleasing to God. To these the author now calls his readers. The first he mentions, utilizing OT language, is literally "the sacrifice of praise." This expression is used a few times in the OT to indicate a particular category of literal sacrifice (e.g., 2 Chron. 29:31), but it also becomes a figure of speech for a grateful heart (e.g., Ps. 50:14, 23). This continual "sacrifice" is to be made **through Jesus** (lit., "him") and it is further defined as **the offering presented by** (lit., "the fruit of") **lips that confess him as Lord**. In these last words GNB goes somewhat beyond the text, which reads, literally, "confessing to his name" (cf. RSV: "that acknowledge his name"). Barclay's translation is appropriate: "which publicly affirm their faith in him." In this instance, the "sacrifice of praise" first called for will be the readers' faithfulness to their Christian profession. Only in this way can they show their thankfulness to God for what he has done. There are, however, other **sacrifices that please God**, the spiritual counterpart of the sacrifices of the old covenant. These include such things as **to do good** and **to help one another** (lit., "sharing"). The readers are not to forget these common Christian virtues. This, and not through the sacrifice of animals (cf. 9:8 f.), is the way that faithfulness to God is to be manifested.

Additional Notes

13:10–11 / It is possible, but hardly probable, that v. 10 is an allusion to the Eucharist or Lord's Supper, which of course non-Christians were not allowed to partake of. Yet our author never clearly alludes to the Eucharist (as, for example, he might have done in referring to the Melchizedek story in chap. 7; cf. Gen. 14:18), and the language of the **altar** (and implied sacrifice) would, at least at this early time, be strange in an allusion to the Eucharist. See R. Williamson, "The Eucharist and the Epistle to the Hebrews," *NTS* 21 (1975), pp. 300–12. It is much more likely that the reference to "foods" in the preceding verse turned our author's mind to remember that the priests, although allowed to eat of most of the sacrificed animals (cf. 1 Cor. 9:13; 10:18), were not allowed to eat of the sin offering on the Day of Atonement (Exod. 29:14; Lev. 4:11 f., 21; 16:27). But it is precisely the true sin offering (cf. v. 12) that the priestly representatives of the old order cannot partake of as long as they remain concerned with the preparation rather than the fulfillment.

This text has prompted some commentators to think of the readers as converted priests (cf. Acts 6:7), but this must remain highly speculative since the argument would have been intelligible to ordinary Jewish converts. **Altar** (*thysias-tērion*), used figuratively here, is the common NT word and is used in reference to the literal altar of the Temple in 7:13. The language of "serving the tent" is used earlier, esp. in 8:4 f. See note on 8:5 for the verb "serve" (*latreuō*), and the "tent" or wilderness tabernacle. See A. Snell, "We Have an Altar," *RefThR* 23 (1964), pp. 16–23. **Right** translates *exousia* ("authority") a very common NT word found only here in Hebrews. Much of the actual wording of v. 11 is drawn from the LXX of Lev. 16:27. The present tenses of the verbs may again hint at the actual existence of the Temple and its ritual at the time the author writes. GNB's **Most Holy Place** translates *ta hagia* (lit., "the holies"). For the use of this expression in referring to the Holy of Holies, see 9:8, 12, 25. Only the **High Priest** could bring the sacrificial blood into the Holy of Holies, and that one day in the year (see 9:7). On the importance of **blood**, see note to 9:7. The **camp** (*parembolē*) refers to the encampments of the nomadic Israel. **Outside the camp** refers to unhallowed ground. See H. Koester, " 'Outside the Camp': Hebrews 13:9–14," *HTR* 55 (1962), pp. 299–315 and J. N. Thompson, "Outside the Camp: A Study of Hebrews 13:9–14," *CBQ* 40 (1978), pp. 53–63.

13:12-13 / The word for "suffer" (*paschō*) is also used in the NT to refer to the death of Jesus (cf. 9:26; 1 Pet. 3:18). See note on 9:26. "Outside the gate" is equivalent to **outside the camp**. Outside the city gate meant, of course, outside the wall. Thus, the true sacrifice for sin, to which the sacrifice on the Day of Atonement pointed, was accomplished not on the hallowed ground of the Temple precincts, but outside the holy city. This in itself suggests the separation between Christianity and Judaism as well as the present irrelevance of the sacrifices of the Temple. See J. Jeremias, *TDNT*, vol. 6, pp. 921 f. GNB's **purity . . . from sin** translates the verb *hagiazō* (lit., "sanctify"), which occurs often in Hebrews and usually with the meaning of cleanse from sin or make atonement. See note on 2:11. **The people** (*laos*) are understood to be the people of the new covenant (cf. 8:10; 10:30). The words **outside the camp**, as in v. 11, are drawn from Lev. 16:27. This call to "go out" to the crucified Jesus, **outside the camp**, may mean to leave the protection of Judaism as a legal religion in the Roman Empire. The affirmation of Christianity meant full exposure to persecution. Thus, for the readers, remaining loyal to their Christian profession would mean "bearing his reproach (*oneidismos*)." Almost the same expression occurs in 11:26 (see note) in the description of the faith of Moses. For a reference in our epistle to the abuse suffered by Christ, see 12:2.

13:14 / For the importance and background of the word **city** (*polis*), see note on 11:10. The reference here to a city that is **permanent** or abiding may be intended to remind the readers of the argument presented in 12:27 f. The verb **looking for** (*epizēteō*) occurs in only one other place in Hebrews, where it describes the heroes of the OT as "looking for a [heavenly] country of their own" (11:14).

13:15-16 / A few important manuscripts (e.g., P⁴⁶; Sinaiticus, first hand) omit **then** *(oun)*, perhaps by accident. See Metzger, *TCGNT*, p. 676. The spiritual application of the language of the sacrificial cultus, which we have encountered frequently in Hebrews, is common in the NT. 1 Pet. 2:5 is a good example: "Come as living stones, and let yourselves be used in building the spiritual temple, where you will serve as holy priests to offer spiritual and acceptable sacrifices to God through Jesus Christ." The expression "the fruit of lips" is, like the immediately preceding language, drawn from the OT (cf. Hos. 14:2; Isa. 57:18). Contemporary use of this phrase is attested at Qumran (see 1QH 1:28; cf. 1QS 9:4 f.). After the word "confessing," our author writes "his name" in the dative case. This is similar to passages in the Gospels where what is confessed is expressed by the preposition *en* ("in") and the dative (e.g., Matt. 10:32 and Luke 12:8). See Michel, *TDNT*, vol. 5, pp. 207-12. The Greek noun underlying **do good** (*eupoiia*) occurs only here in the Greek Bible. **Help one another** translates the common NT noun for "fellowship" or "sharing" (*koinonia*), in Hebrews found only here. The notion of being "well pleasing to God" (*euaresteō*) is found several times in our epistle (11:5 f.; 12:28; 13:21). Paul uses language similar to that of Hebrews in Phil. 4:18 where, referring to the gifts brought by Epaphroditus, he writes: "They are like a sweet-smelling offering to God, a sacrifice which is acceptable and pleasing to him" (cf. Matt. 9:13). On this figurative use of "sacrifice," see Behm, *TDNT*, vol. 3, pp. 180-90.

43

Obedience to Church Leaders and a Request for Prayer

HEBREWS 13:17–19

Obey your leaders and follow their orders. They watch over your souls without resting, since they must give to God an account of their service. If you obey them, they will do their work gladly; if not, they will do it with sadness, and that would be of no help to you.

[18]Keep on praying for us. We are sure we have a clear conscience, because we want to do the right thing at all times. [19]And I beg you even more earnestly to pray that God will send me back to you soon.

In this final exhortation, the readers are enjoined to obey their leaders—a common enough motif in the NT, but one that has special significance for these particular readers, given their inclination to abandon their Christian faith and to return to Judaism. Obedience to their leaders will assure safe arrival at the goal God has marked out for them. This is followed by the first personal information about the author, given via a specific request for prayer. The request and the reference to the author's relation to the readers now give the character of an epistle to this impressive theological document.

13:17 / Our author now exhorts his readers to **obey** their leaders and to **follow their orders** (lit., "submit [to the leaders]"). They must recognize the responsibility that lies upon the shoulders of these leaders. In fulfilling their charge, the leaders keep watch (GNB adds **without resting**) as those who must **give** (GNB adds **to God**) **an account** (GNB adds **of their service**). For clarity, GNB paraphrases the next terse words. The point is that the readers are to be obedient and submissive to the authority of their leaders in order that they may accomplish their task with gladness rather than **sadness** (lit., "not groaning"). But obedience to the leaders is not merely for the sake of making their work easier. The failure to submit to them cannot benefit the readers. Indeed, the implication of this understatement is that disobedience and insubordination will put the readers in peril.

13:18-19 / Our author now asks prayer for himself (the plurals in v. 18 are probably rhetorical rather than literal; cf. v. 19). That this request comes without any transition suggests that the author has been related directly to the readers as one of their leaders. The statement about **a clear** (lit., "good") **conscience** implies criticism of the author from some quarter or another—criticism of which the readers have become aware and that may be having a negative effect on them. The author takes the whole matter seriously as we can see from his language **we are sure** ("we are convinced" or "persuaded"). This criticism would appear to involve conduct rather than doctrine (although the two are always related), and thus the author assures his readers of his proper motivation.

We want to do the right thing at all times may be rendered more literally "in everything wanting to conduct ourselves well." Unfortunately we can only speculate as to the circumstances that are alluded to here. Are they directly related, for example, to the specific request of verse 19? This is suggested by the literal wording of the latter: "I beseech you more earnestly to do this, in order that I may quickly be restored to you." For some reason the author has apparently been hindered from returning to the community of the readers. He is clearly in difficulty of some kind. In light of verse 23 this is probably not imprisonment, unless he is confident of imminent release. The author's special relationship to the readers is apparent in his earnest request for prayer to be restored to them. He longs to be in their midst again.

Additional Notes

13:17 / This reference to obeying the present **leaders** (*hēgoumenoi*) brings to mind the challenge to "imitate the faith" of former leaders (13:7; see note there). The verb underlying "submit" (*hypeikō*) occurs only here in the NT. GNB's **without resting** is intended to bring out the nuance of the verb *agrypneō*, "to watch over," which suggests constant vigilance or wakefulness (cf. Eph. 6:18; Luke 21:36; cf. the cognate noun referring to "sleepless nights" in 2 Cor. 11:27; 6:5). The perspective here, indeed, is very similar to that of Paul in 2 Cor. 11:28: "Every day I am under the pressure of my concern for all the churches" (cf. 1 Thess. 2:19 f.). The word **souls** (*psychē*) should be taken in the broader sense of whole persons or beings, as it is in 6:19 and 10:39 (see note on the latter passage). The responsibility of stewardship held by the leaders is a familiar biblical theme (cf. Ezek. 3:17–21; Luke 16:2). This is the only occurrence of the verb "to groan" (*stenazō*) in Hebrews. GNB's **of no help** translates the classical word *alysitelēs* ("unprofitable"), which in the Greek Bible occurs only here. For parallels involving a call to obedience to church leaders generally, see 1 Cor. 16:16 and 1 Thess. 5:12 f. It is possible, of course, that the present exhortation implies some particular insubordination of which the author has heard (is 10:25 relevant?). F. F. Bruce speculates that the leaders were those of a wider Christian community from which the readers may have been tempted to withdraw.

13:18–19 / Here our author writes very much as Paul does on occasion. The request for prayer concerning personal needs is of course common in the Pauline letters (cf. Rom. 15:30; 2 Cor. 1:11 f.; Eph. 6:19; Col. 4:3). The expression "a good conscience" is found several times in the NT, but with the adjectives *agathē*, "good," or *kathara*, "pure," rather than *kalē* as here (e.g., Acts 23:1; 1 Tim. 1:19; 3:9; 2 Tim. 1:3; 1 Pet. 3:16, 21). A passage very similar to the present one is found in 2 Cor. 1:12 where, after a request for prayer, Paul speaks of his untroubled conscience. For the word **conscience**, see note on 9:9. GNB's **at all times** translates *en pasin*, which may also be translated "in everything" (cf. KJV, NASB, NIV, RSV, JB; agreeing with GNB is NEB). The verb **beg** or "urge" (*parakaleō*) occurs with the same meaning in v. 22 (cf. 3:13 and 10:25 for the word used in a different sense). The verb for **restore** (*apokathistēmi*) occurs in Hebrews only here.

44

A Concluding Prayer

God has raised from death our Lord Jesus, who is the Great Shepherd of the sheep as the result of his sacrificial death, by which the eternal covenant is sealed. May the God of peace provide you with every good thing you need in order to do his will, and may he, through Jesus Christ, do in us what pleases him. And to Christ be the glory forever and ever! Amen.

Our author rounds out his letter with a magnificent closing prayer in which he picks up a number of the key motifs in the epistle. The prayer is notable for its beauty and comprehensive scope. Its powerful impact will be apparent to all who have read the letter and noted the deep pastoral concerns of the author's heart.

13:20-21 / GNB's first sentence is in fact a part of the prayer, an address to God based upon his saving work in Christ. GNB compensates by postponing the words **may the God of peace**, which belong at the beginning of the prayer, to the beginning of the second sentence. The address **the God of peace** is a formula common in the Pauline epistles (e.g., Rom. 15:33; 16:20; 2 Cor. 13:11; Phil. 4:9; 1 Thess. 5:23; 2 Thess. 3:16). God is further addressed as the one who raised Jesus **from death** (lit., "the dead"), although the phrase **our Lord Jesus** does not occur until the end of the address, just prior to the first petition, in a climactic position. This passing reference, in the midst of a calling upon God in prayer, surprisingly constitutes the only explicit reference to the resurrection of Jesus in the entire epistle (although of course the resurrection is presupposed in the references to the ascension that are so important to our author). The words that form the immediate object of **raised from death** are **the Great Shepherd of the sheep**, language that finds a NT parallel in the reference to "the Chief Shepherd" of 1 Peter 5:4 (cf. "shepherd of the sheep" in the LXX of Isaiah 63:11) and the words of Jesus in John 10:11 (cf. Mark 14:27). His designation as the **Great Shepherd** is **the result of** (lit., "by") his work of atonement.

GNB's **his sacrificial death by which the eternal covenant is sealed** is a paraphrastic rendering of what is literally "by the blood of the eternal covenant." In this pregnant phrase the author at once alludes to the earlier, detailed description of the sacrificial meaning of Christ's death (chaps. 7, 9–10) and to the accompanying powerful argument about the inauguration of a new covenant (7:22–8:13). The author's choice of the adjective **eternal** is deliberate. For if the old covenant gave way to a new covenant, assurance is needed that the new covenant is definitive and not merely a transitory reality. This is not to deny that OT language is utilized here. For our author, the new covenant established by Christ is none other than that "everlasting covenant" spoken of in Isaiah 55:3, Jeremiah 32:40, and Ezekiel 37:26. This is the "better covenant" of which Christ has become mediator (cf. 7:22; 8:6 f.) and with the concept of an **eternal covenant** we may recall the "eternal salvation" mentioned in 9:12.

The actual petition is that this great God, who has already done so much, would now meet the needs of his people by supplying them with **every good thing** for the purpose of doing **his will**, and remarkably that he would at the same time **do** (lit., "doing") **in us what pleases him**. The shift to the first person pronoun **us** provides a sensitive identification of the author with the readers. In that the readers are called to do the will of God and God does that will in us, the passage is reminiscent of Philippians 2:12 f. It is to be noted that the agency of that activity of God in us is expressed: **through Jesus Christ**. This is in complete accord with the view of Christ and his work throughout the book (cf. 7:22). GNB's **to Christ** is added to the text, but it is clear from the wording of the original that the doxology is directed to him. Most of the NT doxologies are directed to God (e.g., Rom. 11:36; 16:27; Gal. 1:5; Eph. 3:21; Phil. 4:20; 1 Tim. 1:17; Jude 25), and only a few, like the present one, are directed to Christ (e.g., possibly 1 Pet. 4:11; 2 Pet. 3:18; Rev. 1:6). This doxology serves as the climactic ending which corresponds to the exalted Christology set forth in the opening chapter of the book and, indeed, the Christology that constitutes the basis of the exposition in the intervening chapters. In light of the treatise to which the author is now putting the final touches, this doxology to Christ is both appropriate and moving. Although the **Amen** is formulaic, it is also the only fitting response to things so wonderful.

Additional Notes

13:20-21 / This concluding prayer and doxology bear some resemblance to the doxology at the end of Romans (16:25–27), which is also to some extent built upon themes expounded in the body of the work. F. F. Bruce notes the structure of the prayer is that of a collect: it is expressed in the third person, contains an invocation, an adjective clause pointing to the ground upon which the petition depends, main and subsidiary petitions, a plea to the merit of Christ's work, a doxology, and an Amen. There are several relatively unimportant textual variants in these verses. A majority of later manuscripts add the word "work" to the words **every good**; an unintelligible third person pronoun is found before "doing" (GNB's second **do**) in some manuscripts, perhaps by dittography (i.e., accidental repetition by a scribe), and thus the shorter reading is to be preferred; some manuscripts harmonize the pronoun **us** to agree with the earlier second person pronouns; and some manuscripts omit the words **and ever** at the end of the doxology, where the shorter ending is probably to be preferred. On these variants, see Metzger, *TCGNT*, p. 676 f. The verb for **raised** is not one of the usual NT words (*egeirō* or *anistēmi*), but *anagō* (which is used of Christ in Rom. 10:7), perhaps by suggestion from the LXX of Isa. 63:11, where Moses, described as the shepherd of the sheep, is brought up "out of the sea." This is the only occurrence of the words **shepherd** (*poimēn*) and **sheep** in Hebrews.

For the expression "blood of the covenant," see Zech. 9:11. On **covenant** (*diathēkē*), see note to 7:22. **Good thing** (*agathon*) is also used absolutely by our author in 9:11 and 10:1, where, however, it refers to the "good things" of the eschatological order inaugurated by Christ's finished work. The readers are called to do the will (*thelēma*) of God in 10:36; here the prayer is made that they might be equipped to do that will. **What pleases him** is literally "what is pleasing before him" and reflects Semitic idiom. This is synonymous with "the sacrifices that please God," in v. 16.

Commentators differ as to whether the doxology is directed to God or to Christ, since the wording leaves some ambiguity. That doxologies are usually directed to God in the NT writings, that God is the acting subject of these verses and the object of praise in v. 15, together with the fact that the readers are Jewish Christians, argue that God is in view. On the other hand, and more compelling, are the facts that the nearest antecedent to the pronoun "whom" is Jesus Christ, that Jesus assumes extraordinary importance as the Great Shepherd by whose blood the covenant and its gifts are made possible, and that the author assumes the deity of Christ in chap. 1. Thus GNB's translation seems justified (thus too NIV, NEB, JB). See C. E. B. Cranfield, "Hebrews 13:20–21," *SJT* 20 (1967), pp. 437–41; R. Jewett, "Form and Function of the Homiletic Benediction," *AngThR* 51 (1969), pp. 18–34.

45

Postscript and Final Benediction

I beg you, my brothers, to listen patiently to this message of encouragement; for this letter I have written you is not very long. [23]I want you to know that our brother Timothy has been let out of prison. If he comes soon enough, I will have him with me when I see you. [24]Give our greetings to all your leaders and to all God's people. The brothers from Italy send you their greetings. [25]May God's grace be with you all.

Although the epistle has come to its end with the concluding prayer, as so often happens in the letters of the NT our author has yet a few more words for his readers. Again we get a few bits of tantalizing information, which are followed by a word of greeting and a final benediction.

13:22 / The author first adds a note to his readers, whom he again (cf. 3:1, 12; 10:19) addresses as **brothers** (GNB adds **my**), to urge them **to listen patiently** (lit., "to bear with" or "listen willingly") to what he has written. He now describes his epistle as **this message of encouragement** or, more literally, "my word of exhortation," a phrase that is widely accepted as a good characterization of the work as a whole. As we have seen, Hebrews is essentially a series of exhortations, a kind of sermon in written form. These exhortations are based, to be sure, on very solid theological argumentation, but the latter always supports a practical concern or application. Our author has himself done in this work what he at one point urges his readers to do: "encourage one another" (10:25). He notes further that he has written "briefly" (GNB translates **not very long**), the implication being that he is able to elaborate these matters at greater length when the occasion presents itself (cf. the restraint in 9:5b and 11:32). In the meantime he covets the readers' attention to the important document he is sending to them, though it seem lengthy and difficult.

13:23 / The readers are now informed (**I want you to know** is lit. "know") about the release of **our brother Timothy**. It is probable, though not absolutely certain, that this Timothy is the disciple of Paul whom we know of elsewhere in the NT. In any event, he is apparently well known and beloved to the readers. It is also probable, but not absolutely certain, that the message about Timothy is, as GNB puts it, that he **has been let out of prison**, since the literal "set free" could mean the experience of some other kind of freedom. Where he was imprisoned is unknown (the NT nowhere records an imprisonment of Timothy), although Rome or Ephesus are good possibilities for Timothy the disciple of Paul. The author is hopeful that Timothy can meet him before long and accompany him on a visit to the church, apparently already planned.

13:24 / The author now sends greetings (**give our greetings** is literally "Greet") **to all your leaders**. The reference to **all** here may suggest those of a larger church community than that simply of the readers, but this is far from certain. These greetings are in line with the author's encouragement for the readers to respect and submit to their leaders (v. 17). His greetings extend, however, to **all God's people** (lit., "all the saints"). He has furthermore a special greeting to the readers from **the brothers** ("the saints," but implied from the preceding verse) **from Italy**. Unfortunately these last words are unclear in that the greetings may, on the one hand, be sent from Italians in Italy to Christians elsewhere or, on the other, from Italians living abroad to their brothers in the homeland. The most natural reading is the latter, although the former cannot be ruled out. If we could be positive about the location of the addressees, this uncertainty, of course, would not exist. But that determination cannot be made on the basis of this verse alone.

13:25 / The last words of an epistle are commonly a brief benediction such as this. This one happens to be in verbatim agreement with that of Titus 3:15 and very close to that of 2 Timothy 4:22. The determinative word is **grace** (*charis*), that one word that is quintessential to the Christian gospel and to every message given to the church by God's spokesmen—including this letter of exhortation by an anonymous author to Jewish Christians who have come to the new covenant through the grace of Jesus Christ.

Additional Notes

13:22 / It is possible that in this postscript the author, if he had dictated the letter as a whole to a scribe or secretary, here takes up the pen himself. This phenomenon is often evident in the Pauline letters (cf. 2 Thess. 3:17; Gal. 6:11; Col. 4:18; 1 Cor. 16:21). **Beg** (*parakaleō*) is the same verb used in v. 19. The verb underlying **listen patiently** (*anechō*) occurs only here in Hebrews. The phrase "word of exhortation" (*logos tēs paraklēseōs*) occurs also in Acts 13:15, where it describes Paul's sermon at Pisidian Antioch—a sermon that was based on the interpretation of certain OT texts so as to bring out their significance for the present. Since this is also what our author does for his readers, perhaps we are to think of the phrase as having this special connotation. When 1 Peter is described as a "brief letter" (5:12) the words may be taken more literally than here. Our author has tried to keep the length of the work under control despite the significance of what he writes and asks the readers' indulgence in this regard.

13:23 / Since our author shows some contact with Pauline theology, he was probably a member of the larger Pauline circle, and thus the likelihood that this Timothy was the disciple of Paul is increased. The verb **let out** (*apolyō*) occurs in Hebrews only here. In the passive, as here, it can mean simply that Timothy has "been dismissed," "taken leave," or "departed," perhaps having finished some responsibility. See BAGD, p. 96. If, as we have argued, the letter is addressed to a community of believers in Rome, then Timothy's imprisonment or other hindrance must have occurred elsewhere. He apparently has some distance to travel to meet the author.

13:24 / The word for **leaders** (*hēgoumenoi*) occurs also in vv. 7 and 17. The technical term "saints" (*hagioi*), describing those who have been set apart by the saving grace of God, is also used by the author in 6:10 (cf. 3:1 where the adjective "holy," *hagios*, is combined with "brothers"). See Proksch, *TDNT*, vol. 1, p. 100–110. The word **greet** (*aspazomai*) is an intimate term in that culture, implying an embrace. See Windisch, *TNDT*, vol. 1, pp. 496–502.

13:25 / A few minor textual variants occur in this verse. Many manuscripts have understandably added an Amen to the benediction. For discussion of these variants and the very interesting variations in the subscription added to the letter, many of which include "to the Hebrews, written from Italy through Timothy," see Metzger, *TCGNT*, p. 677 f.

Abbreviations

AngThR	*Anglican Theological Review*
Ant.	Josephus, *Antiquities*
ASV	American Standard Version
BAGD	Bauer, Arndt, Gingrich, and Danker, *A Greek-English Lexicon of the New Testament and Other Early Christian Literature* (1979)
Barclay	*The New Testament: A New Translation* (1969)
BibTheo	*Biblical Theology*
CBQ	*Catholic Biblical Quarterly*
cf.	compare
chap. (chaps.)	chapter (chapters)
CTJ	*Calvin Theological Journal*
DCT	A. Richardson, ed., *Dictionary of Christian Theology* (1969)
EBT	J. B. Bauer, ed., *Encyclopedia of Biblical Theology* (reprint of *Sacramentum Verbi*, 1970)
EJ	C. Roth, ed., *Encyclopedia Judaica* (1971)
EQ	*Evangelical Quarterly*
ET	English Translation
ExpT	*Expository Times*
f. (ff.)	and following verse or page (verses or pages)
GNB	Good News Bible
HTR	*Harvard Theological Review*
Interp	*Interpretation*
JB	Jerusalem Bible
JBL	*Journal of Biblical Literature*
JE	I. Singer, ed., *Jewish Encyclopedia* (1901–06)
JSJ	*Journal for the Study of Judaism*
KJV	King James Version
lit.	literally
LXX	Septuagint (the pre-Christian Greek translation of the OT)
Moffatt	*The New Testament: A New Translation* (1922)
NASB	New American Standard Bible
NCBCS	New Century Bible Commentary Series
NEB	New English Bible
NIDNTT	C. Brown, ed., *The New International Dictionary of New Testament Theology* (1975–78)

NIV	New International Version
NovT	*Novum Testamentum*
NT	New Testament
NTL	New Testament Library
NTS	*New Testament Studies*
OT	Old Testament
Phillips	*The New Testament in Modern English* (1959)
RefThR	*Reformed Theological Review*
RestQ	*Restoration Quarterly*
SBLM	Society of Biblical Literature Monograph
SBT	Studies in Biblical Theology
SJT	*Scottish Journal of Theology*
SNTSM	Society of New Testament Studies Monograph
Strack-Billerbeck	*Kommentar zum Neuen Testament aus Talmud und Midrasch* (1922–38)
StudTh	*Studia Theologica*
TCGNT	B. Metzger, *A Textual Commentary on the Greek New Testament* (UBS, 1971)
TDNT	G. Kittel and G. Friedrich, eds., *Theological Dictionary of the New Testament*, trans. G. W. Bromiley (1964–72)
UBS	United Bible Societies
VoxEv	*Vox Evangelica*
v. (vv.)	verse (verses)
War	Josephus, *Jewish War*
WPCS	Westminster Pelican Commentary Series
WTJ	*Westminster Theological Journal*
ZNW	*Zeitschrift für die Neutestamentliche Wissenschaft*
ZPEB	M. C. Tenney, ed., *Zondervan Pictorial Encyclopedia of the Bible* (1975)

For Further Reading

Commentaries

Bruce, F. F. *Commentary on the Epistle to the Hebrews*. NICNT. Grand Rapids: Eerdmans, 1964.

Buchanan, G. W. *To the Hebrews*. AB. New York: Doubleday, 1972.

Davidson, A. B. *The Epistle to the Hebrews*. Edinburgh: T. & T. Clark, 1882.

Davies, J. H. *A Letter to the Hebrews*. Cambridge: Cambridge University Press, 1967.

Delitzsch, F. *Commentary on the Epistle to the Hebrews*. Translated by T. L. Kingsbury from German original of 1857. 2 vols. Edinburgh: T. & T. Clark, 1871. Reprint. Minneapolis: Klock & Klock, 1978.

Héring, J. *The Epistle to the Hebrews*. Translated by A. W. Heathcoat and P. J. Allcock from French original of 1955. London: Epworth, 1970.

Hewitt, T. *The Epistle to the Hebrews*. Tyndale NTC. London: Tyndale, 1960.

Hughes, P. E. *A Commentary on the Epistle to the Hebrews*. Grand Rapids: Eerdmans, 1977.

Jewett, R. *Letter to the Pilgrims: A Commentary on the Epistle to the Hebrews*. New York: Pilgrim Press, 1981.

Moffatt, J. *A Critical and Exegetical Commentary on the Epistle to the Hebrews*. ICC. New York: Scribner, 1924.

Montefiore, H. W. *The Epistle to the Hebrews*. Harper's NTC. New York: Harper & Row, 1964.

Peake, A. S. *Hebrews*. Century Bible. New York: Henry Frowde; Edinburgh: T. C. & E. C. Jack, 1914.

Westcott, B. F. *The Epistle to the Hebrews*. 2d ed. London and New York: Macmillan, 1892. Reprinted. Grand Rapids: Eerdmans, 1952 and later.

Although this bibliography is otherwise restricted to works available in English, the following two commentaries in German and French are so important that they demand to be noted.

Michel, O. *Der Brief an die Hebräer*. 13th ed. KEKNT. Göttingen: Vandenhoeck and Ruprecht, 1975.

Spicq, C. *L'Épître aux Hébreux*, 2 vols. Paris: J. Gabalda, 1952–53.

Surveys of Recent Scholarship on Hebrews

Batdorf, I. W. "Hebrews and Qumran: Old Methods and New Directions." In *Festschrift to Honor F. Wilbur Gingrich*, edited by E. H. Barth and R. E. Cocroft, pp. 16–35. Leiden: E. J. Brill, 1972.

Bruce, F. F. "Recent Literature on the Epistle to the Hebrews." *Themelios* 3 (1966): pp. 31–36.

———. "Recent Contributions to the Understanding of Hebrews." *ExpT* 80 (1969): pp. 260–64.

Buchanan, G. W. "The Present State of Scholarship on Hebrews." In *Christianity, Judaism and Other Greco-Roman Cults* (Studies for Morton Smith at Sixty), edited by J. Neusner, vol. 1, pp. 299–330. Leiden: E. J. Brill, 1975.

Johnsson, W. G. "Issues in the Interpretation of Hebrews." *Andrews University Seminary Studies* 15 (1977): pp. 169–87.

McCullough, J. C. "Some Recent Developments in Research on the Epistle to the Hebrews." *Irish Biblical Studies* 2 (1980): pp. 141–65.

Background

Anderson, C. P. "Hebrews among the Letters of Paul." *Studies in Religion* 5 (1975–76): pp. 258–66.

Bruce, F. F. " 'To the Hebrews' or 'To the Essenes'?" *NTS* 9 (1963): pp. 217–32.

Dahms, J. V. "The First Readers of Hebrews." *Journal of the Evangelical Theological Society* 20 (1977): pp. 365–75.

Dey, L. K. K. *The Intermediary World and Patterns of Perfection in Philo and Hebrews.* SBLDS, vol. 25. Missoula, Mont.: Scholars Press, 1975.

Eccles, R. S. "The Purpose of Hellenistic Patterns in Hebrews." In *Religions in Antiquity*, edited by J. Neusner, pp. 207–26. Leiden: E. J. Brill, 1968.

Mackay, C. "The Argument of Hebrews." *Church Quarterly Review* 168 (1967): pp. 325–38.

Manson, T. W. "The Problem of the Epistle to the Hebrews." *Bulletin of the John Rylands Library* 32 (1949): pp. 1–17. Reprinted in *Studies in the Gospels and Epistles.* Edited by M. Black, pp. 242–58. Manchester: Manchester University Press, 1962.

Weeks, N. "Admonition and Error in Hebrews." *WTJ* 39 (1976): pp. 72–80.

Williamson, R. "Platonism and Hebrews." *SJT* 16 (1963):415–24.

———. *Philo and the Epistle to the Hebrews.* Leiden: E. J. Brill, 1970.

———. "The Background of the Epistle to the Hebrews." *ExpT* 87 (1976): pp. 232–37.

Yadin, Y. "The Dead Sea Scrolls and The Epistle to the Hebrews." *Scripta Hierosolymitana* 4 (1957): pp. 36–55.

Theology

Barrett, C. K. "The Eschatology of the Epistle to the Hebrews." In *The Background of the New Testament and Its Eschatology*, edited by W. D. Davies and D. Daube, pp. 363–93. Cambridge: Cambridge University Press, 1954.

Brooks, W. E. "The Perpetuity of Christ's Sacrifice in the Epistle to the Hebrews." *JBL* 89 (1970): pp. 205–14.

Bruce, F. F. "The Kerygma of Hebrews." *Interp* 23 (1969): pp. 3–19.

Campbell, J. C. "In a Son: The Doctrine of Incarnation in the Epistle to the Hebrews." *Interp* 10 (1956): pp. 24–38.

Carlston, C. E. "Eschatology and Repentance in the Epistle to the Hebrews." *JBL* 79 (1959): pp. 296-302.

Cleary, M. "Jesus, Pioneer and Source of Salvation: The Christology of Hebrews 1–6." *The Bible Today* 67 (1973): pp. 1242–48.

Davies, J. H. "The Heavenly Work of Christ in Hebrews." *Studia Evangelica* 4 (1968): pp. 384–89.

Filson, F. V. *'Yesterday': A Study of Hebrews in the Light of Chapter 13.* SBT, series 2, vol. 4. London: SCM, 1967.

Giles, P. "Son of Man in the Epistle to the Hebrews." *ExpT* 86 (1975): pp. 328-32.

Harrison, E. F. "The Theology of the Epistle to the Hebrews." *Bibliotheca Sacra* 12 (1964): pp. 333–40.

Hellyer, L. "The *Prōtokos* Title in Hebrews." *Studia Biblica et Theologica* 6 (1976): pp. 3–28.

Hoekema, A. A. "The Perfection of Christ in Hebrews." *CTJ* 9 (1974): pp. 31–37.

Johnsson, W. G. "The Cultus of Hebrews in Twentieth-Century Scholarship." *ExpT* 89 (1978): pp. 104–8.

_____. "Pilgrimage in Hebrews." *JBL* 97 (1978): pp. 239–51.

Milligan, G. *The Theology of the Epistle to the Hebrews.* Edinburgh: T. & T. Clark, 1899.

Nairne, A. *The Epistle of Priesthood.* 2d ed. Edinburgh: T. & T. Clark, 1915.

Robinson, W. "The Eschatology of Hebrews: A Study in the Christian Doctrine of Hope." *Encounter* 22 (1961): pp. 37–51.

Schaeffer, J. R. "The Relationship Between Priestly and Servant Messianism in Hebrews." *CBQ* 30 (1968): pp. 359–85.

Scott, E. F. *The Epistle to the Hebrews: Its Doctrine and Significance.* Edinburgh: T. & T. Clark, 1922.

Silva, M. "Perfection and Eschatology in Hebrews." *WTJ* 39 (1976): pp. 60–71.

Smalley, S. S. "Atonement in Hebrews." *EQ* 33 (1961): pp. 36–46.

Stewart, R. A. "Creation and Matter in the Epistle to the Hebrews." *NTS* 12 (1966): pp. 284–93.

_____. "Sinless High Priest." *NTS* 14 (1967): pp. 126–35.

Stott, W. "The Conception of 'Offering' in the Epistle to the Hebrews." *NTS* 9 (1962-63): pp. 62–67.

Tasker, R. V. G. *The Gospel in the Epistle to the Hebrews.* London: Tyndale, 1950.

Vanhoye, A. *Our Priest Is Christ: The Doctrine of the Epistle to the Hebrews.* Rome: Pontifical Biblical Institute, 1977.

Vos, G. *The Teaching of the Epistle to the Hebrews.* Edited by J. G. Vos. Grand Rapids: Eerdmans, 1956.

Wikgren, A. "Patterns of Perfection in the Epistle to the Hebrews." *NTS* 6 (1960): pp. 159–67.

Williamson, R. "Hebrews and Doctrine." *ExpT* 81 (1970): pp. 371–76.

————. "The Eucharist and the Epistle to the Hebrews." *NTS* 21 (1975): pp. 300–12.

Other Notable Works

Barth, M. "The Old Testament in Hebrews: An Essay in Biblical Hermeneutics." In *Current Issues in New Testament Interpretation* (Essays in Honor of O. A. Piper). Edited by W. Klassen and G. F. Snyder, pp. 53–78. New York: Harper & Row, 1962.

Caird, G. B. "The Exegetical Method of the Epistle to the Hebrews." *Canadian Journal of Theology* 5 (1959): pp. 44–51.

Combrink, H. J. B., "Some Thoughts on the Old Testament Citations in the Epistle to the Hebrews." *Neotestamentica* 5 (1971): pp. 22–36.

Hagner, D. A., "Interpreting the Epistle to the Hebrews." In *The Literature and Meaning of Scripture*, edited by M. A. Inch and C. H. Bullock, pp. 217–42. Grand Rapids: Baker, 1981.

Howard, G. "Hebrews and the Old Testament Quotations." *NovT* 10 (1968): pp. 208–16.

Hughes, G. *Hebrews and Hermeneutics.* SNTSMS, vol. 36. Cambridge: Cambridge University Press, 1979.

Kistemaker, S. *The Psalms Citations in the Epistle to the Hebrews.* Amsterdam: W. G. van Soest, 1961.

Manson, W. *The Epistle to the Hebrews: An Historical and Theological Reconsideration.* London: Hodder & Stoughton, 1951.

McCullough, J. C. "The Old Testament Quotations in Hebrews." *NTS* 26 (1980): pp. 363–79.

Rendall, R. "The Method of the Writer to the Hebrews in Using Old Testament Quotations." *EQ* 27 (1955): pp. 214–20.

Sowers, S. G. *The Hermeneutics of Philo and Hebrews.* Zurich: EVZ, 1965.

Swetnam, J. "On the Literary Genre of the 'Epistle' to the Hebrews." *NovT* 11 (1969): pp. 261–69.

————. "Form and Content in Hebrews 1–6" *Biblica* 53 (1972): pp. 368–85.

————. "Form and Content in Hebrews 7–13." *Biblica* 55 (1974): pp. 333–48.

Synge, F. C. *Hebrews and Scriptures.* London: SPCK, 1959.

Thomas, K. J. "Old Testament Citations in Hebrews." *NTS* 11 (1965): pp. 303–25.

Thompson, J. W. "The Structure and Purpose of the Catena in Heb. 1:5–13." *CBQ* 38 (1976): pp. 352–63.

Subject Index

Scripture Index

APOCRYPHA

NONCANONICAL BOOKS